D0220741

Tradition and Trauma

Modern Hebrew Classics
David Patterson, Series Editor

This series presents in English formative works of lasting significance that appeared in Hebrew during the fifty years between approximately 1889 and 1939 as well as more recent critical work. The series, edited by David Patterson, emeritus president of the Oxford Centre for Post-graduate Hebrew Studies, acquaints the English reader with the quality of modern Hebrew writing in its period of renaissance.

Tradition and Trauma: Studies in the Fiction of S. J. Agnon,
edited by David Patterson and Glenda Abramson

A Dream Come True, *Eliezer Ben-Yehuda,*
translated by T. Muraoka, edited by George Mandel

The World of Israel Weissbrem, *translated by Alan D. Crown*

Out of the Depths, *Joseph Chaim Brenner,*
translated by David Patterson

Tradition and Trauma

Studies in the Fiction of
S. J. Agnon

EDITED BY

David Patterson
and Glenda Abramson

Westview Press

BOULDER • SAN FRANCISCO • OXFORD

Modern Hebrew Classics

All rights reserved. No part of this publication may be reproduced or transmitted in any form or by any means, electronic or mechanical, including photocopy, recording, or any information storage and retrieval system, without permission in writing from the publisher.

Copyright © 1994 by Westview Press, Inc.; Chapter 10 copyright © 1994 by David Aberbach

Published in 1994 in the United States of America by Westview Press, Inc., 5500 Central Avenue, Boulder, Colorado 80301-2877, and in the United Kingdom by Westview Press, 36 Lonsdale Road, Summertown, Oxford OX2 7EW

Library of Congress Cataloging-in-Publication Data
Tradition and trauma : studies in the fiction of S. J. Agnon / edited
    by David Patterson and Glenda Abramson.
        p.   cm. — (Modern Hebrew classics)
    Some of the studies were presented originally as papers at a
conference entitled "Tradition and Trauma, on the Centenary of the
Birth of S. J. Agnon, 1888–1970," which took place at Mount Holyoke
College, on 16–17 April 1988.
    Includes bibliographical references and index.
    ISBN 0-8133-2024-0. — ISBN 0-8133-2025-9 (pbk.)
        1. Agnon, Shmuel Yosef, 1888–1970—Criticism and interpretation—
Congresses.   I. Patterson, David, 1922–   .   II. Abramson, Glenda.
III. Series.
PJ5053.A4Z9225   1994
892.4'35—dc20   93-43704
                                                                                                                    CIP

Printed and bound in the United States of America

The paper used in this publication meets the requirements
of the American National Standard for Permanence of Paper
for Printed Library Materials Z39.48-1984.

10   9   8   7   6   5   4   3   2

Contents

Preface

In the academic year 1987–1988, while serving as professor of Jewish studies at Mount Holyoke College, I convened a conference entitled "Tradition and Trauma, on the Centenary of the Birth of S. J. Agnon, 1888–1970," which took place at the college on 16–17 April 1988.

The centenary of the birth of Agnon, the sole Hebrew writer to receive a Nobel Prize for Literature (1966), provided a convenient vantage point to review the man and his writings. For an author to be regarded as a "classic" within his own lifetime reflects a rare and distinguished talent. But Agnon was a legend for two whole generations, and he remains unquestionably the outstanding fiction writer in modern Hebrew literature. Subtle, enigmatic, and elusive, his stories hold intense fascination for ordinary readers and literary critics alike. Hence, the conference attempted to explore core aspects of his unusual appeal.

During the two days of the conference, papers were delivered by Aharon Appelfeld, Arnold Band, Nitza Ben-Dov, Esther Fuchs, Anne Golomb Hoffman, Miri Kubovy, David Patterson, Naomi Sokoloff, and Judith Romney Wegner. The introductory remarks were given by Dean Joseph Ellis and the concluding remarks by Mount Holyoke President Elizabeth Kennan. The four sessions were chaired, respectively, by Howard Adelman, Judith Baskin, Shmuel Bolozky, and Don Weber.

In addition to the papers delivered at the conference, this volume includes papers by David Aberbach, Glenda Abramson, and Edna Amir Coffin. Glenda Abramson kindly consented to become joint editor of the volume.

Sincere thanks are due to the president and staff of Mount Holyoke College, who contributed so much to the success of the conference, and to the staff of the Oxford Centre for Postgraduate Hebrew Studies for their help in preparing the manuscript for publication.

David Patterson

1

Introduction:
A Legend in His Time

David Patterson

The purpose of this introduction is to prepare the ground for the detailed studies that make up the remainder of this volume. In this chapter I will attempt to explain, in some measure, why, on the centenary of his birth in 1888 in the town of Buczacz in Galicia, Samuel Joseph Agnon remains so highly regarded and still occupies a central position in modern Hebrew literature.

Agnon achieved the unusual distinction of being widely recognized as a "classic" while at the height of his powers. His literary reputation was firmly established even prior to the Second World War, and for more than sixty years his fame has been legendary. Until his death in 1972, his creative powers continued unabated, not only in the production of new stories, but also in the reworking of copious unpublished material, much of which has since been published posthumously. For the Hebrew-reading public each new publication spelled surprise and delight; every line was scrutinized and avidly debated in the hope that it might furnish one more clue toward a fuller understanding of his enigmatic personality. Agnon's status is unique. In spite of his being a writer of world stature and unquestionably the outstanding figure in contemporary Hebrew literature, whose voluminous writings made an immense impact on many of the most tal-

ented authors in Israel, he remains insufficiently known beyond
the confines of Hebrew-reading circles, owing perhaps to the
extraordinary difficulty of translating his work convincingly.

Indeed, for the English-language reader confronting Agnon's
work for the first time, the reaction may well be, What is all the
excitement about? Is this man really so great an author? Since
Hebrew readers entertain no such doubts, the logical conclusion
is that the secret must lie, at least in part, in Agnon's use of language. The quality of his prose loses much of its tension in translation. Hence the impact exerted on the English-language reader
is correspondingly reduced. This element of style is so central to
the appreciation of Agnon's writing that some brief remarks on
the development of modern Hebrew prose may prove instructive.

Throughout the nineteenth century, modern Hebrew literature tended to be written in a deliberate neobiblical style, which
exercised considerable constraints on the free expression of ideas.
The characteristic feature of biblical prose is its remarkable brev-
ity, an artistic economy of high order. A relentless unfolding of
consecutive events is coupled with a dramatic absence of super-
fluous information. It is a skeleton narrative, which bites into the
imagination to supply the flesh and blood. The sheer economy is
its greatest source of strength. But as a medium of expression for
the modern story or novel, which is expansive, discursive, and
heavily dependent upon description and extraneous detail, biblical narrative is sadly inadequate.

Long before Agnon appeared upon the literary scene,
Hebrew writers had concluded that biblical Hebrew was too in-
flexible an instrument for their purposes. But what was the alternative? Even as Agnon was growing up, Hebrew was being
revived as a vernacular, and the center of Hebrew writing was
gradually shifting from Eastern Europe to Palestine. These
changes culminated in a veritable literary renaissance after the
creation of the State of Israel in 1948. The physical transference
of Hebrew writers from Europe to the Middle East engendered
radical changes in topography, landscape, environment, accent,

and semantic usages, all of which exerted profound influence on Hebrew literature. The fusion of ancient and modern connotations along with the secularization of the holy tongue caused serious difficulties for many authors but also yielded striking innovation in the realm of metaphor and image.

Gradually the different strata of literary Hebrew ranging over millennia were fused together in the attempt to produce a flexible instrument of expression that could grapple with the demands of a changing reality. Some of the more talented authors began to shape a kind of Hebrew that would be able to cope with a wide variety of subject matter. This creation of a Hebrew that is timeless, yet loaded with association, is one of Agnon's great achievements. Although his style is at once distinctive and as immediately recognizable as a signature, it remains firmly grounded in the traditional strata of Hebrew literature and, as such, highly reminiscent and suggestive. Agnon's language is pregnant with association to the Mishnah, the Midrash, and the late-medieval Hebrew moralists; yet it remains unmistakably characteristic. The first impressions of apparent simplicity soon give way to a realization of the overtones, references, and allusions arising from the author's familiarity with the vast corpus of Hebrew literature. The ancient vocabulary of Hebrew is loaded with associations of all kinds, and the skillful juxtaposition of words and phrases can be made to yield a variety of nuances.

Of all the ingredients drawn from the various strata of Hebrew literature, however, the dominant influence on Agnon's style is, perhaps, the Midrash. Now Midrash is, in essence, commentary upon the Hebrew Bible, and it comprises a voluminous literature composed over many centuries. It consists broadly of an attempt to expound the Bible in the widest terms of reference. Its glance sweeps from heaven to earth and earth to heaven, and it is rich in imagery and metaphor. In style it is diffuse and repetitive, but there is a certain tension and discipline in the language, and it has a rhythmic appeal. It is indicative, for example, that such authorities as Maimonides in the twelfth century and Nahman Krochmal in the nineteenth each defined Midrash as poetry! However unlikely such a definition of the Midrash might at first appear, on further reflection the range of its imagination, its sheer sweep, its use of metaphor, symbol, and allusion, its fusion of opposites, constitute the very essence of poetry. Certainly, the connection is germane to an understanding of Agnon's style.

This subtle use of Hebrew sources lies at the heart of the difficulty in translating Agnon's work convincingly. The histories and associations of so much of his vocabulary and phraseology create an illusion that begins to dissolve as soon as the Hebrew text is rendered into English. Every language has its own magic, its own particular charms. Every language has its natural rhythms, which cast its particular spells. Only too often in the English translations of Agnon's writings, the magic is broken and the wonderful enchantment fades into the light of common day. Until there emerges a translator of sufficient merit and superior talent who can perform extraordinary feats of translation, the reading of Agnon's work in English may yield a certain element of disappointment. In his case, the medium is, indeed, the message.

But thematically as well as linguistically Agnon's writings can be read at different levels. He is a superb storyteller who unfolds a tale magnificently. Readers, however, are never quite sure whether they understand the work correctly. One of the most penetrating of his earlier literary critics was the late Professor Barukh Kurzweil, who suggested many interpretations of Agnon's symbolism. Agnon himself remained tantalizingly ingenuous and used to say, "All I do is write a simple story, and along comes Professor K. and tells me what it means!" For the unsophisticated reader much of Agnon's writing consists of simple and appealing stories and folktales, delightfully unfolded. The more perceptive reader will gradually become aware of an increasingly disturbing significance and depth, which reveal a quality of an entirely different order, a quality that suffuses his work with a subtle coloring most difficult to imitate.

The charm exerted by Agnon's stories on two generations of readers stems partly from the nature of his subject matter. Many of his tales are rooted in childhood reminiscence of his native Galicia. The spiritual depth and richness of Jewish life in Eastern Europe, with its wealth of folklore and religious tradition, its warmth of human relationships, its piety, simplicity, and respect for learning, provide the background for much of his work. An element of wistfulness and nostalgia for a world gone by pervades the stories, although they are far from appearing old-fashioned or merely quaint. Other stories again, some more realistic in flavor, depict the life of the early settlers in the Land of Israel in the first decades of this century, or the decline of Jewish life in Europe following the ravages of the First World War. Both groups of stories, nostalgic and realistic, have picaresque and even epic elements. Many of them are painted on a broad canvas with a wide sweep and are characterized by a rich variety of episodes, presenting a kaleidoscopic view of many aspects of Jewish life. They portray an extraordinary gallery of characters and a veritable plethora of themes, which reflect the author's fertile and inventive imagination. It is little wonder that thematically their appeal to the emotions of the Hebrew reader has proved so powerful. The longing for origins and roots is a natural feeling among Israel's largely immigrant population, and Agnon's stories help to furnish a sorely needed sense of continuity.

But there is a further aspect of Agnon's work, which provides a clear explanation of his popularity. In spite of his obsession with the past, Agnon was as authentically in tune with his present as is any of his fellow writers in contemporary Hebrew literature. Particularly during the last three decades of his life— although his earlier work displays like tendencies—Agnon's stories were infused with a feeling of nightmare, a grotesque and semimagical atmosphere of mystery and enigma. His works reflect the anxieties of our age of transition, in which division among the instructed has nullified authority and led to widespread loss of faith. Religion, science, medicine, politics, provide neither adequate guidance nor real solace. Humanity's spirit is sick; society is suffering from a nervous breakdown. Violence and brutality mirror the disintegration of established order. The problem facing the modern individual is how to live in a society that is no longer properly supported by tradition. The acute crisis of faith gives rise to a sense of insecurity and guilt, to an obsession with death. Serious literature, which serves as a sounding board for the mental and spiritual stresses of the age, expresses its anxieties in terror dreams. Where the fears are not expressed directly, the literature resorts to symbolic or allegorical forms. The result is frequently a kind of fairy tale in which the individual predicament is made to represent the predicament of humankind and the readers are invited to identify with a situation that might just as easily apply to themselves. The extraordinary influence of Kafka, for example, on so many writers in so many languages, and the remarkable rise of existentialist ideas are no mere literary quirks. They provide the clearest illustration of the modern writers' attitude to their experience. Nor is it surprising that some of the prevailing symbols in modern literature are shabbiness, squalor, and ineffectuality—the marks of a world that has seen better days.

The longing for the better days, for a society infused with simple piety, kindliness, and faith, for a generation that possessed real strength and ability to act in a meaningful way, constitutes a frequently recurring theme in Agnon's stories. Whereas in former times pious men could bring the dead to life, today even the living are dead. The harmony of life has disappeared. Hence the fruitless hunt in "Ido and Enam" for the lost harmonious language of humankind. Hence the frequent resort to symbolism in the shape of missing letters, mislaid keys, books that have been burned or stolen, and houses abandoned by their inhabitants. Time and again the enigmatic themes indicate loss of innocence, spiritual confusion, and the impotent urge to restore some remnants of the past before all is lost. And in resorting to the poetic devices of implication, metaphor, and symbol to clothe his ideas, the author has wisely selected the language of the Midrash, which itself is poetry.

The preoccupation with the general feeling of disintegration and spiritual decay and the resort to dreamlike, nightmare fantasy and symbol place Agnon firmly in the mainstream of modern literature. But his originality resides in his specific reference to the problem in terms of Jewish heritage and tradition. The general malaise is common to humanity, but the detailed application is in Jewish terms. This very concentration on the spiritual area, where his knowledge and experience are so intimate and deep, lends a particular strength and efficacy to his stories. The wider context of decline and disintegration is pinpointed in the traumatic experience of the Jew. Changing times have whittled away his strength. In his encounter with the world, the universe, and God, he is adrift and helpless. Beneath the misty, dreamlike surface of many of his stories, where the fixatives of time and place dissolve and lose cohesion, despair, tragedy, and death lurk in dark ambush and reflect a pessimism of disturbing depth. One positive element alone remains constant—Jerusalem herself, which in Agnon's stories is endowed with a personality of her own, and which becomes a symbol for all that is meaningful and permanent and harmonious in life. It is as though the holy city alone contains the seeds that might restore that wholeness of spirit and oneness with the world that are slipping through the nerveless fingers of our unhappy generation.

The various studies of Agnon's writings contained in this volume reflect careful analysis, detailed research, and weighty erudition. They illustrate, each in its own way, the major importance of a writer who remains, perhaps, the central figure in Hebrew literature in this century, and one who has made a worthy contribution to world literature at large. It is hoped that the following chapters will help to explain in some measure the fascination and enigma of Agnon's writings and to foster an understanding of his work among the English-reading public.

Passion Spins the Plot:
Agnon's "Forevermore"

Naomi Sokoloff

In tragic life, God wot,
No villain need be! Passions spin the plot
We are betrayed by what is false within.
                    —George Meredith

Agnon's "Forevermore" ("Ad 'olam"), a short story riddled
with ironies and contradictions, features as its protagonist a
scholar who has single-mindedly devoted twenty years to re-
searching the history of an ancient city, Gumlidata.[1] Having
completed his work and finally found a publisher for his study,
Adiel Amzeh suddenly discovers the existence of a previously
unknown manuscript on his topic. Held in the possession of a
nearby leper colony, this document beckons Amzeh, who yearns
to clarify a puzzling detail about the final siege of the city.
Renouncing his long-awaited opportunity for public recognition, the scholar repairs to the leper house and examines the
manuscript. Reading and rereading with rapt fascination,
Amzeh remains among the lepers forevermore.

---

1. The story appears in *Elu ve-elu* (1974 ed.), and in English translation by Joel
Blocker and Robert Alter, in Alter (1975), pp. 227–249E. Page numbers followed by "E" in this chapter refer to that English version.

A noble quest for knowledge despite adverse circumstances, or a foolhardy loss of perspective? Both interpretations have been offered to account for Adiel Amzeh's actions. The claim for purity of vision, which draws its inspiration from a traditional midrashic image, relies in part on a perception of the Jews in their devotion to Torah as an isolated people, degraded in exile, and spurned among the nations. Many critics, indeed, have seen in this story an allegory built around the protagonist's name, which means "this people, an adornment to God." The letters *'ayin* and *gimmel,* which appear recurrently as initial letters of names, have been seen as dividing the characters into groups of good and evil figures. Also working for the positive interpretation of Amzeh's predicament, a number of explicit comments made by the narrator and the secondary characters lend credence to the idea of noble sacrifice. Wisdom herself, personified, whispers in Amzeh's ear, "Sit my love, sit and do not leave me." But then again, is this a figure of purity or an emblem of seduction luring the scholar to false values?

A number of compelling factors counteract the pro-Amzeh arguments. First, the book that Amzeh pursues is not holy scripture, but rather description of a highly repugnant, idolatrous society devoid of redeeming spiritual values or law. Further deflecting power away from the sympathetic reading is Amzeh's characterization, which more closely resembles caricature than hagiography and which shows him to be ludicrously obsessed by an idée fixe. Moreover, those letters so crucial to distinguishing good from bad are sometimes scrambled, like the virtuous and wicked qualities of the characters themselves. Finally there is no pat distinction and no simple allegory so much as there is a nagging sense of undecidability. Every noble sentiment thus is in some way eventually undercut.[2] My discussion in this chapter

---

2. Moked (1984), for example, argues the case for Amzeh's nobility of spirit, as does Tsemach (1968). In her article on "Forevermore" (1985b), Esther Fuchs argues that ironic and caricatural description of Adiel Amzeh emphasizes his

will focus on one aspect of the text, elements of plot, to support an ironic assessment of Adiel Amzeh. This approach to the protagonist lost in endless reading ultimately fosters a metanarrative reading that emphasizes the nature of texts, narrative impulses, and reading itself.

As Peter Brooks has pointed out in *Reading for the Plot: Design and Intention in Narrative,* plot is the principle of interconnectedness that, by linking discrete incidents, episodes, and actions, helps confer coherence onto those narrative components of a text. Plot is often conceived of as the outline, or armature, of a story; it is not, however, a static organization but a structuring operation actuated by reading and elicited by meanings that develop temporally through sequence and succession. Brooks observes that the term "plot" in English enjoys a semantic range that can include the idea of order and also indicate the concept of shaping or formulating as a dynamic activity. Plot may mean:

1. a small piece of ground, a measured area of land
2. a ground plan, as for a building; a chart or diagram (hence also the verb "to plot"—for example, to plot a graph)
3. a secret plan to accomplish a hostile or illegal purpose
4. a series of events, the action in a narrative drama.

The first two definitions are based on an idea of boundedness, demarcation, of marking off and ordering. The third suggests plot as scheme or machination, and it may have something in

---

monomaniac fixation on his work. Tochner's essay on "Forevermore" in his collection *Pesher Agnon* (1968), attempts to decode each of the many names and characters in the story within an ideological framework and thus to explicate the story as a polemic against modern biblical scholarship and Hebrew literature. Alter (1975) argues persuasively that such approaches are misguided and that in fact "Forevermore" offers an antiallegory. The proliferation of *'ayin* and *gimmel* invites allegorical reading, but the deployment of this device is inconsistent, so the story remains enigmatic, not to be reduced to such interpretation.

common with the first two categories insofar as to adopt a stratagem is to set out or delineate a particular course of action. In any
event the last kind of plot, the literary term, combines the possibilities implied here of design as both pattern and intention. Plotting as Brooks is concerned with it is what "makes a plot 'move
forward,' and makes us read forward, seeking in the unfolding of
the narrative ... the promise of progress toward meaning."[3]

An overriding feature of the primary plot in "Forevermore"
is digression, that is, the series of interruptions that prevent the
central character from achieving his stated goal of publishing his
research. Amzeh is waylaid first by Adah Eden, a nurse who col-
lects magazines for the lepers. A visit from her delays his attending a decisive meeting with his financial benefactor, Gebhard
Guldenthal. Then he dallies to hear a story she recounts about
how the Gumlidata manuscript arrived in the hands of the lepers. From there he goes to the leprosarium and, as he reads, his
publishing hopes indefinitely deferred, the contents of the
manuscript are recounted at length and thus deflect the reader's
attention, along with Amzeh's, away from the entire story line
about the protagonist's life. A large number of Agnon narratives
feature comparable antiprogressive patterns. Repetition, circularity, episodic fragmentation of narrative line, and disconnected
events prevail in texts as diverse as *The Bridal Canopy* and *The
Book of Deeds,* and the thematic implications that accompany this
formal feature vary in various texts.[4] In "Forevermore," this kind

---

3. Brooks (1984), p. xiii. See also pp. 5–6.

4. The disturbed causal-logical connections and the frustration of linear development in Agnon's fiction often undermine any sense that purpose or meaning
in human life corresponds to the will of the individual. There is, however, considerable debate about how to interpret this phenomenon. Some critics have
argued that it reflects the personalities of weak, indecisive characters; others
claim it is symptomatic of upheavals in the modern world, which have shaken
the foundations of faith; yet others think it hints at Agnon's own belief that
God's will prevails and not human intentions. For a variety of views, see
Kurzweil (1963), Band (1968), Shaked (1976), and Miron (1987).

of narrative design provides ironic plot.[5] The main character perceives the events of his life as a kind of progress, but the reader, by contrast, does not. The fiction therefore offers a regressive plot masquerading as progressive because the protagonist views it as such. In the poem "Modern Love," to which my title alludes, George Meredith wrote, "Passions spin the plot." Amzeh's passion for futile and directionless study here spins his plot into an antiplot, inverting the very concept of plot from the normal sense of forward-moving action to one of disruption and deflection. Early on in the story Agnon succinctly sums up the oddity of Amzeh's life in a sentence that anticipates the deviation of narrative line to come and calls attention to matters of plotting. Articulating the assumption that time progresses in linear fashion and that progress of events is expected to accompany this advancing motion, the text notes that such is not the case with Adiel Amzeh. "Yatsu shanim ve-sifro lo yatsa" (p. 316), it remarks—that is, years went by and his book didn't appear, but literally, years went out and his book didn't come out. The same verb, *y-ts-a,* to leave or go out, is used twice to emphasize the scholar's anomalous lack of progress.

In short, this plot structure creates a pattern of distractions and interruptions that lead finally to a misguided subordination of social ties to an abstract ideal. The central constellation of tensions set up in this way—between action and inaction, text and the context of its transmission—is brought out and adumbrated by other aspects of the plot. The stories within the story, which constitute two of the major distractions in the primary plot, raise questions related to those addressed by that same overarching plot and the narrative as a whole.

The first embedded narrative, concerning how the book on Gumlidata arrived in the lepers' hands, is presented as part of Adah Eden's conversation with Amzeh. In brief it goes like this:

---

5. My comments here draw on Esther Fuchs's discussion of ironic plot in *Omanut ha-hitamemut* (1985a).

When the Goths destroyed Gumlidata, they captured a noble-
man who possessed a copy of the city chronicles. Shortly there-
after the captive contracted cholera and his captors abandoned
him to die. Taken in by some itinerant lepers, the man was at first
dismayed to find himself in their company. Later, however, he
came to be grateful for the refuge they provided him. Joining
their community, he recounted to them the glories of Gumlidata. After their deaths his book was acquired by succeeding
generations of lepers, who passed it down through the ages. The
function of this inserted narrative is clearly to provide a parallel
to Amzeh's own experience. In a sense the events narrated anticipate his end: In each case a story survives, a book continues to
exist—but at the cost of an individual's life, which is repressed
and buried in the isolation of the leper colony. The immediate
narrator, the nurse, attributes a positive value to her tale. "Men
live and die," she concludes, "but their instruments remain and
live on" (p. 242E). In this fashion she sets up an interpretation
that might be applied also to Amzeh. In effect, however, her
evaluation helps build toward the concluding irony of the story.
Any comparison of her tale with the experience of the protagonist produces a false analogy: The count's life depended on the
lepers, but Amzeh does not go to the leprosarium to save himself. Even had the detail he sought out been a crucial one with
which to validate his entire research, it would not have de-
manded urgent attention and might have waited till the following day. The reader, then, must judge Amzeh by weighing his
loss more than his gain.

The second frame story, the account of Gumlidata's siege,
provides another parallel to the main plot, but this is even more
pointedly an alternative to, than an echo of, Amzeh's fate. Here
the Hun girl Eldag has been captured and held in Gumlidata,
forced to serve as a concubine to the aging, repulsive Count
Gifayon, Glaskinon Gitra'al of the house of Giara'al. She cannot
abide the old man's "groaning and drooling" or "the nauseating
smell of the city and its sacrificial altars" (p. 245E). Consequently she tries repeatedly to escape but fails. Eventually,

though, when she relinquishes her attempts to flee and grants the count exceptional sexual favors, she gains the trust of her captors. Due to their relaxed watchfulness, she even finds opportunity to roam about the city alone. One day she takes a wild donkey to a particular place where a small breach has opened in the city wall. She has clothed the animal with a bizarre garment made of calves' eyes, called an Izla, which happens in its shape to resemble the Valley of Cranes—the very place where the walls' foundations are weak. Sending the beast through the opening, Eldag surmises that her father will associate the animal with her. Originally she was lost when riding on a donkey, and he should realize, therefore, that this is a signal for him and his allies, the Goths, to commence their attack. Subsequently this does indeed happen; the invaders enter Gumlidata through the shaky fortifications, destroy the city, and save the girl.

Most significant about this account is that it is a story of captivity and an attempt to break out of enslavement. Unlike Adiel Amzeh, Eldag comes up with a workable plot, a scheme to save herself from slavery. As an instance of action and attainment, it stands in stark contrast to the distractions and digressions that cripple the scholar—a figure who is described as a "slave" to his work (p. 232E). This is also a segment of text that recovers various senses of plot mentioned earlier. The girl schemes as she takes the initiative to bring about a turn of events; her plot, moreover, is enacted at a particular portion of ground that is plotted out, as it were, on the Izla—the garment that functions as a kind of map for the Goths because it is shaped like the Valley of Cranes. These varied definitions of plot converge here to provide a counterpoint to Amzeh, who is not capable of carrying out a plan or breaking out of the narrow strictures of his life. He welcomes enclosed space; his universe is his house, and within that house, the book he has been writing constitutes his entire reality. At the end he trades this limited existence for the even narrower confines of the leper house, and he fails to reach out to a wider sphere of living by publishing his findings. (It should be noted that *le-hotsi la-or*—to publish—in the Hebrew means literally to bring out to light, so this phrase contributes to the opposition between enclosure and openness that functions throughout the story as a central thematic element.)

The Eldag episode then serves fundamentally as an example of a well-conceived, forward-moving plot and as a stimulus for speculation on how Amzeh might better have lived his life. In the classical novel, the subplot often suggests a different solution to the problems worked through by the main plot; it may serve as a way of illustrating and warding off the danger of short circuit, of too easy a solution, and in this way assure that the main plot will continue through to the end.[6] Here, by contrast, in a profoundly ironic text, this secondary, subordinate plot shows what the character might have done right. It presents the short circuit of decisive action that would ward off disabling distractions.

As this episode helps put into relief tensions between digression and linear plot, distraction and decisive action, it also emphasizes the central issue, discussed previously, of communicative circuit. The Eldag tale concentrates on communication. The Hun girl escapes enslavement, not through action alone, but by getting a message to her people, and so breaking out of her isolation. Her ingenuity at creating signs capable of conveying an urgent missive (the iconic reproduction of the valley in the form of the Izla/map, the transformation of the donkey into a visual message), undermines the conclusion Adah Eden reaches that story takes primacy over the teller. On the contrary, the act of transmitting and reaching an audience proves to be indispensable. The very fact that the story within a story functions as a principal organizing structure of the overall plot is significant in its own right. The nature of a frame story is to provide a context that subsumes another and serves as a referential framework for it. Any move from inner to outer tales suggests a movement of reference from fiction to reality, or from the remote to the immediate, and it also puts into relief the act of storytelling as a contractual relationship between narrator and narratee.

---

6. On the function of subplots, see Brooks (1984), p. 104.

In "Forevermore," concern with the process of transmitting narrative takes on overt prominence because of the central thematic opposition set up from the start: public recognition versus the worth of scholarship, the text itself and its audience. Here, by telling a story within a story, Agnon calls attention to the notion that narration is a preeminently social act that confers currency on stories society accepts as negotiable instruments. In other words, people listen to narrative, fictional or factual, which they perceive as meaningful and worthy of recognition. To survive, a story must have a listener. The manuscript about Gumlidata was making no impact on the world except in a severely circumscribed milieu. When Adiel Amzeh comes along, he functions dramatically as the one who, by reading, makes this story come to the attention of the current reader. By the same token, Adah Eden's anecdote about the count reminds the reader of much the same thing—it brings knowledge of the manuscript out into circulation, wider by one, than it had before. Her frame story, moreover, does not lead so much to information about the siege as to another narrative frame: how the count told his tales to others and under what circumstances. He had trouble preserving the story and succeeded only at the cost of limiting his audience to the lepers. The doubling of frame story within frame story can easily bring the reader not to Adah's conclusions—that the teller is less significant than the tale—but to a sense of regress. What remains invariable is the telling and the dependence of the tale on the teller.

Amzeh's essential problem is precisely that he fails at communication. This doesn't bother him, because he thinks he is engaged in something more worthwhile: the attainment of verifiable historical truth. He believes that the web of words in which he is tangled will lead him to fact and to decisive answers. However, his unquestioning faith in referentiality is misplaced. Ultimately the story about Gumlidata is of doubtful factuality. It is based on a book of chronicles, written to perpetuate a glorious, heroic version of events from the Gumlidatan point of view. Furthermore, both the narrator and Adah Eden say that everyone in the city died during the conquest, and this information puts into question the authority of the scribe or storyteller transmitting any account of those events.

The obtrusive use of *'ayin* and *gimmel* in the text as initial letters of multiple words complements this understanding of Amzeh's convictions as poor judgment and misguided faith in referentiality. The bizarre repetition of the letters has the pronounced effect of highlighting and reinforcing the artifice of the work as a whole. Heightening an emphasis on sound, the author calls attention to the words themselves that make up the text and disallows any perception of language as simply a medium to convey an extratextual reality. In this way Agnon deliberately imposes fictionality on all levels of the narrative and, significantly, on the chronicles of Gumlidata. Therefore, whereas Amzeh believes that his sources and research represent historical, empirical inquiry into facts about the phenomenal world, the reader realizes the all-encompassing textuality and antimimetic nature of his endeavor.

These issues come into play pointedly at a moment of crisis. When Adah Eden disrupts Amzeh's plans to meet with his patron, the scholar begins to stutter. That is, his words are broken off in the middle. Consequently her interpretation is met with yet another kind of breakdown that recapitulates in miniature the overall pattern of the plot: Once more, interruption is accompanied by emphasis on communicative failure. The stammering suggests Amzeh's surprise, of course, but it also suggests more. The new information introduced by the nurse, the revelation of new evidence about Gumlidata, serves as an indication that the scholar's work so far has not been firmly based in social fact or even well informed of all the pertinent existing evidence. Indeed, it is hinted, his book is itself a kind of empty language or stammering. Highlighting this impression Agnon plays on the root *g-m-g-m* (to stutter) as Amzeh's stutter draws attention to the same letters in *Gum*lidata. Similarly the narrative calls attention to the interplay of *'ayin* and *gimmel* at a moment when the root

'-l-g (to stammer) appears repeatedly.[7] This portion of the story also deals with translation and in so doing contributes to much the same conclusion. Based on conjecture and rearrangements of letters, not grounded in empirical proof, the scholar's theories prove to be largely a play of sounds, signifiers without established connection to signifieds. In short, his research has been exposed as an edifice of words, a verbal construct or fiction. However, instead of recognizing it as such—thanks to Nurse Eden's intervention—and reevaluating his entire enterprise, the protagonist dashes off to the leprosarium to acquire yet more information of dubious factuality. Lost in a world of endless learning, generating more and more readings and interpretations, Amzeh never escapes the circle of signs into historical fact. Intellectually he remains trapped in the prison house of language.

Making his predicament even worse, the communicative circuit he has neglected for the sake of this questionable pursuit of truth does not simply dissipate and disappear. The entire issue of communication reinscribes itself in the story at this point because the protagonist cannot operate in a social vacuum. Rather, he trades a healthy context for a more restrictive and devastating one. Amzeh, who fails to finish composing his version of Gumlidata's history because of constant revising, rereading, and reconsidering, at the end is faced literally with decomposition; he is threatened with contamination by that manuscript, which has been handled by generations of lepers. Disintegrating, falling apart from handling by generations of lepers, this writing more closely resembles pus on skin than ink on paper. In a grotesquely graphic conception of the transmissibility of narrative, Agnon here presents text as contagion.

The ending to "Forevermore" must be understood then to

---

7. The Hebrew reads: "Nit*'aleg* 'alav leshono ve-hithil me*gamgem* ma ma ma, im im shamati yafeh *gum gum gum* li … li didata" (p. 322, emphasis added here to indicate repeated configurations of letters). Later (p. 324) the narrative refers to "*tsehok 'ilgim*" and, in close proximity, the word "'*elg*adata," calling attention to the pattern *'-l-g.*

deviate from expectations of narrative conclusion as outcome
and closure. The outcome of events, of course, yields a failure to
come out, and the result is also to undermine any sense of resolution. On the one hand, the character's fate seems like an emblem of closure par excellence. Enclosed in the leper house,
Adiel Amzeh stays there forevermore, temporally and spatially
sealed off from the demands of society that he shunned. The
"ever after" of fairy tale and folklore, the convention of the perfect happy ending, remains the last word here. (The final sentence reads: "... he did not put his work aside and did not leave
his place and remained there forevermore.") And yet this denouement does not represent a state of renewed equilibrium, a
restoration of an original positive circumstance enriched by in-
terim adventures, events, and obstacles overcome. Instead
Agnon presents a built-in contradiction: a character who, in
search of ennobling wisdom, lives a degraded existence, and
who, finding an answer he sought with difficulty, has nonetheless
missed out on essentials and been seduced by trivialities. In short
the result here is an ongoing state of irresolution and finality
without termination, a state that suggests an abdication of
closure.

This conclusion is directed toward misreading by the narrator,
who sees Adiel Amzeh's end as fortuitous. Learning, the narrator
claims, "bestows a special blessing on those who are not put off
easily" (p. 249E). This evaluation should not be taken at face
value, though, not only because of Amzeh's straitened circumstances, but also because the narrative as a whole puts into relief
the limitations of this narrator's vision and the artifice with
which he imposes meaning onto events. His comments here, for
example, draw attention to the fact that he has set up a particular
design for the story from the start. As a result the text heightens
attention once again to narrators, in conversation with an audience, as ones who design plot. "Forevermore" thereby detracts
from the vision of story as something independent from the context of its own formulation. For example, this dynamic is evidenced most clearly by an aside the narrator makes, to the effect

that had Gebhard Guldenthal seen Adiel Amzeh at work, he might have observed the radiance of a man truly devoted to wisdom. These parenthetical remarks end as the narratorial voice says, "But you see my friend, for the sake of a little moralizing, I have gone and given away the ending at the very beginning of my story" (p. 234E). Only ostensibly has he given away the denouement—that is, that Amzeh will choose pursuit of knowledge over public recognition. In actuality, as has already been said, the ending turns out to be considerably more complex. The effect of the narrator's comment, then, is simply to point out that this figure has a particular meaning or moral in mind for his story (to wit: Wisdom is more precious than worldly success). The narrator makes evident his role as someone who shapes a text, who tries to tell a tale in order to convey a particular message and design.

The treatment of the ending is especially important because the moment of closure is a highly sensitive one in the structure of narrative. If plot grants meaning over time, endings enjoy special status as the legitimizing authority on which beginnings and middles depend for their retrospective meaning. Readers assume that the end of a story will confer understanding on what has come before, and they read in confidence that what remains to be read will restructure the provisional meanings of what has already been read. For this reason it is possible to speak of the "anticipation of retrospection" as a chief tool in making sense of narrative.[8] In his consciously anticipatory comment, Agnon's narrator makes this dynamic explicit and lays bare the armature of his narrative. The author, Agnon, thereby also puts into relief the artifice of his own construction of narrative, while calling attention to the very issue of narration as a dominant concern in the text as a whole.

These remarks have taken us, then, from reading along with Adiel Amzeh in order to discover the "whodunit" of Gumlidata's last days (that is, who laid the siege and where) to a

8. Brooks (1984), p. 23.

metanarrative reading that focuses on the nature of texts and narration. The first kind of reading—reading for the plot in a simplistic sense—is often assumed to be primary in fiction. To be
sure, readers of fiction always read at least in part to do detective
work, to construct a hypothetical *histoire* (that is, the narrated
events) out of the available *discours* (the narration of events). This
is the reason Todorov assigns privileged status to the detective
story as a genre.[9]

In that genre the work of detection is overtly present for the
reader, and it serves to reveal the as-yet-unrevealed story of a
crime. The two orders of the text, inquest and crime, clearly illustrate the distinction between *discours* and *histoire,* and this kind
of fictional pattern therefore lays bare the nature of all narrative.
Agnon's "Forevermore," though, suggests that reading as detective work is not enough; it is necessary but not sufficient. As the
story clearly delineates Amzeh's limitations in his strategies for
finding knowledge (that is, in his own detective work), "Forevermore" as a whole provides an alternative model of texts and
reading as a path to gaining wisdom. The reader is challenged to
ask why the fiction is built the way it is and what it conveys
thereby, rather than to give weight first and foremost to narrated
events. If we read for the plot, that is, to find out what happened
to Adiel Amzeh, we miss out on the strategies of deferring and
digressing, the crucial structures that put into relief important
facets of characterization here and that in themselves contribute
fundamentally to a thematic focus on textuality.

The story in effect offers an allegory of reading. In a sense all
fictional texts are about reading at some level, and many guide us
toward the conditions of their own interpretation. This work by
Agnon more directly than many other texts raises these questions, because it explicitly concerns a search for meaning, authority, closure, narratability, referentiality, and audience. As
such it invites the reader to be aware that one should not take

---

9. Todorov (1977).

narrators naively at their word, that it is important to be aware of the fact of narration, of who tells what to whom and why.

These ideas move us beyond the formalism of describing narrative organization to the issue of narrative desire: desire as a central thematic focus and desire as impetus for narrating. The two phenomena converge in "Forevermore," for this is a narrative replete with multiple narrators, circumstances of narration, and motivations to narrate: there is the count who told his story of the siege to express his gratitude to the lepers, and the nurse who, though a comically bumbling, rambling narrator and a dilatory agent of digressive plot, tells her tales to highly effective, pragmatic ends (by distracting Adiel Amzeh she succeeds in getting him to turn aside from his appointment with Guldenthal and donate magazines, books, almost his entire library to the leprosarium); there is Amzeh who suffers a pathological inability to get his story out; finally there is the author, who tells his own tale via digressions, distractions, and multiple narrators, at once dramatizing Amzeh's distractability, identifying with his protagonist's vagaries, and warning against them. The essential question then arises: why this complexity, why the indirection, the subtleties, the obfuscation? Agnon's text turns on the fundamental irony that an author who creates a caveat against the unreliability of narrators and their hidden motives should create such a slippery narrative, deliberately teasing his readers into oversimple and mistaken interpretations.

Partly this art must be seen as the expression of a personality that needs distance from people, that seeks always to be sly, elusive.[10] Deceits and ironies, hallmarks of Agnon's fiction, in "Forevermore" dramatize and stylistically recreate the thematic em-

---

10. Aberbach (1984) outlines a psychological portrait of Agnon that would justify this view. His study, however, proposes to establish parallels between the psychological makeup of the author and of the characters in his works. I would argue that careful distinction should be made between author and character, so the story should not be viewed (as Hochman [1970], for example, does) in terms of a simple *ars poetica* that supposes identification between Amzeh and

phasis on unreliable narration. In part, also, we should note that the undecidabilities of the text force the reader, like all narrators, to write a story, making sense out of the available evidence. Leaving the reader with the burden of decoding baffling events, reconstituting them in an interpretation, the text in this way generates a reenactment of tensions that are its own essential concern. The resulting story, the reader's story, must always be formulated with some uneasiness.

Lest my own reading of this text seem too pat or pretend to account for all the puzzling elements of "Forevermore," let me take note of yet another odd, disquieting irony. Perhaps the greatest undecidability of all, a condensation of previous tensions between in and out, text and world, occurs at the end of the text at the important moment of possible closure. Amzeh, locked away in the leprosarium, finds that other scholars have begun to publish his ideas and hypotheses. Though his book never reached the hands of the living, since no material objects are allowed to leave the leper house, somehow the information has leaked out. The narrator explains the phenomenon this way: "When a true scholar discovers a thing that is right, even if he himself is isolated and hidden away in the innermost chambers of his house, something of what he had found reaches the world" (p. 249E). This explanation again insists that transcendent truth is a supreme value that works its way out to society. Another reading is also possible. It could be that the ideas that occurred to Amzeh were not so special and occurred to others as well. In that case his life has been a waste, his sacrifice unnecessary. It may be, too, that the manuscript he pursued was not truly indispensable for his work. Given all the evidence up to this point, I am inclined toward the ironic reading of Adiel Amzeh, but I do not

---

Agnon. A more promising avenue of inquiry would be, in Brooks's formulation, to follow the "superimposition of [a] model of the functioning of the psychic apparatus on the functioning of the text" (Brooks [1984], p. 112)—in other words, to investigate both the nature of composition in a narrative and the motivation for the telling of a tale.

discount the possibility that at this point the text may begin to deconstruct itself. The impasses of meaning here threaten to dismantle the binary oppositions of transcendent truth/contextualized discourse that have guided my discussion till now. Perhaps the final details of the fiction collapse the categories of understanding fundamental to an ironic reading of the scholar's sacrifice.

By way of conclusion I would like to suggest as well that this text, in its production of complex and intricate plot, which to a large extent concerns plotting, is revelatory of Agnon, the author himself, as a shaper of narratives. Agnon is a writer known for his many tales—some personal and some collective or religious—that attempt to recover a lost world. Many exhibit nostalgia for a more traditional time or for childhood and a religious milieu that have disappeared. In this regard, to some degree, the author resembles his protagonist. By no means a ridiculously simplistic, laughably monomaniac Amzeh, Agnon is nonetheless a writer whose work throughout is marked by its preoccupation and fascination with the past. In "Forevermore" that whole kind of enterprise is reconsidered. Self-conscious about the issues at stake—the pitfalls attendant on a passion to recuperate the past in writing—the author both reveals and conceals himself at once, simultaneously exposing a dream and protecting it, announcing his cynicism and masking it with pieties.

Presenting the ludicrous scholar to provide comment on the function and possibilities of writing as a means to restore lost worlds, "Forevermore" therefore also offers a perspective on Agnon's brand of artistry, whose point of departure is the lack of sacred texts in modern life. This is an art that Agnon saw as an outgrowth of, but an inadequate substitution for, religion. Imaginative tales cannot pretend to replace sacred writing, but the telling of them becomes significant in an effort to maintain textual tradition, to draw on the sources, and to keep a genuinely Jewish Hebraic influence alive. Not a return to the past, such writing does justify the artist as a shaper of community. So, although the allusive reference to Ecclesiastes, "for whom do I work?"(p. 242E),[11] echoes with futility for Adiel Amzeh at the end of his story, for Agnon himself the question can be answered somewhat more positively, perhaps with doubt but without the same profound sense of grief. The author's complex relationship to his narration and plot construction in "Forevermore" clues the reader in to these issues, and this consideration of plot may serve as a point of departure to recuperate and reintegrate some of those major aspects of the text mentioned at the outset of this chapter but not specifically dealt with here: the uses of allusion, the confusion of sacred and profane in the imagery of the story, the deliberate but inconsistent invitation to allegorical reading, which fosters puzzlement about what kind of hermeneutics to pursue in explicating the text. The metanarrative reading is not incompatible, for instance, with an understanding of "Forevermore" as a satiric look at modern scholarship or secular fiction. Agnon may be expressing his reservations about both those endeavors as they grasp at excavatory knowledge—archaeological or historical—rather than seeking out the sanctity and spirituality imbued in tradition.[12] Viewing this story from the angle of plot is also not incompatible with an understanding that the text expresses a frustrated search for meaning. While Amzeh ascertains trivial answers to ease trivial dilemmas, his bigger problems go unsolved, and the perplexing uncertainties of the text as a whole defy easy answers. Because of the disallowing of simple allegory the narrative functions here—much in the mode of many Kafka narratives—as *aggada* without *halakha,* lore in search of law.[13] All of these considerations, as they emerge out of careful examination of plot in "Forevermore," may help illuminate Agnon's contradictory relation, as a modern writer, to tradition.

---

11. "lemi ani 'amel?" p. 334.

12. The shortcomings of scholars and writers is a persistent theme in Agnon's fiction.

13. This is Walter Benjamin's formulation of Kafka's aesthetic. For discussion see Alter (1977), pp. 60–61.

❧ 3 ❧

Negotiating Jewish History:
The Author, His Code,
and His Reader

Arnold J. Band

"I tell you, 'Rabbi Binyomin,' that Mendele's style is not the last word in Hebrew fiction."

In a retrospective article written in 1933, the addressee of this statement, "Rabbi Binyomin,"[1] recalls his meetings with Agnon in Jaffa in 1908–1911, when both were young, aspiring writers. In one memorable scene, the two are walking along the Mediterranean shore when Agnon protests that Mendele's style, for all its monumental stature, does not lend itself to the description of nuanced psychological states and, as such, is not "the last word in Hebrew fiction."[2] The implication, of course, is that he (Agnon) will do better. Radler-Feldman, recording this event after Agnon had published the four volumes of the first edition of his collected works in 1931, implies that Agnon had indeed succeeded in forging a new prose idiom in Hebrew, something

---

1. The Hebrew author Yehoshua Radler-Feldman.
2. Yehoshua Radler-Feldman, *Mishpehot soferim: partzufim* (Tel Aviv, 1960), p. 280.

that transcended Mendele, even though in 1908 when Agnon expressed these aspirations, "Rabbi Binyomin" thought his claims presumptuous.

Although the sequence of events in this reminiscence might not be entirely accurate, the statements and descriptions of personalities and sentiments have a ring of authenticity and coherence. Mendele, after all, was the giant of modern Hebrew prose fiction in those days, and every young writer had to confront this looming figure. Some aped him, but others like Brenner, Agnon, Gnessin, and Shofman found their own individual style and voice. "Rabbi Binyomin's" analysis of the situation is, in general, precise; Agnon's prodigious energies, his dandyish playfulness, his friendship with Brenner, the favorable reception of two of his Jaffa stories, "Agunot" (1908) and "Vehaya he-'akov le-mishor" (1911), are all attested to in many other sources of the period. What "Rabbi Binyomin" seems to fail to comprehend, however, is the complex seriousness of the young writer's aspirations.

When Agnon protests against Mendele, he is not merely seeking a more adequate linguistic medium to express psychological realism. Mendele's Hebrew style was the quintessence of the Europeanization of Hebrew prose. Despite his richly textured Jewish ambience and his dazzling mastery of Hebrew sources, his syntax and modes of narration are those one would recognize in the great nineteenth-century European authors. As a dedicated proponent of *Haskalah,* his use of this Europeanized style was, in itself, an ideological statement. In rebelling against Mendele, Agnon was not only exploring new modes of expression: He was making a statement about Jewish history.

We should not forget where and when he said what he said and wrote what he wrote. This was Jaffa of the Second Aliyah, the concrete embodiment of secular Zionist aspirations, young pioneers returning to the ancestral homeland to rebuild it from its desolation. Agnon was an anomaly in Jaffa. He was not a pioneer; he never worked on the soil; he came from the Galician province of the Austro-Hungarian Empire, not from Russia, the homeland of most pioneers in Jaffa. To fix Agnon's ideological position among his contemporaries of the Second Aliyah, it is interesting to compare him to the two other figures in "Rabbi Binyomin's" essay: "Rabbi Binyomin" himself had no doubts about the viability of the Zionist enterprise and was busily engaged in a variety of colonizing activities. On the other hand, the writer Josef Hayyim Brenner, also a Galician, was the paragon doubter but nonetheless chose to immerse himself in a host of political and literary activities in addition to writing his own fiction. Agnon's stance was marginal, fraught with ambiguities, and led to no easily definable commitment. His choice of both style and theme in this period was crucial for the development of his career and reveals much about his attitude toward Jewish history. What interests me in this chapter, therefore, are the ideological implications of the choice of his style.

The question of style emerges not only when we study a text but also when we address any of the large questions seriously. When asked to identify what is Agnon's forte as a writer of fiction, we are usually hard-pressed to answer. No careful reader would claim that Agnon's plots are particularly inventive, or that his characters are well-drawn and memorable. And although his psychological remarks are often insightful and his landscapes evocative, these narrative features would never suffice to justify the unflagging critical attention he has enjoyed. Agnon's oblique but demonstrably pervasive preoccupation with some of the more profound issues of modern Jewish life and his deft weaving of a texture of polysemous motifs generate a textual density that sustains repeated close reading. The latter, in turn, alerts the reader to what is specifically, unmistakably Agnonic: the playful dialogue the author conducts with his implicit reader through a carefully modulated narrative voice that speaks in an ingenious style that sounds like speech but is unlike any other discourse in modern Hebrew fiction.

Agnon's style has, to be sure, inspired numerous studies,

mostly tracing his sources in biblical or postbiblical literature. Frequently, this style is characterized as "midrashic," a term so vague and varied in common parlance as to be useless. One can, of course, identify the unmistakable "Agnonic" style as being derived from late-rabbinic models, that is, texts of the past three centuries deriving from rabbinic or Hasidic milieus in Eastern Europe, where the authors spoke Yiddish, which left its imprint on their Hebrew diction and syntax. Rather than trace sources, I would ask, Why did Agnon choose to adopt and cultivate this peculiar style that must convey to the sensitive Hebrew reader the connotations of the world of pious East European Jews? This question is, unfortunately, rarely raised today, for not only is Agnon's style routinely recognized as that of pious writers, but also many readers learn the stylistic norms of East European Jewry primarily through Agnon's writing. This style, however, was not the only one available to Agnon when he first adopted it in 1911 after several years of experimentation with other styles; it actually represents a radical departure from the developing norms of Hebrew style at that time. When we remember that such powerful models as Mendele, Brenner, Bialik, or Berdiczewski were still alive and publishing, and that the use of Hebrew, or even a particular type of Hebrew, was an ideological statement, Agnon's choice begins to assume its proper historical dimensions.

Both individual Agnonic texts and the totality of his fictional works (and, all the more so, his anthologies of traditional materials having to do with such matters as the Days of Awe, or the Revelation at Sinai, or Hasidic tales) are evidence of his "negotiations" with Jewish history. "Negotiation" and "appropriation" are two of the more colorful terms that have insinuated themselves into our critical vocabulary in the past decade and merit usage only upon examination and qualification. Usually they are employed when one wants to describe an author's use of material taken from earlier authors. By talking of "negotiation" or "appropriation," we both restore the author and treat him as an active agent rather than a passive receptor of "influences." Despite their often mindless faddishness, these terms represent a conceptual gain. This gain, however, might be offset by the potential metaphorical obfuscation: Because they derive from the world of property acquisition or capital exchange, they evoke overtones of their origins. I prefer "negotiation" to "appropriation," as the latter implies an act of domination, even violence, in which the object appropriated, here the text, is inert and cannot possibly resist or shape the act of appropriation. "Negotiation," in contrast, assumes that there is an active, ongoing process in which the "other side" is active. It forces us to remember what we often forget, that all texts have to be activated by a reader. The process of negotiation, then, is dynamic and complex. The author—Agnon, for instance—"negotiates" with a text that he has already activated by his reading. What makes the Agnonic text so intriguing is that a careful reading brings you to the conclusion that the author is supremely conscious of his negotiations with the text and, inasmuch as these are historical Jewish texts, the concrete manifestations of what we ordinarily call Jewish history, he is negotiating with Jewish history.

For the reader, then, reading an Agnonic text is also a "negotiation with Jewish history," and should be perceived as such. And since Agnon is so patently conscious of the historical contexts of his linguistic sources and fictive situations, we should also strive to acquire some expertise in these historical contexts. An awareness of this interpretive requirement should free us of some of the subjectivism that is an inevitable component of the interpretive act. In dealing with the text of an author so linguistically manipulative as Agnon, such awareness and added historical controls are not only advisable, they are imperative. Aside from the author's well-known habit of revising his texts for successive publications, we are forced to read his fictions through the voice of one of the most conflicted, yet controlled, narrative voices any modern writer has created. We should realize that almost every story has more than one published version, that the narrator's perspective—and personality—might change from work to work, from version to version of the same work, and even from phrase to phrase in the same sentence.

In suggesting that Agnon "negotiates with Jewish history," I do not imply that Agnon tried to render faithful representations of specific moments in Jewish history. The contrary is true; he was too shrewd a writer to succumb to that temptation. His writing career, we should remember, embraced one of the most turbulent periods in Jewish history. To have lived through that period in some of the most important centers of Jewish historical experience—Galicia, Jerusalem, Germany—and to survive it as a writer in control of his materials is, in itself, a tour de force of the human imagination. I would argue that Agnon succeeded in doing so precisely because he fashioned a mode of narrative discourse that was not based on the norms of Hebrew discourse that we usually associate with the regeneration of modern Hebrew literature. These norms, to be sure, could not be fashioned after Hebrew speech norms at the beginning of this century because few people spoke Hebrew then, even in *Eretz Yisrael* (the Land of Israel) of the Second Aliyah. Since, however, Hebrew was in an advanced stage of "revival" and had already established a viable modern literary tradition by 1905, there were what one might call evolving "quasi-speech" norms, and the major Hebrew prose writers strove to shape and/or approach those norms. In general, Hebrew writers from the last decade of the nineteenth century on linked Hebrew with the national revival movement and, specifically, the creation of a Hebrew community in Palestine. Agnon, in contrast, persisted in refining his highly literary style that enabled him to keep his distance from the worlds of experience that he wished to describe, to recast in his own distinctive language. Until we realize that this mannered style is both a resistance to the hegemony of a ruling culture and a device for containing the centrifugal, contradictory sentiments of the modernist sensibility, we will not fashion an adequate interpretive control.

In order to assess the import of Agnon's negotiation with Jewish history, I shall examine one of the stereotypes of Agnon research, the comparison drawn between his writings and those of Kafka. Since I have dealt with aspects of this comparison else-

where and for different purposes, I shall refer to my previous research on this topic to illustrate my argument.[3]

Agnon's name was first connected with Kafka's in the early
1930s. In 1931, Agnon published the first four volumes of the
"Berlin edition" of his collected works and thereby solidified his
reputation as a modern version of the traditional teller of Jewish
pious tales. In late 1932, he startled his readers by publishing a
new cluster of five stories, titled enigmatically *Sefer ha-ma'asim*
(The book of deeds). Most readers found them impenetrable, as
the stories suspended the realistic canons of time, space, and causality in ways which went far beyond even his most fantastic
quasi-Hasidic tales. Several critics who knew both German literature and the extent of Agnon's library suggested that he had
been reading Kafka. Though my recent studies have convinced
me that the picture was much more complex, that the text behind *Sefer ha-ma'asim* is probably Freud's *Traumdeutung* (*Interpretation of Dreams*) rather than Kafka's stories, the Kafka suggestion
was plausible.[4]

Kafka was, of course, not a well-known writer in the early
1930s, certainly not the oft-cited prooftext he is today, but the
attribution was logical, given the literary situation in Jerusalem
and Tel Aviv. By the late 1920s and early 1930s there had formed
in those two cities a colony of sophisticated German-reading
émigrés, many from Berlin and Prague, some of them Kafka's
close associates. Hugo Bergmann, for instance, came in 1920

---

3. Some of the material in the following pages can be found in a different context in my article "The Kafka-Agnon Polarities," in *The Dove and the Mole (Interplay 5)*, ed. M. Lazar and R. Gottesman (Malibu: University of Southern
California Press and Undena Publications, 1987), pp. 151–160.

4. My remarks on Agnon's reading of Freud's *Interpretation of Dreams* were delivered at two conferences: the Interuniversity Conference on Hebrew
Literature, Beersheba, February 1988, and the Agnon Centenary Conference,
Hebrew University, Jerusalem, June 1988. Since these were the first specific
connections between Agnon's writing and a text of Freud's, Agnon's text has
gained wide currency.

and was prominent in cultural circles; Leo Hermann, the editor of *Selbstwehr,* the Zionist newspaper published in Prague, which Kafka read faithfully, migrated in 1926. Among the refugees who came after the *Anschluss* and *Kristallnacht* were Max Brod, Kafka's friend and literary executor (1939), and the two Weltsches, Felix and Robert (1940). Together with such luminaries as Gershom Scholem, who came in 1923, and Martin Buber, who came in 1933—and, to be sure, many other lesser-known intellectuals—they formed one of the first centers of Kafkaists. Their personal libraries contained at least the three novels, published in the late 1920s, some of the short stories, and, if they left after the *Anschluss* or *Kristallnacht,* the first edition of *Gesammelte Werke,* 1936–1937. To be sure, those libraries contained many other treasures, such as the *Gesammelte Werke* of Sigmund Freud.

Agnon, though an *Ostjude,* was part of these circles because he had spent the period from 1913 to 1924 in Germany; he was an Austrian citizen because he came from Galicia; and he had shrewdly capitalized on the romanticization of the *Ostjude,* which began to surface in Germany in the first decade of this century. Although Agnon protested that he had never read Kafka except for "Der Verwandlung" ("Metamorphosis"), and that his wife read these works, he probably knew more than a little of Kafka and Freud since his wife read to him from these two writers in the 1930s.

When one observes both Agnon and Kafka from the perspective of general history, the comparison is far from gratuitous: Both were born in the 1880s (Kafka in 1883; Agnon in 1888) and reared in the homes of relatively successful businessmen, both in marketing, in the last decades of the Habsburg Empire. Whereas Kafka's Prague was far more Westernized than Agnon's Buczacz, connections of the latter with Lemberg and Vienna were well established; the latest newspapers were available and political life was intense. If one were to compare the news of the Jewish world published in *Selbstwehr,* the Zionist weekly whose centrality in Kafka's life has been demonstrated by Hartmut

Binder, with the Hebrew and Yiddish newspapers that Agnon was reading (and in which he published), one finds a remarkable commonality of content and concern: reports of Zionist activities; the settlement of Palestine; anti-Semitism, as in reports of pogroms in Russia; blood libels throughout all of Eastern Europe; and, between 1911 and 1913, the Beilis Trial, which reopened the festering wounds of the Dreyfus Affair. The improved communications available with the building of the railroads and the telegraph contributed mightily to the formation of an international sense of Jewish solidarity: the Kishinev pogrom (1903) or the death of Herzl (1904), for instance, were widely covered, and the news was immediately available in Jewish homes everywhere.

During Agnon's stay in Germany between 1913 and 1924, mostly in Berlin, but also in Leipzig, Munich, Frankfurt, and Bad Homburg, the intellectual circles of our two writers actually intersected in some places. Agnon probably read "Der Verwandlung" during this period, and it is inconceivable that Kafka did not come across the name of Agnon, as the latter was very popular in the circles of German Jews who were Zionists and disposed to harbor a strange nostalgia for anything that smacked of *Ostjudentum,* as manifested in Buber's *Der Jude.* The latter certainly reached Kafka, who published in it "Ein Bericht für eine Akademie" (A report for an academy) in 1917. Agnon published six stories in *Der Jude* between 1917 and 1924, several of which had been translated from the Hebrew manuscript by Gershom Scholem. One of the six, "Aggadat ha-sofer" ("Die Erzählung vom Toraschreiber" in its German translation),[5] appeared in the same volume, though not in the same issue, as "Ein Bericht für eine Akademie." Agnon also published stories in three anthologies that were very popular in the same circles: (1) *Chad Gadja: Das Pesachbuch,* ed. Hugo Bergmann (Berlin, 1914); (2) *Treue: Eine Judisches Sammelschrift,* ed. Leo Hermann

---

5. "The Story of a Torah Scribe."

(Berlin, 1915); and (3) *Das Buch von den Polnischen Juden,* ed. S. J. Agnon and A. Eliasberg (Berlin, 1916).

The grounds for comparison between Kafka and Agnon are historically attested. We should not, however, rush into the facile comparisons that usually assert that Kafka "influenced" Agnon because some of his most significant works were published in German in the period 1912–1914 and Agnon spent the years 1913 to 1924 in a German-speaking environment. Agnon had, in fact, written a story in Yiddish in 1907 with the intriguing name "Toten-Tants," which manifested many of the calculated indeterminacies of Kafka's mature style—and this before Kafka had published anything. Both writers had read widely in neoromantic German and Scandinavian authors; both had read and admired Dostoyevski and Flaubert. Although grounds for comparison exist, historical research suggests that we should avoid misleading and simplistic notions of "influence." There are, to be sure, major differences between these two writers, as there are between any two writers. The major difference in their backgrounds was their mastery of the texts and texture of Eastern European Jewish life. In this crucial area, Agnon was the prodigiously erudite insider, whereas Kafka was the sympathetic, perceptive outsider. The difference, I shall demonstrate, manifests itself most sharply in their attitudes toward language.

This essential difference did not seem to trouble many critics, even the prestigious Hebrew critic, Barukh Kurzweil—also a Prague Jew. In many articles and books published in Israel, Kurzweil argued that under the deceptively pious surface of Agnon's prose lurk serious religious doubts. He compared Agnon repeatedly to other modern writers such as Kafka, Musil, and Joyce; more than any other student of Agnon's prose, he disabused the Hebrew reader of the naïve view of Agnon that prevailed through the 1940s. Kurzweil correctly noted the obvious fact that although Kafka was only marginal to the Jewish tradition, Agnon was fully in the tradition, despite all his doubts. And yet, by slighting the differences in attitude toward language— and their implications—Kurzweil essentially constricted and subverted the grounds for comparison. Furthermore, his critical perspective was usually theologically oriented and deliberately avoided literary history.

Following Kurzweil, many critics have offered lavish comparisons between Kafka and Agnon. We should, however, establish some guidelines for research in this area by defining what is possible and productive. What, we should ask, are the perimeters of our investigation? Do we compare—or contrast—all of Agnon with all of Kafka? Obviously this is impossible because much of Agnon bears no resemblance whatsoever to Kafka's normative mode of expression. Even if we were to go beyond the twenty-odd stories of *Sefer ha-ma'asim* (ordinarily recognized as "Kafkaesque," though my recent research indicates that it is rather more Freudian) to include such formidable pieces as "Shevu'at emunim" ("Betrothed"), "Ido ve-'enam" ("Ido and Enam"), "Ad 'olam" ("Forevermore"), "Hadom ve-khiseh" ("The Stool and the Throne"), and the "kelev meshugah" ("mad dog") portions of the novel *Temol shilshom* (Only yesterday)—altogether some seven hundred pages of dense fiction—we would still be left with several thousand pages of stories, novels, quasi-historical compilations of tales, collections of rewritten customs intermixed with anecdotes, eulogies, commemorative pieces, and so on. When we speak of Agnon's "resemblance" to Kafka, we are actually referring to about 10 percent of the former's work.

To focus on the problem of style choice and its implications we turn to two stories, one by each writer, both first published in 1912—not that these stories are thematically related, but that each, in its own way, was crucial in the artistic development of the author: Agnon's "Vehaya he-'akov le-mishor" ("And the Crooked Shall Become Straight"), and Kafka's "Das Urteil" ("The Judgment"). In each case, the story represents a "breakthrough"—to use Politzer's term concerning Kafka—a breakthrough from fragments and experimentation to a sudden mastery involving decisions regarding stylistic and thematic features that mark the author's work for the rest of his career.

Kafka's "Das Urteil," written during the night of September 22–23, 1912, deals with the clash between a son, Georg Bendemann, and his seemingly ailing, aged father, who, by the end of the story, condemns his son to death by drowning. Bound by this injunction or command (*Urteil*), Georg jumps off the bridge near their apartment. In this story we already find the seemingly lucid sentence that, upon examination, is often indeterminate; the obsession with guilt and trials; the subject-object inversion; the varied and often contradictory identifications; and the unique fusion of disparate experiences—all characteristic features of Kafka's art.

Here, as in some of Kafka's other well-integrated stories, a central, generalized concept is presented as the title, for example, "The Judgment" or "Metamorphosis," and the narrative is a taut examination of the term, situation by situation. The term may have several mutually contradictory meanings, and the story is then a narrative concretization of the frustrating, yet exhilarating, complexities of language. Elsewhere, I have traced the term *Urteil* to both the Jewish High Holiday Prayer Book and the famous Beilis Trial (1911–1913). Echoes of the Rosh Hashanah or Yom Kippur service illuminate the process of judgment, the figure of the father or of all systems of authority, which, by their very nature, must fail, despite their oppressiveness. Where the term *Urteil* appears in the service, it is attributed to the divinity envisaged as a domineering king and judge of the world, the source of all authority and thus of guilt, too. Muffled echoes of the Beilis Trial can be found in the text: the friend in Russia, the scene of an overturned shop, the priest raising his hand, the obsession with unmotivated guilt. Given Kafka's family background and his recently rekindled Jewish consciousness, an event so central to the consciousness of Prague Jewry as the Beilis Trial in Kiev could not have left him unaffected. Identification with Mendel Beilis, or even a remote though prolonged observation of his plight, could have provided Kafka with the validation of his own feelings of insecurity and loneliness, an objectification of his oedipal torment, corroboration of his doubts about the validity and viability of language, and a moral justification for the be-wildering dialectic between self-corrosive guilt and subtle im-posture, which marks so many of his protagonists.

In this story, as in most of his stories and novels, Kafka scrupu-lously suppresses any reference to specific persons, places, or events. When a specific place is named, Russia, for instance, it is not as a realistic item but as a symbolic detail away from the pres-ence of the protagonist. The German also avoids reference to recognizable literary texts; it evokes no historical echoes. This "clean" style is the product of deliberate artistic choices: the tight, Flaubertian technique that leaves nothing to choice; the plot strategies that take the reader from an apparently bourgeois setting into the abyss lurking beneath it; in all, a departure from the limitations of realistic prose narrative.

Agnon, in writing "Vehaya he-'akov le-mishor," also made several decisions concerning his craft that determined the direc-tion of his writing for the rest of his long career. Though six years younger than Kafka during the writing of this crucial story, he had already published about seventy pieces in Hebrew and in Yiddish, both in Buczacz and Jaffa. Most of these were, to be sure, embarrassingly clumsy and were published only because the editor of a provincial newspaper often has to fill space. Those published in Jaffa attest to experiments in more serious writing, usually macabre, neoromantic tales of frustrated love, bizarre deaths, strange women—all conveyed in an agitated, often lush Hebrew prose style. Agnon himself obviously realized that this was not the medium he was seeking since, after the success of "Vehaya he-'akov le-mishor," he scrapped most of what he had previously written and either rewrote or totally discarded every line he had published. Few of these seventy items were ever re-published in the many collections of his works.

Instead of paring down contemporary prose style to the threshold of meaning as Kafka would do, Agnon adopted the late-rabbinic style his grandfather might have used, but kept it under scrupulously tight control. The lexical, morphological, and phrase syntax are clearly late rabbinic. The sentence, however, is an ingenious fusion of the modern and the traditional: Although carefully measured and modern in its strategems, it nevertheless echoes the syntax of more folkish genres, the Hasidic tale, for instance. The Hebrew reader cannot escape the fusion of these two registers, the traditional and the modern. In that Agnon deliberately shaped this style after experimenting with other styles prevalent in his youth and after the massive efforts by Mendele Mokher Sefarim[6] to Europeanize Hebrew prose, his choice of a style that was historically regressive in certain aspects implies a deliberate literary and ideological position. In that no Hebrew writer can escape consciousness of the various historical strata of the Hebrew language that are present and meaningful in modern Hebrew prose, linguistic choice involves some sort of attitude toward specific periods in Jewish history and what they mean in the modern period. For instance, the choice of a biblicizing style by *Haskalah* writers implied a revolt against rabbinical norms, whereas the choice of a composite classical rabbinic fused with biblical style by Mendele implied a distancing from *Haskalah* norms. Agnon, whose knowledge of Hebrew of all periods was prodigious, was obviously conscious of the historical provenance and implication of any phrase or syntactical structure he might use. The "negotiation" with Jewish history is obvious in every line. Agnon could thus generate the tension he sought between historical-linguistic resonance (so important in an ancient, text-oriented culture) and a controlled reticence, which often conceals more than it tells. The sensitive reader is thus forced to share the implied author's ambivalence about the world he has chosen to describe.

The technique worked wonders even in the first story in which it was used: "Vehaya he-'akov le-mishor." The author faced a crucial choice in writing this story: In the society described, mid-nineteenth-century Galicia, the norms of traditional piety and the bourgeois ethic are at odds. The hero,

---

6. Shalom Jacob Abramowitz, 1835–1917.

Menashe Hayyim, a pious shopkeeper of some means, is forced into bankruptcy by a new competitor. To recoup his capital, he reluctantly takes to the road as an itinerant beggar armed with a letter of recommendation certifying his identity, his former position in society, and his rectitude. This seemingly bizarre technique for recovering lost capital was not unheard of in earlier centuries but had become the butt of satire by the nineteenth century. Begging for funds even for acceptable charities like family support and dowries for indigent brides were stock subjects of satire in the works of such seminal authors as Mendele. Agnon wrote his story against the background of Mendele's works, which had been published in a three-volume edition the previous year. Agnon's story is thus a deliberate deviation from Mendele's narrative technique: It is more attentive to psychological realism or to bourgeois attitudes and strives to achieve effects that are less formally rabbinic, less balanced in their syntax. By refusing to avoid both late-rabbinic or Hasidic locutions and Yiddish speech patterns, he shaped an ambiguous, flexible style that does not let the reader know exactly what the author thinks about Menashe Hayyim's beggary, which is kept in the background while the hero's reactions to situations are foregrounded. With this style Agnon could fuse the pious with the bourgeois and neutralize the satirical Mendelean bite.

Since Menashe Hayyim is conceived as a person and not a type, he can lose both status and identity, themes Agnon learned from his reading in European literature. The hero succumbs to temptation once he has recouped some of his money and sells his letter to another beggar. As one might anticipate, he then loses his money and all his possessions and must return to the road to beg, sans letter of recommendation. The beggar who bought the letter naturally dies and is buried as Menashe Hayyim: The latter's wife, now a widow, remarries and bears children, which she could not do before when married to Menashe Hayyim. When the hero finally returns home, he finds his wife both married and a mother.

Here, too, Agnon dwells upon the conflict inherent in the situation: According to Jewish law, Menashe Hayyim should reveal that he is alive, thus embarrassing his wife and condemning her child to bastardy; but since he loves his wife—a bourgeois-romantic sentiment—he leaves town beset by the guilt of his concealment. He spends the last days of his life living in a cemetery, where, by chance, he finds the cemetery guard inscribing his name on a handsome gravestone that his wife, thinking that the beggar carrying the letter was indeed her husband, had ordered to memorialize him. Several days later, happy in the thought that his wife still loved him and that he had resisted the temptation to reveal the truth, thereby ruining her life, Menashe Hayyim dies and the guard, who knew the story, places over his grave the stone ordered by his wife for the beggar's grave, which she thought was his.

Even in bald plot outline, this novella does not sound like the pious tale it was taken to be by most critics for over thirty years: The quasi-rabbinic style and the pious milieu succeeded in deflecting the reader from topoi obvious today, such as the loss of identity and the descent into hell, let alone the ambiguous ending in the graveyard or the hero's impotence. Kurzweil noticed in the early 1950s that there are, indeed, many discordant elements in the story; but following his theological bias, he read the story and much of modern Hebrew literature as a literary manifestation of secularism. The story, for him, implies an accusation against the cruelty of God, who lets the hero descend into a world of chaos for no glaring sin, if any at all. The hero is forced to leave his home and wife and to depart on a journey from which there is no return, since his return can be effected only by a miracle. But there are no miracles today.

Some fifteen years later I argued that Kurzweil did not address himself to the totality of the story, to the title, which—taken from Isaiah 40—implies that "the crooked is made straight," and to the ending, which seems to vindicate the hero and restores the reader's confidence in the possibility of justice in this world. Menashe Hayyim does die happy in the knowledge that he has withstood temptation (to reveal his true identity: that he was still alive) and has been rewarded with the two gifts most important to him, after he had despaired of ever recouping his fortune and his status: assurance of his wife's continuing love for him and confidence that he would have his posterity even if it were merely his name on a tombstone.

More important, Kurzweil, like most critics, has not come to grips with the implications of Agnon's choice of this peculiar style, with what I call his "negotiation" with Jewish history. If we consider the mode of production crucial for an interpretation of the work of art, we must account for this choice, which changed the direction of his artistic enterprise. After four years of experimentation in a neoromantic style with themes taken from the world of Jaffa where he lived, he abandoned both his stylistic and thematic course. He obviously realized that the neoromantic direction did not afford him the opportunities to confront the cultural and psychological problems that possessed him or to exploit his prodigious knowledge of Hebrew. Ultimately, these Jaffa stories were embarrassingly self-indulgent, even frivolous, and remained so unless recast in his new style. (Many, as I have said, were simply discarded.) Here the contrast with Kafka is instructive. Kafka selected situations that were to him intolerable, or absurd, or comically grotesque and struggled to fashion an unmediated linguistic medium, contemporary yet timeless, concrete yet constantly plumbing the depths of human consciousness. Agnon's style beginning with "Vehaya he-'akov le-mishor" immediately directs the reader to a world of texts and textuality, a specific textuality at that, one that embodies in all its features a traditional, recognizable milieu. No competent reader of Hebrew could conceivably miss the multifarious implications of this style.

Realizing he could never fashion a neutral text, "free" of referentiality to previous texts—for such was the nature of the Hebrew language in the beginning of the century and is, to a lesser degree, even today—Agnon fashioned an artful pastiche of an older style so convincing that it took most readers thirty years to realize that under the "pious" text of the novella lay a subtext that qualified, ironized, or even subverted the text. The seemingly pious text can thus be used for a variety of purposes: as a mask hiding or modifying the author's bold or revelatory sentiments on religion or sensuality; or as a mediating barrier that allows the author to distance himself from too direct and immediate responses to the dynamic, demanding events of contemporary Jewish history. Without such a text, Agnon's "negotiation" with Jewish history would have been impossible, since he, as a writer of fiction, would have been overwhelmed by the flood of events.

Though criticized for this style by such formidable figures as Berdiczewski and S. Tzemah, Agnon succeeded admirably in creating a voice that allows for a wide range of authorial attitudes toward the text and the situations created, a subtle modulation between authorial and narrative voice, hence the possibility of a variety of "unreliable" narrators. Applied to the stories that most closely resemble those of Kafka, the manneristic style adds another level of indeterminacy. If, furthermore, one were to speak of Kafka and Agnon in terms of self-referentiality and the concomitant "play" of signification, one could say that Kafka creates the space for "play" by precluding clear signification of the represented world, and Agnon creates space for "play" by precluding clear signification of the textual world. Again, it is the artist's deliberate choice of style that makes all the difference. Two narrative situations may be thematically identical, but if they are conveyed in radically different styles, their impact on the reader has likewise to be radically different.

4

"Mad Dog" and Denouement in *Temol shilshom*

Anne Golomb Hoffman

Agnon's novel *Temol shilshom* (Only yesterday) includes a theme in which a young man paints the words "mad dog" on the back of a stray mutt; the dog then wanders around Jerusalem in search of a reader who can decode for him the mysterious inscription on his back, all the while terrorizing the pious inhabitants of the city's Mea Shearim section. Eventually, in a poetic justice whose logic we shall consider, the dog bites Yitzhak Kummer, the young man who painted the words on his back, and causes that young man's death. That death, which brings the novel to a close, is linked to the coming of rains that end the drought that has been plaguing Jerusalem.

Although this may all seem quite mad, it is important to add that the novel is set in the period of the Second Aliyah, during the years 1905–1914. It captures so well the atmospheres of Jerusalem, Jaffa, the early agricultural settlements, as well as the lure of ideology and the promise of renewal that Zionism offered to the youth of the period, that it has been heralded for its importance as a "social novel."[1]

---

1. Kurzweil considers *Temol shilshom* to be "the most important and successful effort in the area of the social novel in our new literature" (Kurzweil, "Temol shilshom," p. 216). See also Shaked, *Ha-sipporet ha-'ivrit* 2: 206.

Yitzhak Kummer, the protagonist of *Temol shilshom,* leaves his father and siblings in Eastern Europe in order to journey to the Land of Israel to become a pioneer. He arrives in Jaffa and joins up with his peers, most of whom more or less fail to find the work and renewal they seek. In what appears to be a somewhat regressive move, Yitzhak eventually ends up in the extremely pious Jerusalem neighborhood of Mea Shearim, where he has the encounter with the dog already mentioned.

The critic Dan Miron remarks on the incomprehensibility of the ending of *Temol shilshom,* commenting that the conjunction of Yitzhak's death with the end of the drought is more in keeping with a pagan notion of sacrifice than it is with Judaic values. Arnold Band offers a persuasive argument with respect to the painful disproportion between Yitzhak's negligible "sins" and the severity of his death as punishment by noting that even though the novel is set in the early years of this century, Agnon wrote most of it during the years 1943–1945, when the signs of the destruction of European Jewry were unmistakable. From this perspective, the irrationality of Yitzhak's senseless death (the sacrifice of this latter-day Isaac) is a mere reflection of the larger insanity of the Holocaust. I find Band's observations to be utterly persuasive, although I must note that his reference to extra-literary events contemporary with the writing of the novel points up rather than resolves the problem of closure. Miron and Band remain uncomfortable with the ending, but Band's discussion at least offers us an argument from history that provides a context for the painful disproportion of the ending.[2]

Now there is a further problem to be considered here, and that is the puzzle or contradiction in Yitzhak Kummer's death

---

2. In addition to the history of readers' discomforts with closure, the history of the manuscript of the novel points as well to the author's discomforts with the relation of the two plots—that of Yitzhak and that of the dog, Balak. See Sarah Hagar's account of the development of the novel out of the stories of Yitzhak and of Balak, with varying degrees of emphasis and ascendancy accorded to each (Hagar, "'Temol shilshom': hithavut ha-mivneh ve-ahduto").

from a dog bite given by a dog that may or may not be rabid, but that bears the *inscription* "mad dog" painted by the protagonist himself for no apparent reason. Is the dog rabid? Critics have taken the dog's condition for granted,[3] but the question of causality cannot be answered in terms of veterinary medicine or animal psychology. Rather than attempt to conventionalize the novel, it is worth a closer look at the relation of the inscription— "mad dog" or *kelev meshugah*—to the creature that bears it on his back, and the relation of that creature—the dog as text—to the various characters, "readers," we might call them, that he encounters in his wanderings through Jerusalem.

If we examine the position in the text of the onset of the dog Balak's "symptoms," we find it follows upon an extended discussion of the dissemination of that same Balak as text; by this, I mean the account of the subjection of the writing on his back to endlessly unfolding interpretations. A little background here: The critic Bar-Adon points out the centrality of the Hebrew language to Agnon's conception of the Zionist idea and the life of the nation. He argues as well that Agnon perceived a danger to Hebrew's emergence as a language of daily use, central to national identity, amid the languages (French, German, English) that were competing for ascendancy at the time of the Second Aliyah. Bar-Adon has shown the dog to be the key to a sociolinguistic critique, centering on the disputes over the revival of Hebrew and the relation of Hebrew to other languages in the years before the First World War, that is, the period in which the novel is set. In fact, it is possible to construct a walking tour of Jerusalem out of the dog's wanderings, one that would cover the territory of this political-cultural struggle. The dog as a walking

---

3. Barzel, for example, notes that a mad dog will bite and kill (*Bein Agnon le-Kafka,* p. 225); he observes, "The dog in the tradition of Israel is an animal connected to prey and impurity ... the dog, as Agnon understood from his childhood, in contrast to the cat or the rooster, for example, was known to be an outdoors creature, not a domestic animal" (p. 223).

text passes by "readers" in the novel who belong to the constitu-
ent communities of *Eretz Yisrael,* the Land of Israel. Take, for example, the Frenchman, principal of the French "Alliance"
School, who reads the writing on the dog's back from left to
right and calls the dog "Balak" as a result of that misreading.

At one point in his wanderings through the Mea Shearim section of Jerusalem, the dog Balak encounters a sermonizing
preacher, R. Gronam Yekum Purkan, who places the dog in a
talmudic context in order to make the dog the reading of the
generation and the vehicle for his exhortation of the crowd.[4]
"The face of the generation is like the face of a dog" (*Temol
shilshom,* pp. 585–586), he declares, citing a talmudic source
with the passionate conviction that grows out of the speaker's
confidence in his control of text and audience. But in the midst
of this fire and brimstone sermon in which he uses the dog as
mashal, or example, the *mashal* itself "takes on skin and bones" in
a sudden materialization of the text that suggests a writing out of
control, and, in fact, the subject of the interpretation asserts its
primacy over the interpreter, as the barks of the dog make themselves heard over and above the shouts of the preacher.

When the attention of our protagonist Yitzhak is finally
drawn to the writing on the back of the dog that has been terrorizing the pious inhabitants of Mea Shearim, he dismisses it as a
writing that he himself produced, a text that he controls: "And
are we obliged to believe everything that is written?" he asks.

---

4. Sanhedrin 97a: "It has been taught, R. Judah said: In the generation when
the son of David comes, the house of assembly will be for harlots, Galilee in ruins, Gablan lie desolate, the border inhabitants wander about from city to city,
receiving no hospitality, the wisdom of scribes in disfavor, God-fearing men
despised, people [the face of the generation] be dog-faced, and truth entirely
lacking. ... It has been taught, R. Nehorai said: In the generation when
Messiah comes, young men will insult the old, and old men will stand before
the young [to give them honor]; daughters will rise up against their mothers,
and daughters-in-law against their mothers-in-law. The people shall be dog-
faced, and a son will not be abashed in his father's presence."

"But I'll tell you, I myself wrote on his hide, and I know that he's a healthy dog, because if he were mad, I wouldn't have had anything to do with him" (p. 159). But the "text" is out of control now: Yitzhak's dismissal of any danger coincides precisely with the onset of "madness" in the dog. Balak begins to "doubt his sanity" (p. 591) just as concerns about him are allayed by Yitzhak's words. In effect, the writing asserts its independence of its putative author. The result is something of a comedy of readers, as texts (canine, talmudic, homiletic) run amok.

The dog stimulates activity in the novel that surrounds questions of language, the stability of meaning, the capacity of writing to name a thing. Here are some of the directions it goes in: "Pnei ha-dor ki-fnei ha-kelev" (The face of the generation is like the face of the dog); the word play of *kelev* and Balak; the novel cites the practice of tying notes of excommunication onto tails of black dogs, even once writing the actual words of the ban—*Epikoros muhram u-menudeh* (banned and excommunicated heretic)—on the fur of a number of dogs in order to cast out a reformer (p. 276). Newspapers battle in their reports on the dog and their efforts to interpret the significance of the canine phenomenon, so much so that when the Jaffa papers take up the case, their readers assume that the account of the dog is an "allegory" and wonder how to "learn the hidden [meaning] from the explicit," with the result that "the number of interpretations was the same as the number of inhabitants of the city" (p. 459). Along with the obvious satire of readers/interpreters, the dog's wanderings suggest the instability of any text, the breakdown of the kind of authoritarian writing the pious men of Jerusalem espouse and carry out in their posting of excommunications.[5]

---

5. An example of this writing can be found on page 461 of the novel, where the text refers to the writ of excommunication issued against schools teaching in Hebrew. Avraham Holtz has identified Agnon's source for the language of the excommunication as a writ issued in 1914. My thanks to Professor Holtz for sharing this information with me.

The dog violates authorized usages of writing, acting out the upheaval of meaning and authority that such paternal writings are meant to exclude and suppress, and defeating the efforts of two men of Jerusalem, the preacher R. Gronam and the fanatical R. Faysh, to anchor meaning in a text. The sermonizing of R. Gronam and the excommunicating activities of R. Faysh are terminated abruptly in encounters with the dog. This radical loss of speech testifies to their loss of power to nominate, denominate, name, and exclude when they are confronted with the signifier cut loose, the "mad" dog roaming the alleys of Jerusalem.

The subversive and disruptive nature of this inscription—itself the product of an idle impulse on the part of Yitzhak as its author—prompts, perhaps, an inquiry into the intergenerational world of the novel. The narrative voice in *Temol shilshom* is ostensibly allied with Yitzhak and his youthful peers in a manner that connects with the historical context of the novel, that is, the generation of young people who left Eastern Europe for Palestine imbued with the romance of Zionism.[6] This peer sense extends into a pervasive discomfort with the older generation. Yitzhak's intergenerational encounters fall into a virtually paradigmatic alignment of Jerusalem with pious elders and the concept of *Yerushalayim shel ma'alah* (the heavenly Jerusalem) as opposed to the young men who have come to work the land in its physical being, as we can see in this passage early in the novel:

> The old man asked Yitzhak, "What are you doing here?" Said Yitzhak to him, "I am travelling to Eretz Yisrael." The old man was amazed: "And is it the way of a youth to go to the Land of Israel?" Said Yitzhak to him, "To work her land I am going."

---

6. It is well to bear in mind that "for a majority of the 30,000 Jews who departed for Palestine in the Second Aliyah years between 1905 and 1914, Labor Zionism ... was the catalyst," while at the same time it has been estimated that possibly 80 percent of those who made aliyah "returned to Europe or continued on to America within weeks or months of their arrival" (Sachar, *A History of Israel,* pp. 72–73).

The old man became even more amazed. "Is not the Land of Israel made up entirely of synagogues and houses of study? Is not the Land of Israel exclusively for prayer, so what does working the soil have to do with heavenly requirements?" He had figured out that this young man was from the group of the Zionists who were seeking to tear the land out of its holiness and to make it like all other lands. He began to complain about Yitzhak, in the manner of the elders of Israel of that generation, who looked upon us as if we had come, heaven forbid, to turn the world to heresy. (p. 32)

Not only does this passage underscore the departure of the youth from the way of the fathers, but also as it unfolds, the alliance of narrator with protagonist brings to the fore the oedipal rebellion, which supplies the generation's identification of itself.

The opening of the novel, in its delineation of Yitzhak's youthful activities and aspirations as a Zionist, suggests the definition of character through ideology, at least superficially. Ideology here organizes character and names the subject on a conscious level. At the same time, in its portrayal of Yitzhak as naïve and yet inscrutably death-drawn, *Temol shilshom* demonstrates the opacity of the subject in ways that dissolve the certainty of conceptions based on the transparency of consciousness. The narrative voice tells Yitzhak's story without necessarily comprehending the direction it takes, in a manner that suggests the generation's noncomprehension of itself. Yitzhak is the function of a shift—ideological, geographical, political—from Diaspora to Zion. He attempts to affiliate himself with—literally, to become the son of—Zionism. But there is an excess here; there is more going on than can be subsumed into the name, the noun *tzioni,* or Zionist.

Temol shilshom is motivated by a search for identity through the father that produces a series of substitutions; its underlying premise is the failure of the Diaspora father. From one angle, in acceding to his son's schemes, the Diaspora father fails to provide for his son's passage through the Oedipus. Or, looked at from a different angle through the biblical text of the *'akedah*—the sacrifice of Isaac—to which Yitzhak's name (Isaac) alludes, we could say that the father sends the son out to an *'akedah,* or sacrifice, from which he fails to rescue him.

Yitzhak's adoption of or affiliation with Zionism suggests a first effort at paternal substitution. The failure of the substitute "father" can be seen in Yitzhak's gradual disenchantment with the Zionist functionaries, so dazzling to him from the distance of exile, whom he meets first in Europe and then in Jaffa.

Within the novel's opening paragraph, the desire to rebuild the Land of Israel from its destruction and to rebuild oneself through it produces a biblical vision of the land, laborers returning at dusk to sit, one man under his grapevine, another beneath his fig tree, gathering his wife and sons and daughters around him. This vision of the Promised Land offers a radiant alternative to the poverty and impotence of the Diaspora family. What is striking here is the language of "return," derived certainly from the heart of Jewish longings for Zion, but coming from a youth for whom the journey constitutes just as much a departure, a most radical break from the world of his father. Yitzhak imagines a "return" to a world he has never known, or, more accurately, the "return" frames an attempt to enter a family romance announced on the first page of the novel. (The imaginary nature of his wishes becomes clear later on in the novel when Yitzhak visits a *moshav,* an agricultural settlement named Ein Ganim, whose workers bring to life his romantic vision, with some significant modifications: These workers hold fast to their vision and integrate it into the world through labor and self-sacrifice.)

Temol shilshom is a large and panoramic novel that takes in the social scene of a period in the development of the State of Israel. And yet, like the account of the aliyah of Yitzhak Kummer, it contains its end in its beginning. Although Yitzhak is ostensibly seeking to build and be rebuilt through work on the land, his efforts can be read at the same time as a drive to return to origins. One begins to suspect that Yitzhak seeks not so much the missing father as he does absorption into something larger than him-

self that will relieve him of the challenge of an individuality he
has so far resisted.[7]

Consider for example the image of Zion that reveals itself in
the structure of Yitzhak's expectations. On board ship on the
way to the Promised Land, Yitzhak is asked by an old man:
" 'You have relatives in the Land of Israel?' Said Yitzhak to him,
'Who needs them, all of Israel are friends, all the more so in the
Land of Israel' " (p. 33). Yitzhak's reply is intelligible in terms of
the rhetoric of the day, but we should not overlook the manner
in which it shapes a primitive set of expectations, sidestepping or
ignoring actual heterogeneity. Indeed, the text notes that
Yitzhak feels "orphaned" (*meyutam*) on arrival, when he sees the
other immigrants meet their relatives (p. 39). Strikingly, moreover, this experience of feeling "orphaned" on arrival is succeeded immediately by denial, as Yitzhak comments to himself
on the young men who take his bags at the harbor, using language that the text designates as *melitzah:* "Our mother Zion
sent her sons to welcome their brother who has returned to her"
(p. 39). *Melitzah* serves to sustain the level of fantasy; language
buffers Yitzhak, although its ironic discrepancy with the situation at hand is not lost on the reader.

When Yitzhak moves later on to Jerusalem, that move appears
to reverse the direction he has been traveling and so to signal a
major change in milieu and ideology; nevertheless, it is possible

---

7. In this respect, note the argument advanced by A. B. Yehoshua in his essays
on Zionism: "The natural balance between father-God and mother-homeland
has been disturbed in the consciousness of Judaism by the dominance of the father. The sanctity of the land and its apotheosis only intensified fear of it. It was
transformed from mother to woman (the father's wife), and therefore any reck-
less contact, without the father's supervision and permission, becomes incestu-
ous and invites the severest punishment.

"In the *Golah,* relations with the father-God are easier (the mother is distant; only longing is directed toward her). ... As long as she is remote the
mother can maintain her important position, and the father preserves his ex-
clusivity without losing the people, for it retains the homeland in its consciousness" (Yehoshua, *Between Right and Right,* pp. 57–58).

to discern here again the drive for incorporation, the wish to re-
gain fusion. The unique status of Jerusalem in Judaism justifies its
place in the psychic structure that the text generates.

As maternal geography in a literary text, Jerusalem bears
comparison to Joyce's Ireland. Within their respective texts,
Ireland and Jerusalem are forms of homeland, *heimlich* and
unheimlich, to use the terms Freud discusses in "The Uncanny."
Like Agnon, Joyce is aware (and wary) of place as threat of absorption, a consciousness he pushes to satire in his characterization of Stephen Dedalus in *Portrait of the Artist as a Young Man.* It
should be noted that *Bildung* in Agnon's novel places the protagonist in a tension between *two* poles, *two* homelands—the
Diaspora and Zion. While Stephen Dedalus poises himself for
flight into an unknown future out of which he will "forge" an
identity for himself and his "race" (with all the ironies that
"forge" carries), Yitzhak turns to a "new" homeland that is at
the same time the ancient birthplace of his people. In contrast to
Yitzhak, who lacks a mother and is born into exile, Stephen is
born in the motherland and sees exile as the necessary condition
to individuation. He must become father to himself not only to
escape the paternal authority of God and priesthood, but also, on
what is arguably a deeper or more primary level, to avoid the
danger of incorporation into a maternal core.

Juxtaposition of two passages, one early and one later in the
novel, brings out the constancy of drives that is Yitzhak.
Consider Yitzhak's experience on arrival in *Eretz Yisrael:* "That
very night Yitzhak learned what he had not learned in all the
years, all those years in which he had seen the new *Eretz Yisrael* as
one piece [*hativah ahat*], that same night he learned that even
[*Eretz Yisrael*] had made herself *pieces and pieces* [*hativot hativot*].[8]

Compare this early notation of Yitzhak's yearnings to be of a
piece with his brethren to the moment, later in the novel, at
which he recites *Kaddish,* the mourner's prayer, at the Western

---

8. p. 55; emphasis added.

Wall on the anniversary of his mother's death (a moment that is anticipated midway in the novel when Yitzhak's first Sabbath visit to the Wall leaves him feeling like "an infant without sin" [p. 262]):

> Now that he had said Kaddish he was drawn closer as if in and of itself to the holy stones. His heart began to pound and his legs to shake. And with the shaking of his legs and the pounding of his heart his voice went out with the voice of all those standing next to the Wall. ... The stones were swallowed up in darkness, and all the worshippers became of *one piece* [*hativah ahat*] before the Omnipresent [*ha-makom,* lit. "the place"].[9]

The moment seems to supply the reunion or reabsorption that Yitzhak failed to find on first entry into the land of Zion; indeed Yitzhak is *nivlah,* "swallowed up," into corporate unity with other worshippers before the deity, whose appellation here supports further the sense of absorption into place in a concrete sense.[10] The narrative is virtually disrupted at moments such as this by a movement suggestive of desire for union or reunion with a presence that has always been longed for, although it may never have existed.[11]

Indeed, for Yitzhak, the move to Jerusalem reads as the effort to find what Jaffa has not supplied—not only the stern father and the oedipal situation, but less perceptibly perhaps, the move back

---

9. p. 351; emphasis added.

10. This moment of mourning a parent compares with a significant passage in *A Guest for the Night* (*Oreah natah lalun*) in which the narrator enters the Beit Hamidrash to study in memory of his father and experiences boundary loss and the feeling of absorption into something larger than himself.

11. The paternal schema should not lead us to overlook a tension between departure and return that plays a structuring role in narrative, a tension that may be prior to or may somehow underlie the struggle of the individual with paternal institutions embodying the name of the Father. Feminist revisionist approaches to psychoanalysis and literature have turned attention to intrusions into the oedipal plot of questions concerning fusion, differentiation, stability of

into a preindividuated state. The Jerusalem section of the novel is marked by a tension between this regressive moment and, at the same time, the drive to unseat the father, to take the father's place, a move that is manifest in Yitzhak's entry into the house of the fanatical R. Faysh. In the context of his move from Jaffa and the society of peers to Jerusalem, Yitzhak's turn to Shifra, daughter of the fanatical R. Faysh, can be read as part of a turn away from the outward-directedness of Zionism as movement and social ideology. At the same time, there can be little doubt that Shifra is the forbidden object: The text makes it abundantly clear that a functioning R. Faysh would never permit Yitzhak to cross his threshold; furthermore, the interchangeability of Shifra with her mother underscores the placement of the daughter in the forbidden.

It is via the inscription on the dog that this implicitly oedipal drama emerges into action. For it is the dog who topples R. Faysh, the most terrifying embodiment of the father imago. It is only because of the dog's encounter with R. Faysh, resulting in the prostration of that sternly authoritarian figure, that Yitzhak is able to move in and assume two interchangeable women, mother and daughter, taking the place of the father who lies mute, unable to arrest the young man's oedipal triumph. In this

---

character, or meaning in ways that prompt a reexamination of the relation of the subject of language.

It is important to note that we are looking at constructions of gender, of the "maternal" and the "paternal," in language; our statements are the product of the very definitions and oppositions that they attempt to analyze. This is a constraint that we may not be able to escape but that we can at least interrogate. Juliet Mitchell notes that "to Freud, if psychoanalysis is phallocentric, it is because the human social order that it perceives refracted through the individual human subject is patrocentric. To date, the father stands in the position of the third term that *must* break the asocial dyadic unit of mother and child. We can see that this third term will always need to be represented by something or someone. Lacan returns to the problem, arguing that the relation of mother and child cannot be viewed outside the structure established by the position of the father" (Mitchell, "Introduction," p. 23).

respect, then, the dog is the emissary for Yitzhak's aggression against the father. Read this way, a triumph such as Yitzhak's is intolerable; according to the primitive law of retribution, Yitzhak must pay in kind and, in fact, Yitzhak is bitten by the dog whose "madness" his inscription has produced and so pays for his transgression by assuming the paralysis of the father.

Thus the dog is also the vehicle for the other side of this oedipal drama, the redirection of aggression away from the "father" and back to the "son," that is to say, Yitzhak. In this respect, the dog, overdetermined creature that he is, becomes the vehicle for Yitzhak's self-punishment. In effect, one could argue that by inscribing the dog with the words *kelev meshugah,* "mad dog," Yitzhak has written the *herem,* or excommunication, casting himself out for the worst crime of all: the violation of oedipal taboos. (Several times, the text compares Yitzhak's writing on the dog to the old practice of tying excommunications onto dogs, as if to prompt our investigation into the oedipal significance of such writings.) The dog brings about the change in Yitzhak's position from *writer* of the *herem*—a role analogous to that of R. Faysh and the pious men of Jerusalem—to the *object* of the *herem*: he who is cast out. His position changes from grammatical subject of the sentence to its object, from he who writes to the one who is written (or bitten), in a manner that parallels the odyssey of the text that is the dog. The dog is initially the "text" that Yitzhak writes, but in its tireless search for a reader, this "text" takes on a more active role and reaches out to bite Yitzhak.

In a study of the Ashkenazi practice of preserving the cloth used during the circumcision ceremony for later use as a binder for the Torah, Kirshenblatt-Gimblett refers to circumcision as the "cut that binds": "Carrying the child's name and birth date, and even the blood of circumcision, the binder symbolically binds the child around the law each time it is used to secure the Torah scroll."[12] In *Temol shilshom,* a function analogous to the

---

12. "The Cut That Binds," p. 137.

Torah binder can be discerned in the list—the *pinkas,* or communal record—that Reb Alter preserves of the names of all the young men whom he circumcised in Yitzhak's hometown. As *mohel,* or circumciser, Reb Alter served to inscribe Yitzhak in a list, to impose the law that brings him into community. Circumcision signifies the covenant with a heavenly Father and occurs under the authorization of the earthly father, representative of the Law. As the "cut that binds," it names the subject and heralds his entry into an existing network of signifiers. Or, more accurately, since it occurs eight days after birth, it heralds the power and authority of the all-pervasive symbolic order to which the *infans* will gain access, through the acquisition of speech and acquiescence, to the law of the Father. From one angle, the dog's bite undoes the ties that circumcision initiates, in a perverse mirroring of the ritual that the text does not suppress. The bite is the consequence of an inscription that occurs in a moment of *suspension* of the Law in the utter randomness of writing surfaces. Inscription and bite combine to exclude Yitzhak from community, disqualifying him from the social role to which marriage to Shifra, an event that immediately precedes the dog's bite, has admitted him.

After the start of his illness, Yitzhak's condition is brought to the attention of R. Alter by his wife, who dreams that Yitzhak's mother came to her expressing fear that her son had fallen victim to "savage anger" (*haron af*)—a phrase that brings to mind not only its scriptural uses but also the father-tyrant of *Totem and Taboo.* Hinda Pu'ah reports this dream to R. Alter, thinking that he "will laugh at her" (*yitzhak la*): the verb *yitzhak,* or "will laugh," is of course the same as Yitzhak's name, echoing parodically the biblical etymology for the naming of Isaac.[13] Rather than *laugh,* however, R. Alter confirms his wife's worries by telling her that on his list—his *pinkas*—of those he has cir-

---

13. Genesis 18:12.

cumcised, the letters of Yitzhak's name have begun to fade and become illegible.[14]

Reb Alter's list constitutes a writing *into* community, insofar as circumcision, the "cut that binds," initiates the inscription of Jewish males into community. This contrasts with the writing *out of* community that we see in the writing on the dog, an inscription that combines with the dog's bite to reverse the rite of circumcision, thus constituting the cut that severs, excluding Yitzhak from the community he entered with circumcision. Through Reb Alter's reference to an effaced writing—the fading of Yitzhak's name on his list—the novel comments on itself; in this seemingly hallucinatory moment, one inscription writes out another in a struggle for legibility for which Yitzhak is literally the locus.

Within the structures that the text generates, Yitzhak has acted out the Forbidden; his accession to death is a sacrifice, whose purpose is to "restore" the power of the Father. This can be compared with dramas of filial sacrifice in Kafka's stories: "Metamorphosis" ends with Gregor's death out of a love for his family that goes unnoticed by them; although Gregor is swept out with the trash, his death takes its place in a sacrificial scheme insofar as it is linked with the sudden burst of spring that brings new life to the family. This concluding note of redemption and renewal can be compared structurally to the onset of rains in *Temol shilshom* following Yitzhak's death; we can see that Gregor's assumption of guilt, like Yitzhak's, has to do with no sin of his own, beyond entrapment in the web of the oedipal. In "Penal Colony," the officer makes a gift of himself to the machine that is the instrument of law, the "Old Law" according to which guilt is never to be doubted. The machine, of course, is a writing machine, which can be said to inscribe the name of the

---

14. *nitashteshu*, p. 602.

Father in a punishment that the "son" does not survive.[15] These texts suggest forms of oedipal guilt for which no atonement is possible. Sons pay tribute with their lives, repaying the debt of a rebellion whose impact is as cosmic as it is imaginary.

The inherence of this guilt in narrative structure suggests, from a psychoanalytic point of view, something like the refusal of the child to relinquish the primitive desire to be the phallus for the mother, a refusal that makes every encounter with the paternal a struggle to the death.[16] The developmental alternative to these savage dramas comes about through the normalization of the Oedipus complex: The child accepts that he cannot *literally* take the place of the father; through this accession to the law of the Father, the child accepts what constitutes "symbolic castration" and identifies with the *role* or *function* of the father.[17]

---

15. And of course we should not forget Josef K's comment on his own death: " 'Like a dog!' he said; it was as if the shame of it must outlive him" (Kafka, *The Trial*, p. 286). Max Brod cites the point where, in *Letter to His Father*, Kafka connects his use of the phrase to the infinite sense of guilt created in him by his father (cf. Brod, *Franz Kafka*, p. 24). Kafka, *Letter to His Father*, p. 73: "Here, it is enough to remind you of early days. I had lost my self-confidence where you were concerned, and in its place had developed a boundless sense of guilt. (In recollection of this boundlessness I once wrote of someone, accurately: 'He is afraid the shame will outlive him, even.')"

16. "We will take *Verwerfung*, then, to be foreclosure of the signifier. To the point at which the Name-of-the-Father is called—we shall see how—may correspond in the Other, then, a mere hole, which by the inadequacy of the metaphoric effect will provoke a corresponding hole at the place of the phallic signification" (Lacan, *Écrits*, p. 201). The concept of foreclosure or *Verwerfung* is one that Lacan takes from Freud (cf. ibid., pp. 201, 217). John P. Muller offers this explanation of the concept: "In psychotic development castration is foreclosed: the child remains in a dual, symbiotic union with the mother in which the child identifies with being the all-fulfilling object of the mother's desire ... in attempting to *be* the imaginary phallus or completion of the mother the child rejects the limits implied by castration" ("Language, Psychosis, and the Subject in Lacan," p. 23).

17. Freud comments on the unconscious equation of circumcision with castration and sees this as "one of the roots of [Western] anti-semitism: ... If we ven-

In contrast, literature makes available to us a vicarious living-out of the Oedipus in its more radical form. Yitzhak's end testifies to a hidden but persistent insistence on the radical nature of his transgression, which in effect resists any modification or integration. (For example, a well-meaning friend of Yitzhak's takes a *minyan,* or quorum, to the Western Wall to recite psalms, including a particular verse that mentions a dog, ten times, in what can be seen as an effort to weave Yitzhak into the fabric of Jerusalem, but his effort does not offset the savage text of madness [p. 604].) It is this insistence, buried in the structure of the text, that makes necessary the death-as-tribute-to-the-father to which Yitzhak submits. Read back into history, then, the novel traces the dilemma of a generation whose impulse to self-realization, whether on an individual or a national level, carried with it dangerous resonances of early struggles.

In Sophocles' rendition of the myth, Oedipus survives the punishment that we may understand to be castration; he offers himself to the people of Thebes as a horrible example, but in essence a therapeutic one: "Approach and deign to touch me for all my wretchedness, and do not fear. / No man but I can bear my evil doom."[18] In telling the townspeople his story, whether or not they accept it, Oedipus gains access to a dimension of being beyond simple commission of the crime; he has accepted his guilt; he can make a claim to participation in the social order based on that acceptance and the consequent possibility of integration. In *Temol shilshom,* as in Kafka's "Metamorphosis," the split between the fate of the protagonist and the life of the collective goes unaddressed and unresolved; it remains to the reader to

---

ture to carry our conjectures back to the primaeval days of the human race we can surmise that originally circumcision must have been a milder substitute, designed to take the place of castration" ("Leonardo da Vinci and a Memory of His Childhood," pp. 95–96 n. 3).

18. ll. 1413–1415.

piece together the traces of an expiatory plot structure and to consider the place of that drama in human life.

The severity of Yitzhak's end is offset by the survival of the social world (and, particularly, by the example of the agricultural settlement, Ein Ganim); there is also a fairly unpersuasive closing reference on the last page of the novel to a projected sequel that will tell of the "deeds of the rest of our friends" (p. 607).[19] The only significant alternatives that the text offers can be seen in those figures who have, in one way or another, established distance from woman as well as from social movements.[20]

A concluding note on writing: Writing is meant to define, delineate, control madness or aberrance, but the madness *in writing* breaks down the distinctions it is meant to maintain. Felman notes that the presentation of madness in literary texts marks a "radical ambiguity of the inside and the outside, insofar as this ambiguity escapes the speaking subjects";[21] madness brings forward indeterminacies and instabilities that are inherent in writing as well as in the subject but might be overlooked in the interests of more peaceable readings.

---

19. Although Miron expresses the difficulty, for Agnon and reader alike, in reconciling the "absurd and shocking" ending of *Temol shilshom* with "the meaning and value of Zionism and the pioneering enterprise" ("Domesticating a Foreign Genre," p. 10), he offers the penetrating observation that in Agnon's later novels, "the problematic status of closure became the main manifestation of the widening gap between the Jewish religious point of departure and the psychological, social and ethical reality of the contemporary Jew" (ibid., p. 25).

20. These include Y. H. Brenner, who is noteworthy in this appearance for his cynicism, clear-sightedness, and simplicity; the character of Leichtfuss, who is marked by his isolation and self-sufficiency; and the character of the artist, Blaukopf, who draws a separation (*matah vilon*) in order to practice his art. A character named Arzaf is the extreme of this isolationist tendency: His professional activities as a taxidermist testify to his lack of relationship to other creatures (Kurzweil, "Temol shilshom," pp. 201–221, 224). The deadliness of Arzaf's touch and the deathly seductiveness of his appeal to Balak make clear the sinister nature of the alternative he offers.

21. *Writing and Madness*, p. 13.

Yitzhak never masters the discourses—neither Zionism nor the piety of the ultraorthodox men of Jerusalem—to which he attempts to affiliate himself. His writing on the dog, an imitation of the writing of the father, produces a comedy-drama of the instability of the sign that opens up the drama of subjectivity to the text at large. The novel draws us into this drama by taking note, on the one hand, of the contrast between the lasting colors and precise lettering of the signs that Yitzhak makes to order for his customers, and on the other hand, of Yitzhak's idly impulsive writing on the dog, who is himself a creature of random coloration and indeterminate breed (p. 275). And in a further play on this theme (a further *mise en abîme* of the text, we could say), the dog Balak is pictured as something of a frustrated reader, unable to find out the meaning of the inscription on his back that has caused him so much trouble: We are told that Balak bites Yitzhak out of a desire to drink the truth in his blood (p. 593).

In fact, there is a startling similarity between the moment at which Yitzhak writes on the dog and the moment at which the dog bites Yitzhak: Each involves a loss of control and self-consciousness; each is a moment of possession, transport beyond the objective sense of the "I." These moments supply the sense of being of a piece, *hativah ahat* instead of *hativot hativot,* of being *nivlah,* or swallowed up in an experience of boundary loss. Each is a moment *of* writing (as well as a moment *in* the writing) in which the stable distinctions writing is supposed to produce break down. Such moments of madness or excess collapse distinctions between subject and object, demonstrating the danger of too much closeness (whereas sanity, or the reasonable guarantee of a stable writing, assumes a "correct" distance).[22] Such moments of excess in the novel are atoned for or repressed in the closure, whose rigid oedipal scheme of filial sacrifice attempts to contain the madness in writing.

---

22. Lacan, *Écrits,* pp. 246–471.

✦ 5 ✦

The Garment and the Loaf:
Tales of the Unfinished Task

Glenda Abramson

S efer ha-ma'asim (The book of deeds), written between 1932 and 1945, presents nightmarish scenes in the daily life of a man who is suspended between two worlds, of Jewish tradition and of modernism. The contemporary settings of these stories belie their fixation with metaphysical battle and their concealed texture of myth: failed missions, lapses of faith, disobedience, temptation, and guilt. The narrator's world is constituted by surrealistic landscapes, shifting time planes, and locations populated by enigmatic, unreal figures. He knows with certainty neither what he wants nor where he wants to be. Bearing in on his unfulfilled needs and his bewilderment is the world of religious observance and traditional Jewish life, the consistent subtext of even the most "modern" of Agnon's stories. The stories in *Sefer ha-ma'asim* lack inner logic or closure; as narratives they are elaborate conundrums reflecting the hermeneutic confusion of the dream and are therefore slow to yield their meaning without the requisite tools. Moreover, Alter's well-known description of Agnon implicitly highlights one of the problems faced by Agnon's readers:

On Agnon's worktable in his house in Talpiot, one might conceivably find a copy of James Joyce (in translation) or Rilke, but one is more likely to see some yellowed, flaking volume that proves to be an obscure eighth-century homiletical commentary on the Pentateuch, or a collection of Hassidic parables, or perhaps a late medieval mystical treatise. In this respect Agnon continues the tradition of the illustrious rabbinic line from which he is descended, and possesses a voluminous knowledge of traditional Hebrew and Aramaic source materials.[1]

Agnon's novels and the stories in *Sefer ha-ma'asim* are evidence of that capacious intellectual storehouse, for they are chains of allusion to the sources that in many cases provide a key to their interpretation.

Without the same recourse to Agnon's traditional sources his reader must rely on features of the texts that, by their reiteration from work to work, offer an overall clue to interpretation. The duplication in *Sefer ha-ma'asim* of situations, character types, and linguistic features is not surprising in a collection whose protagonist appears to be the same throughout and whose emotional condition demands a repetition of certain actions and patterns of thought. However, an author may also repeat motifs, characters, or events in disparate works, cathectic repetitions that are little different in principle from the recurrence of structural or thematic patterns in Mahler's music, for example, or of figures and objects that have a fixed "meaning" or reference in Chagall's paintings. In Agnon's case the reiteration of themes, motifs, or linguistic formations from one story to another may serve to illuminate both; a character or event that is apparently obscure in one story may be more easily explicated when encountered in an altered context in another. Such is the case with two stories from separate collections, "Pat shlemah" ("A Whole Loaf"), from *Sefer ha-ma'asim,*[2] and "Ha-malbush" ("The Garment"), published in the 1952 collection *Ad henna.*[3]

---

1. Robert Alter, *After the Tradition* (New York: E. P. Dutton, 1969), p. 138.

2. Tel Aviv and Jerusalem: Schocken Books, 1932, pp. 143–155.

3. Tel Aviv and Jerusalem: Schocken Books, 1952, pp. 305–320.

Both of these stories are allegories of sin, guilt, and retribution: A man of extreme passivity sins through hesitation, the vac-
illation that ultimately brings about his horrible judgment and
punishment. The idea of *tikkun,* with its full connotation of
metaphysical restoration, permeates both tales, and both protagonists are offered the choice of salvation, but for one reason or
another they defy a powerful authority by neglecting to accept it
and suffer as a consequence. Both protagonists differ from the
evildoer of fable or fairy tale in that they aspire to good but, in
accordance with the bewildered inertia of Agnon's heroes, they
are unable to achieve it. Despite their thematic similarities, the
stories demonstrate certain generic variations, "Ha-malbush"
being derived from the fable or morality tale whose representative hero is an old tailor, a figure of folklore, whereas "Pat
shlemah" is a modernist story moving through planes of realism
and surrealism, with an unnamed "existentialist" hero.[4] It is
therefore the more "difficult" of the two stories in its symbolic
and linguistic intricacy and its dreamlike shifts of scene. Its multitude of strange people and events has occasioned an appropriate multitude of interpretations. I believe that examining it in
conjunction with "Ha-malbush" serves to illuminate some of its
darker complexities, since "Ha-malbush" moves along the lines
of causality with clearer logical coherence; like a fable it has intelligible linear codings and a form of closure: sin, retribution,
and a moral.

"Pat shlemah" is so well known that a very brief summary
will suffice. A man whose wife is away sets forth to a restaurant
on Sabbath night. On his way he meets a great scholar, Dr.
Yekutiel Neeman, who gives him a bundle of letters to mail. He
also encounters his old friend, Mr. Gressler, and an acquaintance, Mr. Hofni. He reaches the restaurant without having sent
the letters and orders a meal, including a whole loaf. He waits for

---

4. Arnold Band, *Nostalgia and Nightmare* (Berkeley and Los Angeles: University
of California Press, 1968), p. 200.

many hours and eventually upsets the tray on which his meal is brought and the letters are stained by the food. He continues to wait throughout the night, alone with a mouse that gnaws left-over bones and a cat whose eyes shine with an unnatural light. The following evening the narrator sets out from his home again on an identical quest for food.

Although "Pat shlemah" and "Ha-malbush" share repeated motifs, situations, symbolic features, and latent significances, the image of the "whole loaf" is unique to its eponymous story, but not irrelevant to the central principle of "Ha-malbush." Arnold Band sees it as the Sabbath loaf, representing traditional and spiritual wholeness;[5] Kurzweil as the egotistical desire for physical satisfaction;[6] Avraham Holtz, disagreeing with both, observes that not one but two whole loaves (*shtei kikarot*) are required for the Sabbath meal, basing his argument on the injunction, "On the Sabbaths and festivals—a man must slice [the bread of] two loaves."[7] Furthermore, Holtz claims that the presence of a single loaf on a fully laid table is a sign of idolatry. He refers to Isaiah 65:11: "But ye are they that forsake the Lord, that forget my holy mountain, that prepare a table for that troop [*ha-orkhim la-gad shulhan*], and that furnish the drink offering to that number," and to rabbinic interpretations of the verse that, in certain circumstances, regard a single loaf as part of a table set for the gods. Holtz brings to bear on his interpretation Agnon's story "Ha-nidah," in which the loaf is perceived by Rabbi Avigdor as a sign of idolatry. According to Holtz, therefore, the desire for a table set with a whole loaf is a gesture toward idolatry,[8] an interpretation approaching Kurzweil's unequivocal view of the narrator in

5. Band, op. cit., p. 190.

6. Barukh Kurzweil, *Massot 'al sippurei S. Y. Agnon* (Tel Aviv and Jerusalem: Schocken Books, 1963), pp. 86–94.

7. Maimonides, *Mishneh Torah,* Berakhot 7, 4. Avraham Holtz, "Mi-shlemut la-'avodah zarah," *Ha-sifrut* 3, 2 (November 1971): p. 297.

8. Holtz, op. cit., p. 298.

"Pat shlemah" as preoccupied with nothing more than the gratification of his physical needs. Yet Agnon's emphasis on the "whole" loaf suggests that the loaf, even if not designated specifically for the Sabbath (the narrator, after all, goes in search of his meal after the Sabbath has ended), still represents a form of elevation, not necessarily confined to a religious occasion. The desire is for the quality most difficult for any Agnonic hero to achieve: completeness. The story offers us diverse illustrations of *in*completeness: sexual (the narrator's wife has been away for some time), corporeal (he has not eaten for an entire day), and spiritual (he has not satisfied the obligations of the Sabbath). The whole loaf, with its perfect, circular, form and its connotations, remains a tantalizing image of fulfillment for the narrator, while the recounted events of his life suggest divergence and disintegration.

The narrator's fragmentation does not, however, devolve only on his spiritual life, although he has indeed desecrated the Sabbath by failing to prepare in advance for it and by neglecting to provide the three meals prescribed for it.[9] Furthermore, he apparently doubts the authorship of Dr. Neeman's book, a symbol of the Pentateuch (pp. 144–145). These are spiritual defects, but his corporeal life is equally impaired: His home is incomplete without his family and his body is suffering from lack of sustenance. His task, therefore, is to repair both insufficient halves of his self, to amalgamate them, and to achieve the emotional integration required for a correct life. Throughout the story he is as incapable of opting for either exclusive pole, physicality or spirituality, as he is of perfectly integrating them; he is paralyzed by indecision; he neither attains his desired meal nor mails the letters, which represent spiritual affirmation, being deflected on the point of doing one or the other. The meal of which the whole loaf is the centerpiece does not, I believe, represent exclusive spirituality, exclusive sensuality, or idolatry

---

9. Holtz, op. cit., p. 299.

(apostasy). Physicality (the "animal" nature) and the spirit, both represented symbolically and through exaggerated examples in the story, are not mutually exclusive but reconcilable, a reconciliation that is the narrator's task, as it is to temper any excess of body or spirit, to live in peace with both sides of his nature, and to attain the whole loaf. "Pat shlemah" is about his failure to do so through dilatoriness, desire, and, as Kurzweil has pointed out, selfishness.

The narrator is sustained by a vision of himself "sitting at a laden table with a clean tablecloth on it, and waiters and waitresses [*meshartim umeshartot*] attending to me while I ate properly prepared [*metukkan*] food that I had not needed to exhaust myself over" (p. 143). The table is *malé* (full, laden); the clean tablecloth and the waiters indicate a form of ritual. The food is *metukkan,* the first indication of *tikkun* in the story. The language of this passage, in which the whole loaf is not yet mentioned, leads to the conclusion that not only does the whole loaf indicate the desired completeness but also the entire table, laden with the *proper* food. Only when the narrator is finally seated in the restaurant does he speak of a whole loaf (p. 152). *Malé, shalem,* and *metukkan* have similar connotations of perfection and integration and appear to argue against the idea that the table represents a form of apostasy or evil self-gratification. Band reminds us that the righteous in heaven are usually regaled with sumptuous meals.[10] The importance of the story, then, rests not so much on the meaning of the whole loaf, but on the means to its attainment. In the end the narrator receives neither the loaf nor indeed any food at all; his ambivalent indecision has prevented his achieving the peace symbolized by the loaf. Neither his physical nor his spiritual obligations have been realized; he has compounded sin upon sin from the very opening of the story, the circular structure of which suggests that the entire process must begin anew.

---

10. Band, op. cit., p. 191.

Even though the symbol of the "whole loaf" has no parallel in "Ha-malbush," the later story can nonetheless be used to illustrate the central motif of "Pat shlemah" and its overall proposition: The perfection of life is the means toward moral fulfillment in this world and salvation in the next. The failure to attempt this perfection results in punishment and, in the case of the tailor in "Ha-malbush," in death. He has been commissioned by a great lord or prince (*sar*) to make a garment from the choicest fabric (*arig*) in the lord's own workshop. He begins to repair (*letakken*) the garment but due to delays and diversions does not complete it. He is summoned to appear before the lord, fetched to the palace by the lord's cruel servants, and given a short time longer to complete his work. Panic-stricken, he sets to work on it but still finds various reasons to delay. Eventually he spills food on it and rushes to the river to wash it, but it is grabbed by a large fish. The hapless tailor is drowned in his attempts to save the garment. The parable, based on aggadic and midrashic traditions,[11] is clear: the garment is the man's soul, which has been lent him by God. His duty is to maintain it well so that it is returned in the requisite condition in order that its possessor may reach the world to come.[12]

The tale of the commission of a simple workman by an important personage is common in European folklore, refined, for example, in Beatrix Potter's *The Tailor of Gloucester* or the fairy tale *The Shoemaker and the Elves.* In both these tales the commission, which has been interrupted, is completed by some supernatural agency, mice and elves respectively; in both tales the protagonists are good men whose failure to fulfill their duty is through no fault of their own, unlike Agnon's tailor, whose fault

---

11. See Gershon Shaked, "Galui ve-samui ba-sippur," in *Omanut ha-sippur shel Agnon* (Merhavia: Sifriat Po'alim, 1973), pp. 112–131.

12. In "Ha-malbush" the potential reward for the tailor's work is not stated, but he must obey the lord's command. In "Pat shlemah" the reward is implied in the meal, although it is not referred to by the lord-figure, Dr. Yekutiel Neeman.

is willful recalcitrance. Like the narrator in "Pat shlemah," he is an ordinary man, neither good nor evil, aware of the importance of his mission or task, but susceptible to the forces of deflection. In both of the Agnon stories the moral will of the protagonists is subordinated to their immediate wants.

The parallels in both stories are strong, and despite the modernist setting of "Pat shlemah," their linear structure is comparable, with the intimations of ultimate retribution introduced early in both stories and serving as a leitmotif throughout them. The reasons for the retribution are then explored in an interrupted but largely sequential narrative, leading to the retribution itself. However, there are certain structural differences: In "Hamalbush" the commission has been given before the story begins and its opening finds the tailor already working on the garment. "Pat shlemah" opens with the recognition of sins already committed by the narrator before the tale begins, and the redemptive commission is given him within the story. The second important difference is the position of the narrational voice: "Hamalbush" is told about a tailor called Israel (his name is mentioned once, by his wife), whereas the nameless first-person narrator in "Pat shlemah" is recounting his own past experience from a diachronic point far separated from the events themselves, since the story ends as it began, unclosed, with the narrator's setting out for a meal. The circularity of the story heightens its sense of limbo and horror, with the narrator caught in the relentless events, like a mouse in a trap. Although "Ha-malbush" ends with the tailor's death, it is not entirely closed, either, for the authorial voice subsequently interposes with speculations about the tailor's fate after divine judgment.

Both protagonists are offered a second chance. The lord sends the tailor home with added time to complete the repairs, and the narrator encounters Dr. Neeman, who sets him the task of mailing some letters. The narrator is not displeased to see Dr. Neeman, whose scholarship he admires, yet the chapter in which they meet begins: "While I was being *dragged* along [*Im she-ani nigrar ve-holekh*] a certain old man rapped on his window." When the servants of the lord arrive to fetch the tailor, "he was *dragged* along [*nigrar ve-halakh*] with them." The lord is mighty and righteous, Dr. Neeman is saintly and scholarly, but the protagonists meet them reluctantly (*nigrar*), guilt-ridden and aware of their iniquity and the possibility of punishment. Since Dr. Neeman is a portrayal of Moses (as indicated by his name, Yekutiel, his book, and his flowing beard), his letters have the metaphysical weight of religious principles and duties. Their exact contents are unimportant, although critics have seen them variously as the *mitzvot,* or as commandments designating certain spiritual obligations, and as such they correspond to the garment in "Ha-malbush" as a representation of the perfectibility of the soul. The major importance of the letters is in the immediate mailing of them, the mission imposed by the Godlike authority, their having to be *sent* to a place, just as the garment is to be *returned* to the owner of the fabric. Although probably coincidental, it is difficult not to be struck by the similarity of the roots of *iggeret* and *arig.*

Inferences of punishment and death abound in "Ha-malbush" from the start. The tailor's candle burns down and he hears the approach of the lord's servants, whom Shaked associates with the tradition of *hibbut ha-kever,* the beating after death by evil spirits.[13] Also, when he is brought before the lord, the tailor is confined in a narrow dark place that oppresses him, a sure intimation of the grave. The approach of night's darkness, the flickering of the candle, the sound of the lord's wicked servants, and the narrow place are the signs of his ultimate fate for failing to "repair" although "he was given time to repair [*letakken*] and he cannot repair" (p. 307). In "Pat shlemah," as in "Ha-malbush," the notion of ultimate punishment arises shortly after the story opens. The narrator describes the heat of the day and of his house, with a drumbeat reiteration of *esh* (fire) nine times in three lines. Holtz has read this section as Agnon's parody on the

---

13. Shaked, op. cit., p. 121.

Sephardi liturgy for the Sabbath on the first day of Rosh Hashanah, *Ve-hayot bo'arot mareihen ke-gehalei esh* (animals whose burning is like fiery coals).[14] Fire is associated with Mr. Gressler, who may or may not be an incarnation of Satan but who was responsible for burning down the narrator's home and who serves as the alternative to virtue in the story. "Fire" and "furnace" (*kivshan*) constitute the signs of hell's punishment for those who desecrate the Sabbath; the narrator is already threatened with them at the outset of the story. A "house" can be an image for the body,[15] and the narrator's burning house could therefore duplicate his initial description of his burning body: "The fire [*isho*] of a room is a body's fire and the fire of a body is that of a room"(p. 143), reinforcing his foreboding of fiery retribution.

The "fire" theme has a secondary connotation in relation to the narrator's sins, which are manifold, beginning with the disruption of a family. According to Kurzweil, "the normal order of things has been unraveled. The poet [sic: *meshorer*] lives in the isolation of his selfishness. The threat of chaos approaches because the order of things has been violated. The family, the cell of the Jewish society does not surround the poet."[16] The iniquity of a situation so elementally awry has the extended effect of cosmic disruption, "chaos," symbolized by the unnatural heat of the day. The tailor's sinfulness, in contrast, is exclusively related to the garment, which he is incessantly examining in order to discover what it lacks, for in his repair, as in the whole loaf, lies the perfect integration of parts.

The protagonists' various transgressions are, however, superseded by the one that constitutes the framework of both stories, a sin that Band has identified as the sum of all the others in "Pat shlemah": "I did not take trouble [*lo tarahti*] on the Sabbath eve

---

14. Holtz, op. cit., p. 299 and n. 14. This certainly calls to mind the cat whose eyes "blazed with a green light that filled the room" ("Pat shlemah," p. 55).

15. C. G. Jung, *Man and His Symbols* (London: Aldus Books, 1964), p. 78.

16. Kurzweil, op. cit., p. 88.

and I did not have anything to eat on the Sabbath" (p. 143). This sin of failing to prepare food in advance for the Sabbath is stated as an existential fact in "Pat shlemah," but it pertains metaphorically both to the narrator and to the tailor, each of whom neglects to "prepare" his life (or soul). Each is guilty of procrastination, each has broken a promise to a figure of commanding authority representing God, each has flouted the given apparatus of salvation. In "Pat shlemah" this sin of unpreparedness is not confined to the Sabbath but, by extrapolation, refers to the failure of the narrator to discharge all his spiritual obligations. It applies equally to the unmended garment, so that the clarity of the parable in "Ha-malbush" serves as an illumination of the import of "*lo tarahti* ... " to the story of "Pat shlemah" as a whole.

The thematic clarification of the fault of "*lo tarahti* ... " is reinforced by Agnon's linguistic designs, which lead the reader beyond the representational meaning of words to their importance as conspicuous themes. One of his most notable characteristics is his construction of a lexicon of words that, because of the weight of their reappearance in both like and differing contexts, assume the quality of metaphor. Despite their distinct settings, the moral contexts of the two stories are alike and echo each other in their specific vocabulary. For example, the impediment to the protagonists' physical and metaphysical preparation is expressed through the reiterated vocabulary of '*ikkuv* (delay) in both stories. The tailor alludes to his delay by complaining that the lord's servants had not allowed him to dwell (*lehit'akkev*) on his thoughts, but it is those very thoughts later in the story that prevent his returning to the garment. The demonic servants are alert, therefore, to at least one of the tailor's failings. Dr. Neeman's remonstration to the narrator, '*eqev 'iqquv 'ikkuv* (delay follows distortion), could as well be applied to the tailor, particularly in the light of the following description: "The tailor began to cringe [*me'akkem 'atzmo*] before the lord and told him of the many delays [*'ikkuvim*]." Neeman berates the narrator for his failure to return, or restore, his family to Eretz Yisrael, but the story extends the terms of "delay" to his more profound sin, his dereliction regarding the letters. His "crookedness," or spiritual distortion (*'iqquv*), is a result of his delay; the tailor also "distorts" (*me'akkem*), or "twists," himself, with the implication of mendacity, in his attempt to rationalize his own delay. Notwithstanding the self-awareness implicit in the word, he willfully decides not to spend time (*lehit'akkev*) on the garment, but to eat his dinner instead (p. 310). Throughout Agnon's writing the import of *'e-k-v* is negative: a metaphysical delay that must be redressed.

The stories turn on the delaying mechanisms by which both protagonists avoid the prescribed preparation, and which are associated with three elements: the wife, food/hunger, and the "friend." First, both men mistreat their wives, women who are blameless and put-upon. The narrator's wife and children have been abroad for some time, an abnormal situation, which the narrator does nothing to rectify. In fact, Dr. Neeman accuses him:

> "The delay [in bringing back your wife and children] comes from something crooked," he said. He began to scold me. "There's a laziness in you," he said, "so that you have not devoted yourself to bringing them back, with the result that your wife and children are wandering without father and husband while you wander around without wife and children. (p. 144)

Holtz cites the talmudic passage that claims that "those who live abroad are like people without a God"[17] and R. Ishmael's contention that "Israel abroad are idolators."[18] The narrator is therefore guilty of not saving his family from godlessness or idolatry. The unnatural situation of separation from his family leads

---

17. Ketubot 110, 72.
18. Avodah Zarah 8, 71. Holtz, op. cit., p. 300.

directly to the dire consequences of this Sabbath night, but the text implies that his "freedom" (*adam panui hayiti*) has led to previous deviations, particularly in conjunction with Mr. Gressler. Sin is committed by the fact of the narrator's bachelor life and presumed by his friendship with Mr. Gressler specifically while the wife is away. Gressler, who interrupts the narrator's redemptive mission at the very moment of its completion (he encounters him at the post office as he is about to mail the letters), is the inciter or tempter who has already been responsible for the destruction by fire of the narrator's previous home. The story does not reveal whether it had housed the narrator's family, but it was nonetheless an earlier instance of domestic devastation.

Whereas the wife's absence in "Pat shlemah" is both the sin itself and the potential for greater wrongdoing, the *presence* of the tailor's wife in "Ha-malbush" does nothing to prevent similar disaster. She is a long-suffering woman who faithfully carries out her household duties despite her husband's constant griping, and prepares tasty food for him. She appears not to react to his temper and wins the author's approval, evidenced by his description of her as *eshet hayil*. At the story's climax she offers to clean the stained garment, but her husband furiously rejects her help. She is the moral obverse of the tailor, for unlike him she has fulfilled the injunction of "previous preparation": "In the way of housewives, on washday she prepares [*matkinah*] the midday meal the previous night in order to be free to do the laundry" (p. 310). She not only explicitly accords with the injunction but implicitly performs a deed of *tikkun*.

The presence—and absence—of the wives accentuates an additional shared characteristic of the protagonists: their childish responses to their situations. Both suffer fear and resentment of a male authority figure, both avoid reality and adult responsibility, both are easily diverted and drawn to a person who entices them with uncommon delights (*sha'ashuim, ta'anugim* in "Pat shlemah"; drink and gossip in "Ha-malbush"). The female in their lives is mentioned almost exclusively in conjunction with the provision of sustenance, a hint of a child's need for oral gratification. According to Sadan, "The 'meal' serves as a kind of projection of man's desire to free himself from responsibility, to break away from the claims of existence and to return to the primitive condition of foetal dependence [*yankut*]."[19] If so, the whole loaf assumes its Freudian guise of a symbol for the mother's breast.

Hunger, food, and fantasies of eating create a second diversion for both narrators. Edna Afek has noted Agnon's frequently employed method of radical transposition or verb-root metathesis, a technique that was common in medieval poetry and in earlier rabbinic sources.[20] Since Agnon's choice of vocabulary is fundamental to his statement and development of themes, awareness of his linguistic methodology is essential to an understanding of the "concealed narrative" in his work. This applies more substantively to the stories in *Sefer ha-ma'asim* that have the quality of dreams, and that reveal the suggestive distortions and wordplay of dream language, meaningful names, verbal displacement, puns, and concrete symbols such as the four dots (....) representing the tetragrammaton in "Pat shlemah." Agnon's metatheses are too numerous and consistent to be accidental. Words undergo internal shifts throughout a story, demonstrating certain consistent transformations that "strengthen the central motifs."[21] The displacement of letters within a root is therefore not a purely figurative device but is significant to the thematic interpretation of the text. Afek emphasizes certain transpositions in "Pat shlemah" and in "Ha-malbush": in the former, of *ra'av, 'avar, 'evra, 'areivim,* as, for example, in the following: "Because he is a great sage and his words are pleasant [*'areivim*] ... Dr Neeman did not bear a grudge [*'evrato*]. ... On my way I passed [*'avarti*]

---

19. Dov Sadan, *'Al S. Y. Agnon* (Tel Aviv: Hakibbutz Hameuchad, 1978), p. 64.

20. Edna Afek, *Ma'arakhot millim. Iyyunim ba-signon shel S. Y. Agnon* (Tel Aviv: Dekel, 1979), p. 46.

21. Afek, op. cit., p. 46.

behind the House of Study in order to say the Evening Prayer
[*'arvit*]. ... Had Dr. Neeman known I was hungry [*ra'av*] he
would have encouraged me to eat beforehand." Similar examples occur three times more (*'ovrim, ra'av, 'arvit*) in the same
short section (pp. 145–146). Afek has, however, overlooked the
weighted start of the story, *be'erev* Shabbat. She discovers similar metatheses in "Ha-malbush" of *malbush, tavshil, bashel,* but
there, too, the *ra'av- 'avar* transposition applies, as in "the hunger
[*ha-ra'av*] which began to oppress him and the smell of cooking
distracted [*he'eviru*] him from his work." The entire moral standpoint of hunger and food (*r- 'a-v; b-sh-l*) diverting (*'e-v-r*) the tailor from the fulfillment of his duty (*l-v-sh*) and causing him to sin
(*'avera*) is encapsulated in the transposed roots. If Agnon deliberately transposes root letters, his *extension* of a root is no less effective: For example, the pivotal root, *'e-k-v,* denotes the sin of delay; the narrator's nemesis in "Pat shlemah" is a mouse, *'akhbar,*
designating the consequences of such stalling, his guilt or conscience, and his punishment.

The two indicative roots, *r- 'a-v* and *'e-k-v,* therefore have a
causal connection in both stories, hunger as a reason for delay. In
"Pat shlemah" the narrator's vision of his meal displaces his recognition of wrongdoing and later supersedes the fulfillment of
his mission. The recurring fantasy of a heavily laden table tempts
him to the point of indecisive paralysis. Finally his hunger tri-
umphs and he makes his way to the restaurant, the letters still in
his pocket. The tailor delays his stitching to enjoy the meal his
wife has prepared. In the end it is food that destroys all the objects of salvation, the garment and the bundle of letters. There is,
however, a difference in the import of the food itself in both stories. The tailor eats to slake his hunger and continues eating to
the point of digestive discomfort. His food in itself is *no more*
than a diversion. The narrator's meal, which he never eats, is his
vision of unity, the combination of Gressler and Neeman, the
satisfaction of his craving for wholeness. The tailor indeed
achieves the eating of a meal, but he does not enjoy it and it
causes him stomach pain; the narrator does not attain the eating

at all. Both meals do no more than divert attention, *mesi'ot et ha-da'at min ha-'ikkar.*

The third diversion in both cases, the cause of *'ikkuv,* is in the form of a person encountered on the way to the realization of the mission. In "Pat shlemah" this is the strange Mr. Gressler who enters the street like a whirlwind in an anachronistic carriage and pair, intentionally terrifying the passers-by and scattering them in all directions, reminiscent of Ezekiel's warning, "with the hoofs of his horses shall he tread down all thy streets."[22] Gressler's method of transportation places him in the realm of myth; the narrator comments, "I stood amazed; now, when there isn't a horseshoe to be found in the city, a man rides in a carriage and pair" (p. 147). On seeing this apparition the narrator puts the letters and his hunger out of his mind.[23] The character of Gressler (*grässlich* = monstrous)[24] incorporates uncontrolled wildness, a form of cruelty and irresponsibility, but at the same time inescapable allure and affection. He displays also a certain calculation that is reminiscent of the determination of Mephistopheles to procure Faust's soul: Gressler imposes his friendship on the narrator, charming him even when he is resistant to him, obligating him by paying his customs charges when his luggage is held at the port (*'ikkvu et metaltelay, 'ikkuv,* an anticipation of sin), diverting him during his wife's absence, captivating and friendly in contrast to Neeman's righteously angry disapproval. Gressler is the force opposed to the positive pole of Neeman's spirituality, and he is involved in the narrator's failure to obtain the meal and the whole loaf. If the story is an allegory of the battle between the spiritual and animal sides of a man's nature, Gressler very obviously represents the earth, the sensual side

---

22. "Be-farsot susot yirmos et kol hutzotav" (Ezekiel 26:11).

23. "Hisahti et da'ati min ha-igrot ve-khen min ha-ra'av," p. 150; the tailor, similarly diverted, "hisiah et da'ato min ha-malbush," turned his attention from the garment, "Ha-malbush," p. 310.

24. Holtz, op. cit., p. 303 n. 26.

(he is an agriculturalist). The combination of Gressler's friendship, fire, and horses (the latter, according to Jung, symbols of
sometimes uncontrollable instinctive drives erupting from the
unconscious)[25] is a token, if not of evil, at least of the forces inimical to the pursuit of a spiritual life.

In his description of Gressler, Agnon repeats a word that bears
a heavy weight of specific connotation throughout his writing:
makir, which appears five times in three lines (p. 148), indicating
a knowledge that precedes acquaintance or friendship, an instinctive knowledge or a mutual recognition. Throughout this
paragraph the narrator hints at the nature of such knowledge,
"ta'anugim [pleasures], haya mesha'asheni be-divrei hokhmah
[he would delight me with words of wisdom]," a questionable
form of wisdom that undermines every other kind. This is further evidence of a Mephisto-like figure, the possessor of enigmatic knowledge desirable to his initiate. On the night the narrator's house burns, "the firemen made themselves a party and
they grew drunk and filled their vessels with brandy and drink
and when they came to put out the fire they added to it"
(p. 149), a Walpurgis-night scene of demonic merrymaking.
However, the narrator loves Gressler no less for his malfeasance,
leading some commentators to suggest a homosexual relationship between the two, heightened by the narrator's stressing their
friendship while his wife is away. Although the text appears in
many convincing instances to strengthen this assumption, it also
underscores Gressler's engaging nature, his inexplicable attraction for people even at the moment of his greatest cruelty to
them, all of which hints at the irresistible nature of evil.

The narrator and Gressler encounter a strange ratlike person
called Hofni who has invented a better mousetrap and who
bores the narrator with his boasting.[26] Band sees Hofni's inven-

---

25. Jung, op. cit., p. 170.
26. The biblical Hofni, one of the sons of Eli, was indeed a scoundrel, but
Agnon's character does not refer to him.

tion as the technological means toward the repair of the world, a substitute for the essential spiritual restoration.[27] Despite—or perhaps because of—the narrator's dislike of Hofni, whose conversation "gnaws" at him, Gressler invites him aboard the carriage. The character of Hofni remains one of the most enigmatic in the story. If the mouse (or rat) at the end of the story symbolizes the narrator's conscience, Hofni is the one whose purpose is to catch and kill it; he is an extinguisher of conscience and therefore certainly acceptable to Gressler. Hofni is presented as an ironic foil to Dr. Neeman: Both have been responsible for achieving something that has in some way improved the world. "From the day that [Dr. Neeman's book] was published in the world the world changed a little for the better, since a few people mended their ways [*tiknu et ma'aseihem*]" (p. 150). Hofni's invention brings about a similar result: "Mice are a terrible plague and a mousetrap is a great improvement [*tikkun gadol*]."[28] "Writing" is associated with them both, for Hofni insists on recounting to the narrator everything that has been written about him.[29] The name "Hofni" may yield a clue to his function, for if we apply a transposition according to Agnon's models to the root letters of his name, *h-f-n* to *h-n-f* we find the notion of wickedness or sinfulness; if they are further inverted, yielding *n-f-h,* there is again the association with fire and flame, also boasting and self-glorification. Hofni, like Gressler, is inimical to Neeman and his mission. The narrator's encounter with both these figures presages the disaster to come, for it almost ends in his death in the dust, under the horses' hooves.

Hofni recalls the tempter figure of "Ha-malbush," an altogether more subtle and sinister inciter. Like Hofni, he talks incessantly: "How this man does go on and on"—this time about

---

27. Band, op. cit., p. 196.
28. Ibid.
29. Ibid.

communal ephemera.[30] His function as a force of wickedness is suggested by his own rather arcane knowledge. First, he speaks of a colleague of theirs who has outlived his usefulness as an official of a certain guild or society and who is shortly to be dismissed. At his meeting with the lord, the tailor had used as an excuse for his tardiness his duties for the same guild, which take up all his time; his companion's threat is therefore veiled but clear, his words underlining the burden of the story: "If you want mead have mead, a man must not be unbending over eating and drinking, but that same loafer, that same official ... we must be unbending about dismissing him" (p. 317). Second, the friend repeats the ominous statement made earlier in the story that the lord has many garments and will not feel the lack of one (p. 318). Having calmed the tailor with this equivocal reassurance he then tempts him into a tavern, where they drink and pass the time of day. By the time the tailor leaves, he has missed the daily prayers and the garment has been further neglected.

Like the narrator in "Pat shlemah," the tailor is aware of a sense of unease. His thoughts trouble him. From the start of the story he complains about the thoughts that plague him, keeping him from both his work and his prayers: "It is not sufficient that in thoughts there is a certain waste of time but they also divert the mind from essential matters. Take me, for instance, I who have been distracted from the garment by too many thoughts" (p. 311). The narrator in "Pat shlemah" shares the affliction of "thoughts": "For a man's thoughts are bound to delay [le'akkev] his deeds" (p. 146). The tailor's "thoughts" are upon the wicked servants, for his terror of them distracts him from his work, obsessed as he is with visions of the dire consequences of his recal-

---

30. Hebrew: "Kamah yode'a zeh letzaref davar le-davar." It may not be too fanciful to see a morphological connection here between the two tempters: One of the inversions of Hofni (*h-f-n*) gives us *n-f/p-h,* "blacksmith" or "forging." This notion is embodied in *le-tzaref,* "smelting" or "refining."

citrance. The terror of punishment paradoxically prevents his completing his task, and his ruminations about the thoughts themselves similarly waste his time. He is unable to pray, because of his fear of the servants, and like the narrator, he is paralyzed by his guilt and indecision. Both these characters are aware of their sin; they know its expiation but do nothing about it, caught between obligation and temptation and perhaps ambivalent about the good deeds themselves. The tailor is working on the garment without any apparent pride or affection but as a duty, and the narrator in "Pat shlemah" evinces no pleasure in doing a favor for an important man.

Perhaps the least quantifiable sin is that of the imagination, which imposes upon the protagonists further delay and therefore disorder in their lives. The narrator in "Pat shlemah" creates images of completion that he is unable to attain, although he is given the opportunity to do so. He fails to make the causal connection, that obedience to Dr. Neeman will bring him the desired meal. Later his imagination assails him once more in his silent soliloquy regarding the practical value (*to'elet*) of the letters. His conscience warring with his hunger leads his legs to grow "heavy as stone": He neither eats nor mails the letters, while his imagination argues the claims of both. He attempts to tip the balance by forcing his imagination to produce "more than an average man can eat or drink and [appeal] to my taste each item of food and drink" (p. 146). Both men are receptive to any diversion, both are easily deflected by "thoughts" and futile speculation.

Both stories are propelled rapidly to their conclusions, both moving into the surrealism of nightmare, where the protagonists, hesitant and fearful to begin with, are now powerless to act at all. The narrator makes his way to the restaurant. Waiters and waitresses come and go "dressed [*melubashim*] like lords and ladies [*ke-sarim ve-sarot*]." It is difficult not to be tempted by the conjunction of *melubashim* and *sarim;* however, the elegant clothing of the waiters indicates no more than the status of the restaurant. And yet, the narrator continues: "I began to prepare my heart and soul for them" (p. 151).

Although appearing to be helpful, the waiters create of the narrator a Tantalus tortured by the sight of laden trays. They prevent his accomplishing his meal and mailing the letters. The waiters' function recalls that of the wicked servants, to impede and torment the sinner and accentuate his fate. Their instrument, food, is similarly the nemesis of the tailor: The meat from his missed meals, now all added to one pot, has become succulent and fat. The rich gravy spills on the garment: "As he was eating, a little gravy [*ketzat rotev*] spilled on the garment." He almost succeeds in cleansing it in the pure waters of the river, but the fish comes and carries it away.

While the narrator in "Pat shlemah" waits for his meal, the clock strikes ten-thirty, halfway between the hour of the first sin and the judgment, according to the Talmud.[31] The same implication of judgment opens "Ha-malbush," with the tailor's enforced appearance before the lord, and ends it, with the author's conveying to the reader his doubts that the tailor found much good beyond the grave. Shaked has noted that the story's conclusion recalls the Midrash on Jonah[32] that refers to the man who stands before judgment. On checking the time, and perhaps realizing its significance, the narrator in "Pat shlemah" is filled with terror and suddenly remembers the letters. He stands up to rush to the post office (which is now closed [*na'ul*], all possibility of repentance being lost), and in doing so he collides with the waiter, upsetting the tray upon which his long-awaited meal is being brought. Like the garment, the letters are soiled: "They are soiled by mud and gravy [*u-va-rotev*] and wine" (p. 154). Like the tailor, he frantically attempts to repair his failure at the last moment and to act righteously.

The imagery at the conclusion of "Pat shlemah" is reminiscent of that at the start of "Ha-malbush." When the employees quit the restaurant, they leave one small lamp alight, like the sin-

---

31. Sanhedrin 72, 38. Holtz, op. cit., p. 306.
32. Shaked, op. cit., pp. 123–124.

gle candle illuminating the tailor's work, an intimation of his approaching death. The narrator sits in the darkness, as did the tailor. He sits before a table covered by a dirty cloth and laden with bones and empty bottles, an inversion of his vision of plenitude at the beginning of the story. He hears the sound of a key turning in a lock: "They" have locked him in, like the tailor in his dark, narrow room. The grinding of the key is "like the sound of a nail being driven into flesh" (p. 154). Later, the cold water of the river "cuts into [the tailor's] old flesh like a blade" (p. 320). Both protagonists are "pierced" by their retribution. Both doze while the small light flickers, hardly illuminating the darkness. In both stories noises of people approaching are heard from outside, and in both some form of torture takes place in the protagonists' imagination.

No critic has convincingly explained the cat and the mouse in "Pat shlemah." The mouse is commonly held to represent the gnawing of the narrator's conscience; the cat is unexplained, except as part of a grotesque trial of horror. Both are elements of folk- or fairy tales, which generally utilize domestic animals rather than exotic wild beasts for good and evil. Animals that frighten designate human fear and guilt, in addition to a person's violent inclinations.[33] The cat and mouse, like the horses, signify elements of the narrator's self that increasingly threaten his positive tendencies. His terror of the gnawing mouse and his vivid description of its devouring his body reflect the corresponding terror of the tailor at the thought of the cruel and wicked servants who indeed wound him when they fetch him to the lord's palace. Agnon provides a bizarre parody of the narrator's longed-for meal through the mouse's gnawing, as if the entire story is mirrored in the mouse's greed. Also, hunger "gnaws" and consumes the individual, limb by limb. There is a strange echo in "Pat shlemah" of the children's nursery rhyme "Hickory

---

33. Bruno Bettelheim, *The Uses of Enchantment* (Harmondsworth: Penguin Books, 1987), p. 205.

Dickory Dock" in the narrator's hope that the clock will strike and frighten the mouse away. The "gnawing" of the mouse recalls Hofni, who "gnaws" into the narrator's brain. The narrator hears Gressler's carriage passing by outside, but it does not stop. The forces of evil surround him, within and without. He falls to the floor and sleeps and is found in the morning by the cleaners, *meshartim u-meshartot,* the term used to denote waiters and waitresses earlier in the story, and an echo of the lord's servants, *'avdei ha-sar.*

The opening scene of "Ha-malbush" contains every element suggesting the tailor's death and punishment beyond the grave: the darkness, the flickering candle, the distant sound of the lord's servants, the tailor's sleep. The closing scene of "Pat shlemah" repeats these elements: the darkness, the single light, the presence of satanic animals, the sound of Gressler's carriage, the narrator's sleep. But in this story the protagonist does not yet face his heavenly judgment: He arises the next morning, only to begin the entire terrible process again.

The problem of the ordinary man's blunders, his inability—despite his self-knowledge—to prepare adequately for his own salvation, either metaphysically or existentially, underlies these stories. This motif is repeated in both of them through metaphoric and linguistic doublings and similarities of narrative line. Not only are the central themes duplicated, but also precise referents, repeated intertextually in identical form or by permutation, accentuate the intention of the stories and link them as examples of a prevailing preoccupation within Agnon's ideological reservoir.

6

S. J. Agnon and the Art of Sublimation

Nitza Ben-Dov

Verily it is well for the world that it sees only the beauty of the completed work and not its origin nor the conditions whence it sprang.
— Thomas Mann, "Death in Venice"

No doubt literature of the realistic school situates a given hero or heroine in a combination of contexts—historical, political, social, and economic—that constitute a total reality. Yet frequently these cadres may serve as a mask, metaphor, justification, or convenient vantage point from which to observe the thoughts and emotions of one who is detached, albeit not totally, from the aforementioned contexts. A case in point is Thomas Mann's "Death in Venice." The story unfolds against the background of an epidemic that threatens to ravage all of Europe, but its real focus is on the gradual psychological collapse of a great artist. In this ambience of infection and disease in Venice, Gustav Aschenbach, an artist immersed in the contemplation and pursuit of aesthetic beauty, encounters a number of strange and unfamiliar faces. For Aschenbach, these encounters crystallize his radical detachment from both external and internal realities, the latter being chiefly a bleak state of aged, unloved, and unloving bachelorhood. Clearly it is these encounters that precipitate his death, not the pestilential atmosphere of Europe. Aschenbach's encounters force him to confront and acknowledge the creeping decay of his physical, mental, and artistic self—a wrenching recognition for which he lacks a cure, and which kills him.

The theme of artistic endeavor, especially the literary enterprise—the acts of writing and reading, the attempt to discover the artist's sources of inspiration or his daemon, and the creative impulse itself—is one that naturally fascinates the artist and is expressed in his or her work. One could hardly expect those who devote their lives to writing, who write to live and live to write, to do otherwise, since the creative impulse lies at the nerve center of their being. Thus they cannot avoid pondering on paper why it is that they write, and to what end. So as to explore and develop this theme, an author may choose to make the central hero of his work a writer or artist as well. Gustav Aschenbach, for example, is a writer who has reached the end of the road. Harry Lesser, in Bernard Malamud's *The Tenants,* is a frustrated thirty-six-year-old writer struggling to complete his third novel, to which he has already devoted nine and a half years of his life. Writing from the top floor of an abandoned tenement in Manhattan, he stubbornly refuses to vacate the premises until he has finished his novel. The landlord, Mr. Levenspiel, begs Lesser to leave so that he, Levenspiel, can demolish the "rotten house that weighs like a hunch on his back" and set up a profitable, modern six-story apartment building in its place. Lesser refuses to oblige. In one of their fruitless talks, Levenspiel laments this sorry state of affairs and finally asks Lesser: "What's a make-believe novel, Lesser, against all my woes and miseries that I have explained to you?" Lesser, selling the potential virtues of his unfinished "minor" masterpiece, replies: "It exemplifies my best ideas as an artist as well as what life has gradually taught me. When you read it, Levenspiel, even you will love me. It will help you understand and endure your life as the writing of it has helped me sustain mine."[1] It is in that formula for spiritual and

---

1. Bernard Malamud, *The Tenants* (New York: Farrar, Straus and Giroux, 1971), pp. 21–22.

aesthetic fulfillment, treated with a possible edge of self-irony by Lesser, that we nonetheless find the condensed prescriptions for the art and labor of sublimation.

According to Freud, the achievements of civilization are attained through the suppression of instincts. If man is to become a civilized and socially useful animal, he must sacrifice, curb, deflect, channel, and, in Freudian terms, sublimate his libidinous and aggressive impulses. He must elevate his primitive instinctual drives to finer, higher, socially acceptable aims, until the libidinous component is no longer recognizable. Although in most artistic and scientific creations we cannot discern the phases and displacements of the sublimating process, some artists deliberately focus on the twists and turns of sublimation, rendering it the central theme of their work. In order to re-create, in artistic form, the indirect and circuitous route by which we all, according to Freud, learn to sublimate our forbidden desires, many writers introduce apparent digressions into their work. These digressions, which may take the form of a story within a story, the *composition en abîme* parables, daydreams, fantasies, and nightmares, will deflect the reader unskilled in Freudian technique from focusing on that unique psychic energy and force that drove the author to write and that, in turn, motivates the characters in his work to behave as they do.

By resorting to the artifice of displacement, the author achieves two things: first, his work, in content and form, will reflect the detour by which physical gratification is replaced by spiritual fulfillment. Second, his work will reflect the individual and collective attempt to divert our attention from the sublimating process itself.

The channeling of instinctual drives into a higher and artistic form never ceased to preoccupy Samuel Josef Agnon. From his earliest pieces, such as "Agunot," "Aggadat ha-sofer," and "Tishrei," to his swan song, *Shira,* Agnon repeatedly gave expression to the *causa causans* of artistic inspiration. The theme was an intensely personal one for Agnon, one that he must have discovered prior to reading Freud. Those of Agnon's early stories that deal with unquenched erotic thirst that is sublimated into artistic endeavor were written between 1908 and 1912, after Freud delivered his introductory lectures but before his theory became common knowledge. The dates of Agnon's first publications prove that he identified the source of anxiety and found a psychoanalytic solution for it on his own. Yet we cannot deny that Agnon returned again and again to the motif of sublimation precisely at the time when Freud was dissecting the repercussions of sublimation in his *Introduction to Psychoanalysis,* published in 1915, and in *Civilization and Its Discontents,* published in 1930. In this period, from 1913 to 1924, Agnon was living in Germany and reading his way through German culture with the zeal of an autodidact, and it is extremely likely that he now acquainted himself with Freud's work. We can reasonably assume then that when Agnon came across a fine-tuned analysis, development, and scientific affirmation of a theme so central to his work, he may well have been moved to hone and refine a motif that had haunted him from the outset of his career. The process of sublimation, as it resurfaces in Agnon's later works, is a delicate and remarkably original adaptation of the concept of sublimation as understood and taught by Freud.

To illustrate my point, let us now turn our attention to the novella "Ad henna" (Thus far [first published in Israel in 1950 and not yet translated into English]). The plot of the novella unfolds in Europe against the backdrop of the First World War. Its obvious mixture of realism, clearly autobiographical elements, and surrealist interludes suggests that "Ad henna" has a psychological depth that many critics have overlooked in their respective analyses.[2] Aware of the fact that Agnon spent the war years in Europe before he returned to Palestine, these critics assumed

---

2. Barukh Kurzweil and other critics consider "Ad henna" more a document of cultural history than a work of art. See A. J. Band's *Nostalgia and Nightmare: A Study in the Fiction of S. Y. Agnon* (Berkeley and Los Angeles: University of California Press, 1968), pp. 346–347.

that the war was Agnon's primary inspiration for writing "Ad henna," the center of gravity around which all motives and actions in the novella revolved.[3]

Indeed, on the surface, it would seem that the war directly influenced the events that govern the behavior of the protagonist-narrator, Samuel Josef, who is most likely Agnon. By coincidence he is caught in the maelstrom and forced to become the war's unwilling tool. The reader or the critic is at first tempted to conclude that the protagonist's hunger, dislocation, and lack of shelter are a direct function of the war, which has steered him toward a particular course of action. But a closer reading suggests that for Samuel, the war and its attendant maledictions are really peripheral. Though he talks about the war and knows that it is a relentless and pervasive menace, in actuality the war is not the decisive factor controlling his decisions or actions. This is borne out in the bizarre episode of a sleepless night of meanderings, which displaces him in Chapter 8 of the work.

The chapter shifts into high gear when the narrator, who has previously run a number of fruitless errands in various locations in Germany, returns to his room in Berlin, only to find that a new tenant is occupying it. Thus he appears to be a helpless victim of circumstance. In truth, however, he had had no intention of returning to his old room, and the night of his return (described in Chapter 7) as well as the following one (Chapter 8) serve as a catalyst to reveal other, deeper sources of anxiety. The loss of his room is merely the pretext and the fertile ground for the emergence of his angst.

On the night in which Samuel seems to be wandering at random, he runs into both familiar and new faces. These nocturnal encounters, which occur on the dividing line between dream and reality, leave the reader perplexed. What function do they serve in the realistic, factual story? Perhaps we can more easily

---

3. See Nitza Ben-Dov, "Dreams and Human Destiny in *Ad Henna*," *Prooftexts* 7 (1987): 53–63.

grasp their significance if we view them as similar in kind to Aschenbach's fateful encounters with those strangers who forced him to confront the sad realities of his life. Predictably the hero of "Ad henna" is also an artist, a writer of sorts who began, but failed to finish, a work entitled *The History of Vestments* (*Sefer ha-malbushim*), a study of clothes throughout the ages and in all lands.

The writer, with no place to rest his weary head, spends the night wandering in various restaurants and cafés. In one café, at the beginning of the night, he meets an old friend, Josef Bach, whom he hasn't seen since the outbreak of the war. Josef's full name is Samuel Josef Bach, a fact we learn when the narrator informs us that he and Bach have the same first and middle names, "only my friend is known by his middle name and I'm known by my first." Samuel, who knows each member of Josef's family, asks how they are. One by one, Josef Bach recounts how unspeakable catastrophes have befallen them all. Josef, too, is a writer, in the midst of compiling a study tentatively entitled *The Biology of Events* or *The Recurrence of Things*. Surprisingly, the inspiration for his study of historical redundancy has nothing to do with the catastrophes that befell his family. He was inspired by another, unrelated experience, a completely personal one. He says to Samuel: "I was lying in a trench, when something happened to me. I can't really say I had ever experienced that moment, or anything similar to it, before. Yet I had the feeling that the moment, in essence, re-enacted an experience I had already known. ... I began to look into it." Josef tells Samuel that this unaccountable sense of déjà vu unsettled him several times, causing him to wonder: "That first event, is it a new creation, unprecedented, or is it the recurrence of things long forgotten?"[4] Josef, having explained the subject of his book to Samuel, inquires about the progress of Samuel's book. Succinctly, and in a

---

4. S. Y. Agnon, *Ad henna* (Jerusalem and Tel Aviv: Schocken Publishers, 1977), p. 85.

joke, Samuel replies, "I abridged it." "You abridged it?" asks Josef. "Why?" Samuel explains that one day, while packing for a trip, afraid that his voluminous *Sefer ha-malbushim* would prove too cumbersome to take along, he sat down and snipped off the margins of the pages with a pair of scissors. And on that concluding note of merriment the two friends laugh and go their separate ways, Samuel proceeding to another café.

At the closing hour of the second café, Samuel runs into and then joins a group of Jews from Palestine en route to a bakery shop to savor some freshly baked rolls. A Druze of questionable origin—Samuel is not really sure "if he is a Jew, a Syrian, or a Lebanese"—has tagged along with the group. No one ever reaches the bakery to sample the rolls, but Samuel, invited by the Druze, enters his studio and spends part of the night there. What had intrigued Samuel about this Druze, who is also a sculptor (again an artist!) was the latter's description of an epiphanic experience he would like Samuel to share with him at a rarefied hour of the night, "when the night and morning clash and then coalesce in harmony." And the Druze continues and describes to Samuel the scene he is liable to experience in his studio: "If you have ever traveled to Baalbek, you've noticed the ancient statues there at dawn. They burst through the dark as if rising from the bowels of the earth. I'd like to offer you a taste of something like it from my studio, at daybreak."[5] The narrator follows the Druze up to a damp, high-ceilinged room exuding odors of plaster, cold stone, earth, and tobacco. At that point, we learn rather incidentally that the Druze's real motive behind the invitation was to ask Samuel to serve as a go-between between the Druze and a former actress named Brigitta Schimmermann. The Druze, an image-maker, would like Brigitta to stand as model for a statue he would carve capturing her likeness. Half-drunk and practically asleep, the Druze mumbles this desire not to Samuel but to the inanimate statues in his studio.

---

5. Ibid., p. 87.

Who is Brigitta Schimmermann? She is a pretty and charming German lady who dresses with exquisite taste. She is a gentile, a longtime friend of Samuel. They had met well before the war, when she was still unmarried and an actress in a small theater in Berlin. It was the narrator's peculiar field of research—the study of garments throughout the ages and in all lands—that had brought the two together and sealed their friendship. The lovely actress had often consulted Samuel about her choice of clothes. In passing, it is worth noticing here that in Hebrew, the idea of a man courting a woman so as to advise her about her choice of clothes associates neatly with the term *rodef semalot,* in English, a "skirt-chaser," an irony that was surely intended by Agnon.

Brigitta is of capital importance throughout the novel. Were it not for her, the narrator would never have met the Druze or his friend Josef Bach on that sleepless night. It is because of her that the narrator has lost his room to another tenant. Samuel had indeed set out for Leipzig but digresses, as it were, when he decides to visit Brigitta, who has moved with her husband to Lünnenfeld, a town near Leipzig. He stays, or strays, in Lünnenfeld longer than he had anticipated, and when he returns to Berlin, his room is no longer vacant. Hence the causal link between Brigitta, the sleepless night, and Samuel's peculiar nocturnal encounters.

Before we enter the Druze's studio and attempt to explain Samuel's presence there in the latter part of the night, a brief explanation is in order to clarify the thematic and structural centrality of the eighth chapter in "Ad henna." The work contains fifteen chapters, and it would seem that we have undertaken a nearly impossible task—to isolate and explain a single chapter with seven chapters preceding and following it. But Agnon's concentration on the events of a particular night transforms the chapter into a story within a story, and that middle and pivotal chapter can indeed stand on its own. Moreover, in this episode the protagonist encounters entirely new people with whom he shares experiences that are detached from the novella's external plot. Consequently, the interconnection must be made at an-

The Link to Previous Events
The "Cause of all Causes"
Brigitta Schimmermann—a former actress, gentile

The Protagonist
Samuel Josef—a writer
The History of Vestments Throughout the Ages, an unfinished work;
friend of Brigitta Schimmermann and her ex-adviser on clothes

Events on a sleepless night—Two encounters with one hiatus

First Encounter	*Hiatus Between Encounters*	*Second Encounter*
Samuel Josef Bach—a writer, *The Biology of Events,* or *The Recurrence of Things,* a work in progress. Friend of Samuel Josef.	Samuel Josef joins a group of Zionists en route to a bakery to eat "fresh rolls."	Druze—an artist, "image-maker," who longs to cast the image of Brigitta in stone. He offers Samuel Josef "a taste of Baalbek" in his exotic studio.

FIGURE 6.1 "Ad henna"—Chapter 8: a sleepless night.

other level of progression, and Chapter 8 serves as the fulminating point that melds the implicit and allusive elements in "Ad henna," opening the reader's eyes to another dimension of the work. Figure 6.1 is intended to explain the events of the eighth chapter of "Ad henna" and its link to previous events.

Let us then return to the Druze. Who and what does he represent? From the chapter we understand that he was once a barefooted shepherd in Palestine now turned sculptor in Berlin. But how are we to interpret the mutual interest and immediate communion between Samuel and the Druze, to the point that Samuel agrees to follow the Druze to his studio at a strange hour of the night? If the Druze yearns to sculpt Brigitta's body, why does he mumble this longing to himself and his statues rather than address Samuel directly? How does he know Brigitta Schimmermann at all? Perhaps the definitive answer, if there is one, lies buried in the obscure recesses of Samuel's mind, to which neither he nor we have access. But we can nonetheless attempt a partial illumination.

Brigitta is the object of Samuel's illicit desire. That forbidden desire brought him to the Druze's studio. As mentioned earlier, Brigitta is the activating switch that unleashes a chain of events, and because of her persuasiveness, Samuel stays in Lünnenfeld longer than he should have and becomes a homeless vagabond. At the beginning of the night, Samuel says to himself: "Madame Schimmermann had the best intentions, but the outcome does me no good at all. A man should never hold up the departure of a friend." Samuel then associates his delay at Brigitta's home with the infamous episode from Chapter 19 of the Book of Judges, the story of the Levite and the concubine in Gibea. Samuel muses: "Because the father of the concubine delayed the departure of the husband, a misfortune befell his daughter and several thousand Israelites were killed." Even while associating these two unlikely thoughts, however, he whispers to himself: "Yet without you, Brigitta, I would find myself without a roof for the night." Thus Brigitta is simultaneously haven and homelessness and, on occasion, the harbinger of temporary solution to ephemeral problems. These solutions, such as the narrator's momentary shelter in the Druze's studio, fall into a no-man's-land, where dream and consciousness, parable and truth, fantasy and reality, intersect.

To tease, or perhaps to deceive us, Agnon orchestrates the nocturnal episode so that it occurs when Samuel is awake. Ostensibly, the action is taking place in a realistic framework— cafés, restaurants, and studios. But in truth, Agnon has slipped into a surrealistic realm. All the encounters are taking place in the twilight zone, the dreamlike state where Samuel will come face to face with various fragments of his split soul. The two parts of that self, embodied in two encounters, appear separately in different parts of the night. They do not confront each other because Agnon inserts an intermezzo, or hiatus, which is the collective wandering after freshly baked rolls (the attraction to physical pleasures). Thus, the link between the two encounters is not obvious; nor is the link between the Druze and Josef Bach any the more explicit. Each encounter is structurally independent and self-contained. It is only the way in which Bach and the Druze appear—their past and present connection with Samuel, and the location, development, length, and timing of each encounter—which clarifies who is the revealed self and who the inner self; who represents the self in a new guise and who represents the suppressed self; and finally, which of the two is the sublimated self and which the raw and unconscious self.

The encounter with Josef Bach at the beginning of the night is an encounter with the conscious self. That part of Samuel perceives a world in which physical and human evil are omnipresent and beyond human control. The wakeful part of his personality seeks to comprehend and lay down the rules of this cyclical, recurring evil in the book on "the recurrence of things." When compared to a work of such intellectual magnitude, the importance of a book on clothes is minuscule.

The book on the history of vestments is a veiled expression of Samuel's forbidden lust for a gentile woman. Indeed, the book was the cause of their friendship in the first place. When work on it ceases with the advent of the war, not only does it remain unfinished but also the "biology of events" continues to fritter it away. Hence, the symbolic significance of Samuel's cutting away the margins of his book, *Sefer ha-malbushim*. The book on the recurrence of things, or the biology of events, eventually eclipses the book on the history of clothes and drapes its nudity.

The very title of the book on vestments betrays its essential bareness. This becomes clear once we reassess the reason why Samuel began to write the book on vestment at all. Confiding in Brigitta, he says: "I was a young man and my eyes were filled with shapes of many kinds. ... I tried to reproduce them on paper, but thought that I should dress them first. ... I began to look. ... And so I immersed myself in a barren pastime. Now I have to protect it from the moths."[6]

---

6. Ibid., pp. 47–48.

When he was young and impassioned, gazing upon naked shapes in need of clothes, Samuel began "to make" his book. But he soon discovered that the paper and clothes, the raw material of his special occupation, must be protected from moths and he therefore decides to replace them with words and syllables. The substitution of concrete materials by abstract ones—words, the cerebral stuff of literature—will guarantee him a place in eternity. At the same time, the creation itself becomes further and further removed from its primal, forbidden, and socially unacceptable source. But the book on clothes, and the author's materialistic approach to it, belies a real preoccupation with what is underneath; it is a screen or mask for the shapes *under* the clothes. Samuel's exterior focus is disingenuous.

Once the book on vestments is superseded or "covered" by the book on the recurrence of things, the objects of Samuel's lust and longing will have been sublimated as well. When the creator's real desire—the spark that fires his creative energy—is disguised and transformed beyond recognition, the sublimating process is consummated and civilization will have triumphed.

The circuitous road to sublimation is discernible in the writer's singular preoccupation, his study of garments, and in his encounter with Josef Bach, the author of *The Recurrence of Things.* The writing of a historical or anthropological piece on clothes in all their permutations throughout the ages is a respectable pastime, intellectual and quasi-scientific. It is the topic—clothes—which is peculiar and arouses our suspicions. On the surface there is no difference between the book on clothes and the treatise on the biology of events. But appearances to the contrary, there is a crucial difference in approach. Samuel's orientation is decidedly materialistic and sensual. The subject of the book, the quip on why he "abridged" his work, the very act of cutting off the margins of the pages with a pair of scissors, contrast sharply with Josef's more cerebral and loftier orientation. Samuel's only remaining task, now that he has draped the nude images in his mind with clothes, is to drape himself with the personality of an author who writes intentionally or unintentionally, about the same naked subject, but in a different and nobler guise. There *The Book of Vestments* metamorphoses into *The Recurrence of Things,* which is possibly "Ad henna."

In the thick of night, Samuel climbs more than a thousand steps in order to meet the darker side of his personality, the Druze, who is half-drunk and mumbling in his sleep. Samuel does not meet the dark side of his soul in the public arena but in an unidentifiable and otherworldly zone. This Druze does not talk about history, books, or family but about "men and women who haunt us and whom we desperately wish to know. And just as we are about to meet them, something interferes to prevent us from knowing them." The pursuit of these particular men and women becomes so obsessive, says the Druze, that "anyone we do meet irritates us, as if he or she usurped the place of those we sought to know."[7] We soon learn that the Druze's obsession is fixated on Brigitta Schimmermann. During those hypnotic hours before daybreak, the Druze expresses the suppressed desires of his guest, Samuel. Just as Samuel's nonliterary, tactile orientation is betrayed in his joke and in the subject of his book, the same disclosure is made, this time naked as the day it was born, when Samuel confronts his unconscious self, the Druze, disguised as a sculptor. Belatedly, the morning after his sleepless night, Samuel grasps the stratagem of the Druze who wanted to sculpt the body of Brigitta Schimmermann. Samuel engages in a classic projection of his own desires onto the Druze, because that projection enables him to avow his own illicit desire. Just as the model stands naked before the artist, so Samuel's desire for Brigitta is finally exposed.

If we juxtapose Samuel's thoughts with those of the Druze, we find that both of them wish to transubstantiate the same shapes that "fill their eyes"—only one wishes to do it in relative abstraction on paper, the other more palpably in stone. Brigitta appears to us in alternate states of dress and undress as the motifs of vestments and nudity are interchanged.

---

7. Ibid., p. 87.

The Druze, Samuel's darker self, refers to a Canaanite-sounding location, Baalbek (Baal—idol of the Canaanites; in Hebrew *Baal bekhi* means Lord of Tears; it sounds also like the ancient Baalbek in Syria). The Druze himself is described as an *'oseh tzelamim,* an image-maker, or a maker of idols. The pagan worship of Baal, the notions of exile and otherness, all these give off the unmistakable pungency of idolatry. The notion of idol worship is then associated with an adulterous longing for a gentile woman, a desire that the Druze in Samuel yearns to fulfill. The Druze, a member of an ancient and mysterious sect, a minority religion in the Muslim world, externalizes the longing buried in the mind of this Jew from Palestine who hankers after a forbidden woman. The Druze is thus a romantically alluring amalgam. He is otherness, inadmissible lust, mystery.

For Agnon, or for Samuel, these sexual and mysterious elements are simultaneously stimulating and oppressive, and he finds no better outlet for the tension than artistic creation. Thus, in "Ad henna," Agnon draws upon the biblical sources and on the legacy of the Jewish heritage to create a finished product that mirrors a crucial phase in the triumph of civilization, when society forces the individual to restrain his impulses and channel them into socially acceptable domains.

At this point I shall return to Malamud's novel *The Tenants,* since I see a parallel between a secondary figure there, Willy Spearmint, a black writer, and the brown-skinned sculptor, the Druze, in "Ad henna." The two dark artists in these two respective works represent, among other things, the hidden motives of artistic creation that fire the two main "white" characters. In effect the sublimation of raw and pristine sexual energy is a process shared by all four artists, black as well as white. The difference is one of degree. In *The Tenants,* Harry Lesser, the white Jewish writer, is the more sophisticated one, but less in touch with the authentic stirrings of his soul, whereas Willy Spearmint, his black colleague, a live wire of unrestrained emotion seething in his hatred of white America, is a less polished writer but therefore a more authentic creature. Whatever their differences, as part of the sublimating process they both abandon the woman they love. Irene, a white Jewish woman, is the object of both Willy's and Harry's imperfect love as they sacrifice themselves, and her, to finishing their novel. In this respect and others they seem to be interdependent fragments of a single artistic and human entity that cannot live at peace with itself. They are keenly jealous of each other, both as human beings and as struggling writers.

In both "Ad henna" and *The Tenants,* the writers' confrontations with repressed and dark aspects of their personalities have more than individual, national, romantic, and in *The Tenants,* racial implications. Theirs is an encounter with the artist within them. In *The Tenants* their collision has caused the sublimating process to go awry. Neither Harry nor Willy completes his novel, neither retains Irene's love, and their split soul, as the conclusion of *The Tenants* seems to indicate, pays the ultimate price for its relentless state of war—a double murder. In "Ad henna" the situation is different and the encounter does not propel Samuel to self-destruction. Samuel's encounter with the Druze, the sculptor, reveals a desire to fix the image of longing—in this case the image of Brigitta—in eternity and thereby master her by exorcising her. The act of carving Brigitta's image in marble would finally enable Samuel to terminate his fantasies about her and help him break the vicious cycle in which he finds himself entrapped. For if Brigitta started out as something real—a woman of flesh and blood whom Samuel knew before the war— she eventually became a vision, an illusion, a fantasy, and a dream. Only the artistic enterprise can render the illusion palpable and accessible to all. Freud's hypothesis, that art can serve as the vehicle through which one finds the path back to reality, sheds considerable light on the meaning of Samuel's various confrontations with himself.

> An artist ... finds a path back to reality. ... He understands how to work over his day-dreams in such a way as to make them lose what is too personal about them. ... He understands, too, how to

tone them down so they do not easily betray their origin from proscribed sources. Furthermore, he possesses the mysterious power of shaping some particular material until it has become a faithful image of his phantasy. ... If he is able to accomplish all this, he makes it possible for other people ... to derive consolation and alleviation from their own sources of pleasure in their unconscious which have become inaccessible to them; he earns their gratitude and admiration and he has thus achieved through his phantasy what originally he had achieved only in his phantasy—honour, power and the love of women.[8]

The mysterious encounter in the last watch of the night between Samuel and the artist within him is cathartic. Once the object of his longing and lust is externalized, be it on paper or in stone, others can derive benefit from it as well. Both the artist and his audience will learn to "sustain and endure life" once their energy is deflected from the forbidden and is sublimated, be it through the ordinary channel of work or through the creative process of art.

I shall close with a quotation from Agnon in "Ad henna." As we have seen, both the form and content of his novella are structured to reflect the twists and turns, the deceptive displacements, of the sublimating process. The following excerpt is a fine example of that mechanism.

I won't dwell on irrelevant events. Only their Maker really knows why they happen. I don't. Sometimes they are like the shadows connecting dream to dream, dismissed and forgotten even as they come to be, and then we find ourselves looking at dreams as if they were unconnected and rootless. So I'll put aside anything that seems irrelevant to the tale, like the book of my friend Josef Bach on the recurrence of things, or like the fresh rolls we didn't eat, or like the Druze imagemaker who sought me out because he sought to be near Brigitta Schimmermann, be-

---

8. Sigmund Freud, *Introductory Lectures on Psychoanalysis,* trans. James Strachey (New York and London: W. W. Norton, 1977), pp. 376–377.

cause he sought to fix her shape in marble, because she is beautiful, because she is charming, and since he saw us strolling together he thought I could cajole her to stand before him to let
him fashion her image, and after all that he let me be and didn't
ask for a thing. And since he let me be, I'll return to the essence
of the matter.[9]

The essence of the matter is, of course, what Agnon would have
us dismiss or forget. But a naïve reading of this excerpt is no
longer possible. The reader, aware of Freud's notions of sublimation, repression, and avoidance, as was Agnon, knows better.

---

9. *Ad henna,* chap. 9, p. 108.

ᴈᴆ **7** ᴂᴊ

A Guest for the Night:
Epitaph on the Perished Hopes
of the *Haskalah*

Judith Romney Wegner

An interesting feature of *A Guest for the Night,* Agnon's most important work,[1] is its character as historical criticism. It depicts the failure of the multiple responses of nineteenth-century European Jewry to the Enlightenment and its Jewish offshoot, the *Haskalah.*[2] It is the author's testament to the inability of European Jewry to find an adequate replacement for the traditional culture that for centuries had sustained Jewish self-identification and raison d'être in an alien world. Agnon bears witness to the disappointment of the *maskilim,*[3] who had hoped

---

1. For this assessment, see, e.g., Simon Halkin, *Modern Hebrew Literature: Trends and Values* (New York: Schocken Books, 1950), p. 155; Arnold Band, *Nostalgia and Nightmare: A Study in the Fiction of S. Y. Agnon* (Berkeley and Los Angeles: University of California Press, 1968), p. 284; Robert Alter, *After the Tradition* (New York: E. P. Dutton, 1969), p. 143.

2. *Haskalah* denotes the Jewish Enlightenment that followed in the wake of the European Enlightenment. The name comes from the Hebrew root *s-k-l,* meaning "to acquire wisdom, to understand, to make intelligent."

3. This term can mean either "enlighteners" or "enlightened ones," depending on whether the root verb is interpreted transitively or intransitively. Either way, it signifies devotees of the Enlightenment.

to forge a modern Jewish identity compatible with the Age of Reason, as well as to his own profound disillusionment with the failure of the *Haskalah.*

Agnon filters the failure of the *Haskalah* through the lens of the emotional and intellectual contradictions that flowed from the breakdown of ghetto and shtetl[4] barriers and the development of alternative modes of Jewish expression during the nineteenth century. These new modes ranged from the bourgeois acculturation associated with progressive forms of Judaism in Western Europe to utopian socialism and Zionist nationalism in Eastern Europe, and included the revival (principally in Czarist Russia after 1850) of the Hebrew language as a medium of Jewish literary expression. Its revivers used this medium for two related purposes: to propagate a secular-humanist viewpoint based on rationality and morality (the twin gods of the Enlightenment) and to attack the traditional life-style of the shtetl, with its physical and intellectual constraints and its stultifying effect on the development of the human spirit.[5]

Hebrew as the Medium of the
East European *Haskalah*

The development of modern Hebrew literature in Eastern rather than Western Europe was no accident but stemmed from two significant differences between the situation of East and West European Jewry, one historico-political and the other socioeconomic in nature. The first important distinction between Eastern and Western Jews lay in the political structure. The set-

---

4. These were rural towns in which the Jews often formed a majority and were in any case residentially segregated from the peasants of the surrounding region.

5. As depicted, for instance, in Peretz Smolenskin's *Kevurat hamor* (Vienna: 1874).

tlement of Jews in Western Europe had been regulated since the
Middle Ages by a system of residence permits (*hezkat ha-yishuv*).
This system, operated by community leaders with one eye
trained on the reactions of gentile neighbors, effectively controlled the number of Jews who could congregate in one place
and prevented the formation of large, residentially segregated
Jewish enclaves. The consequent dispersal of the Jews among the
gentile population had encouraged some knowledge of local
languages (French, German, English) among the Jews of
Western Europe, even before emancipation brought secular education within the reach of those who aspired to it. Hence,
Enlightenment ideas reached the Jews of Western Europe earlier
than their brethren in the East. Following the first partition of
Poland in 1772 (which brought large numbers of Jews under the
rule of a Russia that had previously excluded them),[6] the policy
of the czars had been to confine the Jews as far as possible within
the area of Russia-Poland known as the Pale of Settlement.
There, Jews were largely isolated in shtetls.

Despite the shtetl's economic dependence as a market town
on the Polish peasantry, not to mention its political dependence
on the Polish nobility (and, later, on the czar, after the failure of
the Polish uprising of 1863),[7] Jewish contact with gentiles was
limited to bare essentials. This prevented many from acquiring
fluency in the local language, thus reinforcing reliance on
Yiddish as their spoken and written means of communication.
Lack of facility in Russian and Polish on the one hand and virtual ignorance of Western European languages on the other
slowed still further the gradual percolation of the Enlightenment
from West to East. Despite the theoretical availability of secular
education to all who desired it (for instance, in Russia from 1825

---

6. Y. Slutsky, "Pale of Settlement," 13 *Enc. Jud.* 24.
7. David G. Roskies, *Against the Apocalypse: Responses to Catastrophe in Modern
Jewish Culture* (Cambridge, Mass.: Harvard University Press, 1984), p. 110.

on), most East European Jews remained insulated from European secular culture. As Michael Stanislawski has noted, "At the end of Nicholas' reign, as at its beginning, the overwhelming majority of Russian Jews lived traditional Jewish lives in autonomous communities insulated and isolated from Russian culture and mores."[8] The only way midcentury *maskilim* could disseminate their ideas to large numbers of Jews, especially to the yeshiva students who made up the Jewish intelligentsia, was by using Jewish languages, that is, Yiddish or Hebrew.

Since Hebrew had long fallen into disuse as a spoken language (and even as a written language for all but the most learned), Yiddish was the normal means of communication among Jews. But most *maskilim* saw Yiddish as the language of benighted obscurantism, incapable of expressing the scientific and humanistic ideas of the Enlightenment. The *maskilim* of Eastern Europe conceived the notion of reviving Hebrew for this purpose—thus, by a curious paradox, employing the most sacred of mediums for the most secular of messages. (Only later, with the rise of Jewish nationalism, did the use of the Hebrew medium become part of a specifically Zionist message.) Thus modern Hebrew literature was born, developing from the first naïve attempts of Abraham Mapu to adapt the language of the Bible to the purposes of the Hebrew novel,[9] through the baroque prose of S. J. Abramowitz (Mendele Mokher Sefarim), Peretz Smolenskin, and others, to the "more mature and satisfying works of the subsequent [turn-of-the-century] period."[10] The fiction of the

---

8. M. Stanislawski, *Tsar Nicholas I and the Jews* (Philadelphia: Jewish Publication Society, 1983), p. 185.

9. Mapu's *Ahavat Tziyon* (1853) is generally designated the first Hebrew novel. See David Patterson, *Abraham Mapu: The Creator of the Modern Hebrew Novel* (London: East and West Library, 1964).

10. David Patterson, *The Hebrew Novel in Czarist Russia* (Edinburgh: Edinburgh University Press, 1964), p. 65.

maskilim was to reach its culmination in the work of Agnon, who as a post-*Haskalah* writer bridged the gap between the Hebrew literature of the nineteenth and that of the twentieth centuries.

The second important difference between the Jews of Eastern and Western Europe lay in the virtual absence in the East of a bourgeois class like that which had developed, for instance, in prerevolutionary France. The medieval social structure of Czarist Russia embraced only two indigenous classes (besides the clergy), namely, the nobility and the peasantry. East European Jews, belonging to neither class, and more comparable socioeconomically with a bourgeoisie, lacked the opportunities that developed in the West for ideological self-identification with the enlightened humanism of the rising intelligentsia. More important, the elite group of East European Jews who had studied at universities in the more advanced cities of Poland, Russia, or even Germany lacked a receptive audience. Their only possible targets were the Jews who still remained in the shtetl or were just now emerging from its intellectual confines. Not surprisingly, the *maskilim* concentrated on subverting the young yeshiva students who constituted the shtetl intellectuals, as well as the rapidly growing urban working class, by exposing the deficiencies and corruptions of the traditional life-style. But these students could be reached only through the languages of the Jews; and disdaining Yiddish, many *maskilim* turned to Hebrew as the only viable alternative.

As the century wore on, and the rise of nation-states in Europe replaced Enlightenment notions of universal brother-hood with exclusive nationalistic sentiments, the *maskilim* turned more and more to the promotion of Jewish national conscious-ness and the movement for resettlement of Jews in Palestine. In addition, the spread of populist movements among the burgeoning proletariat, as the Industrial Revolution moved east-ward, eventually produced a socialist brand of Zionism, which, though stressing universal as well as national ideals, still chose to express itself in the Hebrew language. Thus Hebrew became the medium of various forms of Jewish self-expression in the late nineteenth century.

Cultural Dichotomies and Cognitive Dissonance

Ideological options for post-Enlightenment European Jewry were quite diverse. A Jew could, at the outset, accept or reject the Mendelssohnian attempt to reconcile the rationalism of the Enlightenment with the revelation of the Hebrew Bible. Those who accepted this solution in principle (including those who rejected it in practice) went on to develop new forms of Judaism, such as the enlightened neoorthodoxy of Samson Raphael Hirsch and progressive or scholarly Jewish movements like Reform Judaism and the Wissenschaft des Judentums. But many Jews, rejecting the politics of religious accommodation, found themselves facing irreconcilable ideologies with no satisfactory solutions. A Jew could reject the Enlightenment out of hand and remain within the fold of tradition, accepting the obscurantist constraints upon his intellectual development. Or he might divorce himself from Jewish tradition and espouse Enlightenment values instead, only to risk suffering the trauma of gentile rejection, the limitations of what Jacob Katz has called the "semi-neutral society,"[11] and the consequent disillusionment with those who preached universalism but would not practice it. Jews who tried the latter route experienced a twofold alienation—first from their Jewish roots and then from the secular world that rebuffed their desire for social acceptance. Even those who espoused a more sympathetic ideology, such as socialism or Zionism, would find in time that the reality did not measure up to the ideal.

These disappointments generated cognitive dissonance. The incompatibility of tradition and modernity, and the failure in

---

11. Jacob Katz, *Out of the Ghetto: The Social Background of Jewish Emancipation 1770–1870* (New York: Schocken Books, 1978), p. 201.

practice of cherished ideals, whether of the Enlightenment itself or of a particular ideology substituted for Jewish tradition, produced a sense of alienation—from the sacred, from the secular, sometimes from both. It is with these alienated groups that the fiction of Agnon concerns itself. His writings testify eloquently to the plight of the Jew who, opting for a secular alternative to the hallowed forms of Jewish expression, experiences a profound letdown as he falls into the spiritual abyss that yawns between his traditional background and his newly acquired secular knowledge—between the kerygma of the secular millennium and the discovery that Utopia remains beyond reach.

The unbridgeable gap between traditional Judaism and enlightened humanism forced painful choices on the Jews. To sacrifice tradition on the altar of modernity was to give up the safety of the known for the insecurity of the unknown. The Jew who spurned his sacred faith for secular delights, rejecting time-honored group norms in the newfangled quest for personal fulfillment, traded the certainties of communal regulation for the agony of soul-searching and the hazards of anomie. In the end, as portrayed in Agnon's masterpiece, *A Guest for the Night,* order lapses into chaos and (to paraphrase Arnold Band's graphic figure) nostalgia becomes nightmare.[12]

You Can't Go Home Again

A Guest for the Night tells the story of a year in the life of a Jew who returns in 1929, after a twenty-year absence, to the little town in Galicia where he grew up. The protagonist, cast as an anonymous narrator (who, however, represents both Agnon and the Everyman of the shtetl), makes an abortive effort to revive and relive the comforting security of his youth. His return is motivated by disillusionment with the alternative expression of Jewish identity he adopted when "the little books [of *Haskalah*]

---

12. Arnold Band's *Nostalgia and Nightmare* is the *locus classicus* of Agnon studies.

... made me leave off the study of the Torah."[13] Emigrating to Palestine, he found his dream of Zion unmatched by the reality; his house was burned down by rioting Arabs, so that even in the Jewish homeland he felt alien and rejected. Recast as a Jew in Exile, the narrator returns as a "guest for the night"[14] to his former hometown. There, he confronts the physical and spiritual destruction of a once-flourishing traditional community now in the last stages of decay. The very name of the town, Szibucz (almost an anagram of Agnon's birthplace Buczacz) signifies in Hebrew "breakdown," "disruption," and "confusion." The narrator soon discovers that the few old-timers who still go through the motions of religious observance have lost all sense of its significance. Most of those who seek a meaningful existence have already left town or are on the point of leaving in quest of viable alternatives. The narrator encounters some who remain, or who left but have returned; in every case, they have failed to find a worthwhile substitute for the traditional way. Like the protagonist, they too have learned that "you can't go home again." They have given up an irretrievable treasure for a utopian mirage.

Through his portrayal of these characters, Agnon calls attention to the failure of all the choices the Enlightenment had presented to the Jew. For instance, we meet Schuster, a tailor who, opting for bourgeois assimilation, had emigrated to Germany. There he prospered financially; but his wife could not adjust to Berlin, where "the walls of the houses reach up to the sky and block the air one breathes" (p. 58)—a metaphor for Jewish spiritual suffocation in an incompatible gentile environment. So the tailor returns to a Szibucz decimated by the Great War of 1914–

---

13. P. 109. Unless otherwise indicated, page references are to S. J. Agnon, *A Guest for the Night,* trans. Misha Louvish (New York: Schocken, 1968). The transliterations of Hebrew names given in Louvish's translation have been preserved here.

14. The Hebrew title is taken verbatim from Jeremiah 14:8: *Oreah natah lalun,* literally, "a wayfarer who turns aside to spend the night."

1918, where he has become a failure, reduced to sewing an occasional garment for the rare customer who can still pay for a bespoke overcoat. A second bourgeois way was taken by Leibtche Bodenhaus, whose response to the Enlightenment was to choose German over Hebrew because "in my youth it was the German language that the world thought important" (p. 337). But he has failed to use his knowledge of German for any useful purpose (such as the study of *Wissenschaft*). Instead, he spends his time translating the Hebrew Bible into atrocious German verse—the sole, pathetic contribution he can now make to either Jewish or secular culture.

Those who opted for nonbourgeois alternatives have fared no better. Yeruham Freeman, a prototypical utopian idealist who saw socialism or communism as the modern incarnation of prophetic-messianic universal brotherhood, had gone to Palestine to fulfill his Zionist-socialist ideals (changing his name to the Hebrew *Hofshi,* with its *Hatikvah* overtones of Jewish liberation and autonomy). Freeman is bitterly disappointed to find that even in *Eretz Yisrael* management exploits labor, Arabs kill Jews, and workers starve. Expelled by the British for distributing socialist manifestos to Arabs and Jews alike, Freeman has returned to Szibucz, where he ekes out a living by repairing roads that lead, in Kafkaesque symbolism, only to the grave. Our narrator asks poignantly whether Freeman is repairing the road "from the graveyard to the town or from the town to the graveyard" (p. 84). Either way, socialism has signally failed to liberate Freeman from the bonds of tradition and the limitations of life in Szibucz.

Another path for post-Enlightenment Jews in Eastern Europe was to espouse Zionism of a quasi-messianic rather than socialist stamp. This choice, as we saw, did not work for our narrator, who settled in Palestine only to be burned out by Arabs. Szibucz harbors many more Zionist failures. Yeruham Bach, son of the cantor (the last truly pious Jew remaining in Szibucz), had likewise gone to settle in the Land. But after sending for his old father to join him, he was killed by an Arab (p. 14). His given name Yeruham (like that of the socialist Freeman) conceals an ironic pun; for though *yeruham* means "he will enjoy [God's] compassion," it also evokes the very reverse, by playing on *Lo-ruhama,* the name given to the prophet Hosea's daughter to symbolize God's rejection of Israel upon whom He "will no more have compassion."[15]

For still others in Szibucz, Zionism has failed. A local organizer, asked when he plans to leave for Palestine, answers that he cannot even think of going, because "there is a great deal of work here" (p. 341). The work turns out to consist in traveling around, distributing pamphlets, organizing organizations. This armchair Zionist refuses to visit a group of Jews preparing for kibbutz life on a nearby training farm, because "they do not belong to our organization." Party politics takes precedence over the realization of ideals. Even the dedicated youngsters whom the narrator visits in their clubhouse, the Gordonia,[16] cannot see clearly; in their dark club room, "which is like a blind man whose eyes have died" (p. 100), these young people no longer perceive the spiritual basis of Zionism, thus (from both the Guest's and the author's standpoint) "betray[ing] the religious and moral ideals of the movement and taint[ing] it with corruption."[17] The mentor for whom their clubhouse is named was not the poet Yehuda Leib Gordon, whose work our narrator admires, but rather the socialist Aaron David Gordon, who translated idealistic thought into practical action. This metamorphosis fails to please the Guest, who complains in parable (p. 101) that, whereas Gordon the architect asked for stone to build a temple, Gordon the builder used only brick to construct petty houses. Diaspora Zionists refuse to admit the failure of Zionist ideals in the Land itself, where petty politics divide those who should stand together. Moreover, dedicated youths who do try

---

15. Hosea 1:6.

16. Gordonia, a pioneering youth movement, was founded in Galicia in 1923.

17. David Aberbach, "Agnon and Jewish Nationalism," *L'Eylah* 21 (1986): 17.

to reach Palestine often cannot get in. Such a one is Zvi, who, despairing of an immigration certificate that never comes, eventually takes ship and swims ashore at Jaffa. Captured by the British, he is deported back to Szibucz, where his friends weep for him while "between one time of tears and another they hope for divine mercy" (p. 477). Thus is the Zionist dream reduced once more to a despairing messianic hope against hope.

A Guest for the Night, then, is Agnon's graphic depiction of the *Haskalah's* failure to forge viable alternatives to traditional Judaism. But what of that tradition itself? Can it somehow be retrieved to atone for those who, in various ways, have failed to achieve the messianic task of *tikkun 'olam* ("putting the world to rights")? As Agnon shows time and again, the narrator's Proustian attempt to recapture the vanished world of piety is doomed to fail. The ancient faith and values are gone forever; the gap between tradition and alienation cannot be bridged. The "guest for a night" is a wanderer who literally can't go home again. We see at last the point of the prophetic question that inspired the novel's title: "Why shouldst thou be a stranger in the land, a wayfarer who turns aside to spend the night?"[18] The old home is no more and can never be rebuilt. As Robert Alter has noted, the typical subject of Agnon's stories is "the physically, culturally, and most important, spiritually dispossessed."[19] In *A Guest for the Night* we see "perhaps the greatest single concern in Agnon's writings ... the problem of the modern man who, spiritually, finds himself with no place to live."[20] Having rejected the sacred traditions, communal norms, and secure life-style, he finds himself equally alienated from the alternatives. For the post-*Haskalah* Jew, as Baruch Hochman puts it: "the present is unbearable, and the past will not die; this is the dilemma in which the typical Agnon hero is caught. He tends to be disori-

---

18. *Oreah natah lalun,* Jeremiah 14:8.

19. Alter, *After the Tradition,* p. 148.

20. Alter, op. cit., p. 147.

ented, hanging between the madness and meaninglessness of the
world as it is and his bondage to a past which neutralizes the present even as it alienates him from it."[21]

The Past That Will Not Die

The narrator's bondage to a past that will not die is expressed in
his futile and forlorn attempt to revive the old life of prayer and
study in Szibucz. He cannot recapture the substance, only the
form. The story opens as he arrives home on the Eve of Yom
Kippur, to find the members of his old synagogue performing
the rituals of the Holy Day without any real enthusiasm. Daniel
Bach (another son of the pious Reb Shlomo) expresses the pervasive cynicism of those who still practice the traditions: "I'm a
sceptic, I don't believe in the power of repentance ... and I don't
believe the Almighty cares about the welfare of His creatures"
(p. 4). Bach lost his faith during the Great War, when he stum-
bled on the corpse of a Jewish soldier, blown to bits as he stood
praying in prayer-shawl and phylacteries. In *A Guest for the
Night,* as Sidra Ezrahi has pointed out, the First World War assumes a "mythic significance, recasting the past in the glow of
romantic yearnings for a lost age, while giving a temporal frame
to the troubles of the present."[22]

The figure of the skeptic Bach forms a counterpoint to that of
his father, the cantor, the last pious Jew in town, whose faith per-
sists despite the loss of his other son, killed by Arabs in Palestine.
The novel abounds with similar paradoxes illustrating the di-
chotomy of past certainties and present doubts. Thus, the narrator arrives in town just as a large contingent of his fellow congregants prepares to leave Szibucz for a better life elsewhere. He asks

---

21. Hochman, *The Fiction of S. Y. Agnon* (Ithaca and London: Cornell
University Press, 1970), p. 23.
22. Sidra Dekoven Ezrahi, "Agnon Before and After," *Prooftexts* 2 (1982): 78–
94.

them point-blank, "How can you leave what is certain and go to seek what is in doubt?" They answer, "We are leaving our place because He whose place is on high has left us" (pp. 12–13) —a subtle wordplay on the polysemous meanings of *makom*.[23]

The departing congregants hand the newly returned "Guest" the key to the Beit-Midrash, the old study house that he used to unlock daily to go in and study Torah. But now he finds the place deserted; plaster and whitewash have obliterated the grubby walls and blackened rafters that formerly bore witness to the constant presence of the pious studying by candlelight. The Guest manages to entice a few "students" back during the cold winter months, by supplying logs for the stove each day; but the clientele is sparse, the only "regular" being an old man, Reb Hayyim, formerly a great scholar, now reduced to lighting the candles and sweeping the floor of the Beit-Midrash. The vicissitudes of years of Siberian exile have destroyed his mind. Others, too, have fallen on hard times; Reb Hayyim's wife supports herself by running a small hotel, which has degenerated into a brothel; a woman named Sarah, reduced to poverty, is forced to part with a family heirloom, a Hebrew manuscript of her late husband's grandfather, which no one but the narrator still knows how to read. Even the communal rabbi turns out to be a pompous man who never reads his library of Torah books and is more concerned with the deference due his position than with ministering to his depleted congregation. The vibrant traditional world of yesteryear has vanished irretrievably, leaving in its place a hollow mockery; the sacred has been utterly profaned.

Besides irony, Agnon employs much symbolism. The very name of Szibucz, as we saw, denotes breakdown and decay. The first two people our hero encounters are physically handicapped, symbolizing their crippled minds and spirits. No child has been

---

23. "Manihim anu et mekomenu mipnei she-ha-makom hinihanu." Agnon, *Oreah natah lalun,* p. 18 (in *Kol sippurav shel S. Y. Agnon* [Tel Aviv: Schocken, 1953]).

born in the town for many years, a fact that prefigures the impending doom of a Judaism whose survival depends on the continuity of generations. The people of Szibucz wear worn-out clothes that match the threadbare quality of their lives. The heaviest symbolism of all surrounds the key to the Beit-Midrash. Our protagonist, retrieving it from those who have abandoned shtetl and Torah, hopes it will unlock for him not merely the study house but also the life he gave up years before. But his quest to recapture the past is soon frustrated; he loses the key and finds himself locked out of the Beit-Midrash and all it represents. The past is a closed book that cannot be reopened. Even when the locksmith—a mysterious old man who evokes the prophet Elijah playing on the messianic theme of *"Today!"* that may not come[24]—makes him a duplicate key, the Guest wonders whom to entrust it to when he leaves Szibucz, and how to preserve a tradition whose practitioners are no more. In the end, he offers the key as a circumcision gift to a baby boy born just as he leaves and named in his honor—one more expression of the forlorn hope the Guest will not abandon. But, as David Roskies has pointed out, the "hope of spiritual rehabilitation through a duplicate key to an Old House of Study in a fictional shtetl in Poland is not much in the way of consolation."[25] In sum, the characters and events lead to an inexorable conclusion: No one has found a replacement for two millennia of Jewish tradition, and the old ways have vanished for ever.

Agnon's Writing: Religious or Secular?

Critics agree on Agnon's place at the pinnacle of modern Hebrew literature. But they disagree on whether modern Hebrew literature in general is continuous with Jewish tradition or constitutes a break with it. First, is this literature religious or

---

24. B. Sanhedrin 98a.
25. Roskies, op. cit., p. 132.

secular? Second, does the answer to that question determine whether modern Hebrew literature (or a particular sample of it) represents continuity or a break with Jewish tradition? Both of these questions may be addressed to *A Guest for the Night*.

First, is Agnon a religious writer? Here we must consider what "religious" means. The mere fact that he employs the holy tongue, or even that his style mirrors the classical idiom of late-rabbinic Hebrew, does not dispose of the question. We must also consider Agnon's themes and his treatment of them.

A Guest for the Night abounds with religious themes. Both the form and the substance of the narrator's reflections proclaim the author's intimate acquaintance with the contents of Bible and Talmud. To select just a few from dozens of examples, Agnon cites the following talmudic maxims: With respect to the study of Torah (p. 94), "all your possessions will not equal its value"[26]; with reference to good deeds (p. 98), "for so long as a man lives in this world he can acquire virtuous acts and good deeds, of which a man eats the fruits in this world and the capital remains for the next"[27]; and concerning the gift of prophecy (p. 114), "since the day the vision was blocked, prophecy has been taken away."[28]

Agnon's intimate knowledge of liturgy and ritual emerges throughout the story. Indeed, he makes the narrator's visit last for almost a year partly in order to present the entire cycle of Jewish ceremonial observance, including the Kiddush recitation that precedes the Sabbath meal (p. 127); the requirement of a blessing before and after eating even a mere snack of tea and cake (p. 33); specific references to the daily worship (p. 118); details of festival prayers, above all, the closing service on Yom Kippur (pp. 17–20); the Passover seder (pp. 259–262); the custom of eating dairy foods on Shavuot (p. 285); as well as esoteric details

---

26. Y. Peah 1d, on Proverbs 8:11.

27. M. Peah 1, 1.

28. B. Bava Batra 12a.

like the practice of praying without prayer-shawl or phylacteries on the Fast of Tish'a B'Av (p. 363). Ironically, Agnon puts this custom in the mouth of a gentile of Szibucz, who rebukes an ignorant Jew for getting it wrong.

Besides his desire to portray the traditional observances of the Jewish religious calendar, Agnon may have had another, more subtle motive for making the Guest's visit last not quite a year. In fact, the visit ends after *eleven months.* (He arrives on the eve of Yom Kippur and takes his departure some weeks after Tish'a B'Av but before the advent of Rosh Hashanah.) In other words, the Guest's sojourn in Szibucz lasts for exactly the period of mourning, during which the bereaved must recite Kaddish everyday. And indeed, throughout his stay, the Guest has faithfully mourned the passing of the beloved, traditional world of his fathers.[29]

Not merely religious motifs but also religious sentiments pervade the story. Above all, as he mourns his lost heritage, we feel the desperation of the erstwhile devotee of Torah to recapture the ambience of the study house by reviving its forms, though he cannot resurrect its substance. This, despite our protagonist's opening disclaimer: "I am not one of those who compare the present to days gone by, but when I see the petty standing in the place of the great and the poor in deeds in the place of men of great achievement, I grieve over this generation, whose eyes have not seen Israel's greatness, who believe that Israel never had any greatness at all" (p. 9).

The disclaimer must be taken with a grain of salt; Agnon's whole purpose is precisely to compare the degraded present with the glorious past. So, too, when the narrator complains: "I am not one of those who argue with their Maker, but at that moment I said: Master of the world, Thou who didst create the whole universe, and in whose hands the universe lies, is it difficult for Thee, if I may say so, to give a little pleasure to Thy

---

29. I am indebted to Professor Arnold Band for sharing this insight with me.

sorely tried and loving sons?" (p. 115). Here he surely protests too much, for a principal theme of the book is the narrator's (and author's) implied dispute with the God who has abandoned Israel by letting Israel abandon Him.

Agnon's religious orientation is further expressed in the narrator's assertion that the Jews are God's chosen people, and in the talmudic depiction of Jews as the sons of kings and prophets:

> What is written in these [holy] books? The Holy One, blessed be He, created the universe according to His will and chose us from all the peoples and gave us His Torah so that we should know how to serve Him. ... The Torah surrounds those who study it with goodness and virtue and enhances their favor in the eyes of the world. ... For what reason did the Holy One, blessed be He, choose us and lay upon us the yoke of the Torah and the commandments, for is not the Torah heavy and difficult to observe? ... I will explain it by a parable. It is like a king's crown ... does the king refrain from putting the crown on his head because it is heavy? On the contrary, he puts it on his head and delights in it ... if I am not a king, I am a king's son, and I ought to know. But this man [a talmudic idiom meaning "I"] has forgotten, he and all Israel his people, that they are the sons of kings. The books tell us that this forgetfulness is worse than all other evils—that a king's son should forget he is a king's son. (p. 29)

Although the narrator ascribes these sentiments to "the books," they represent an affirmation of his own (and the author's) traditional stance. At the same time, Agnon expresses his own doubts about the value of clinging to the past, when he puts into the mouth of a young girl, Rachel, the following reply:

> Why should I take on myself the burden of past generations? Let past generations look after themselves and my generation look after itself. ... And as for what you said, that every daughter of Israel should think of herself as a daughter of kings, there's nothing more foolish than that. Today, when the crowns of kings are lying in museums and no one takes pride in them, you come and

say: Every daughter of Israel should think of herself as a daughter
of kings. (p. 30)

The narrator's ambivalence toward traditional Judaism is implicit also in his constant rebuke of those who preserve its forms
but debase its values. Thus, he complains of those who still as-
semble for daily prayer in Szibucz: "They disagree about the text
of the prayers, quarrel over every custom that one of them brings
from his home town as if it had been handed down from Mount
Sinai" (p. 96).

In like fashion, when a poor drayman (the *balagola,* symbolically the lowest man on the Jewish totem pole) gets lost in a
snowstorm, the town's rabbi criticizes the narrator for deciding
to recite *Avinu malkenu*—an invocation of God's mercy—on a
day when this prayer is not normally offered (p. 166). For the
faithful of Szibucz, form has totally eclipsed substance.

These and many other examples suggest a sense in which we
may fairly call Agnon a "religious" writer. His description, not
merely of traditional customs, but also of the emotions that
should ideally inform them, betrays his sympathetic stance. At
the same time, the narrator's searing indictment of the degener-
acy of Jewish life in Szibucz, coupled with his inability to recapture his own lost faith, raises for some critics of modern Hebrew
literature another question: Can Agnon's writing properly be
classified as continuous with Jewish tradition?

Continuity or Revolution?

Three prominent critics of Hebrew literature, Barukh Kurzweil,
Simon Halkin, and Dov Sadan, have debated the relationship of
modern Hebrew literature to traditional Judaism. Kurzweil takes
issue with Halkin and Sadan on the question whether this literature represents continuity or break with tradition. Halkin main-
tains that modern Hebrew literature, as the handmaiden first of
the *Haskalah* and then of Zionism, represents a link in an unbro-
ken chain of Jewish culture. Although recognizing the dishar-

mony between "this new body of Hebrew letters, mainly secular in character, and the religious Jewish folk life from which it sprang,"[30] he does not think its secularity per se disqualifies the literature from representing a continuous development of the tradition. For Halkin, then, Agnon's oeuvre, even if defined as secular, would constitute no break with Jewish tradition.

Dov Sadan likewise rejects the view that modern Hebrew literature represents a break with tradition. But he sees this literature, not as a secular creation of the Enlightenment, but rather as a synthesis that reconciles the conflict between the thesis of Jewish religious tradition and what Sadan regards as the "temporary antithesis" of the *Haskalah*. The Jewish literature that emerges in response to this crisis constitutes a new cultural synthesis, which derives its ultimate inspiration from the religious faith that is the source of all Jewish culture. For Sadan, Agnon's work is part of an ongoing process that by the very nature of the dialectal process represents continuity rather than revolt, regardless of its religious or secular designation.[31]

Barukh Kurzweil takes issue with the characterization of modern Hebrew literature as continuous with Jewish tradition. For Kurzweil, this literature, born of the *Haskalah,* is by definition a secular phenomenon. As such, it can only represent a break with traditional Judaism, whose religious values it deliberately set out to subvert.[32] Moreover, he sees it as an outgrowth of Sabbataian antinomianism and hence a secular perversion of Jewish tradition. However, Kurzweil's antagonism toward modern Hebrew writers does not extend to Agnon. He assigns the latter to what he calls the "tragic" period of Hebrew literature, that is, the aftermath of the *Haskalah,* when Hebrew writers began to realize "that the ideals of Enlightenment humanism

---

30. Halkin, op. cit., p. 33.

31. Dan Miron, "Dov Sadan," 14 *Enc. Jud.* 618–620.

32. Barukh Kurzweil, *Sifrutenu ha-hadashah: hemshekh o mahapekhah?* (Tel Aviv: Schocken Books, 1958), pp. 13, 19.

would not suffice as a new basis of Jewish existence, since the vague hopes of 'progress' they had aroused proved illusory."[33] For Kurzweil, the "tragedy" was made doubly bitter by the fact that just as these writers began to turn back from the values of the gentile world to inner Jewish values, there came the shocking discovery that religious faith, the foundation of Jewish life, had evaporated. Lost faith cannot be restored, no matter how ardently one may desire it; and in Kurzweil's view, the sentimental scribbling of those who yearn to recover Judaism but cannot resurrect their faith should not be called religious literature.

Even so, Kurzweil claims that "tensions between the Jewish past and present" with which Agnon deals "endow this fiction with an intrinsically bi-polar quality ... that ... enables Agnon to treat Jewish reality with an objectivity unprecedented in modern Hebrew literature."[34] Thus, in contrast to his reviling of Zionists and *maskilim* alike as apostles of secularity, Kurzweil sees Agnon as a hybrid, both a religious and a secular writer, who presents "a recapitulation of the sacral Jewish past ... an attempt to transcend the break between the past and the present by creating the possibility of a 'new continuum,' by implying the primacy of the timeless meta-historic over the finitude of history."[35] In the event, for Kurzweil, Agnon's empathy with traditional values (which, in typically orthodox stance, Kurzweil characterizes as "objectivity") saves his work from the twofold taint of damning secularity and discontinuity with the Jewish past.

In closing, I find the question of Agnon's religiosity greatly illuminated by anthropologist Clifford Geertz's seminal definition of religion: "A system of symbols which acts to establish powerful, pervasive and long-lasting moods and motivations in men by formulating conceptions of a general order of existence and

---

33. James Diamond, *Barukh Kurzweil and Modern Hebrew Literature* (Chico, Calif.: Scholars Press, 1983), p. 89.

34. Diamond, op. cit., p. 96.

35. Diamond, op. cit., p. 97.

clothing these conceptions with such an aura of factuality that the moods and motivations seem uniquely realistic."[36]

Geertz's definition captures the ambience of Agnon's work— perhaps encapsulates its essence. Viewing the "Guest" as Agnon's alter ego, his psyche stamped indelibly with his early training in traditional Judaism, one is tempted to claim that Agnon's writing constitutes a religion in itself. But that is another story.

---

36. Clifford Geertz, *The Interpretation of Cultures* (New York: Basic Books, 1973), pp. 87–125, "Religion as a Cultural System."

8

The Ancestral Tale—An Ironic Perspective

Esther Fuchs

The pervasiveness of biblical, talmudic, rabbinic, kabbalistic, and Hasidic allusions in the fiction of S. J. Agnon is obvious to the most casual and unequipped reader. The purpose of the present study is not to establish what critics like Kurzweil, Tochner, and Barzel,[1] among others, have amply demonstrated, namely, that reading Agnon without a keen awareness of Jewish traditional sources is like navigating in a stormy sea without a map and compass. Rather, what I would like to suggest here is that the maps charted by the allusive grid underlying much of Agnon's work often lead even the well-equipped navigator not to the happy shores he may have hoped to reach, but rather to the danger zones he wished to elude. When it comes to Agnon, the work is not completed with the acknowledgment of his indebtedness to Jewish sources and their specific identification; it only begins.

The first part of this article is based on a paper entitled "The Ironic Allusion in Agnon's Ancestral Tales: The Case of Parody," delivered in a special colloquium on "The Poetics and Politics of Allusion in Modern Hebrew Literature," held at the University of Maryland, College Park, 1983.
1. 1975, 1968, and 1975 respectively.

One of the most common pitfalls of allusion hunters is the premise that the Agnonic text not only echoes the themes, structure, and style of traditional Jewish literature but also endorses and promotes their underlying creeds and values. The belief that Agnon's ancestral tales are ideologically continuous with his sources has led some critics to describe these highly combustible materials as authentic traditional tales in which: "everything is harmonized within a dominant pattern of submission, and every discord is resolved within the pattern."[2] The following analysis of the first paragraph of Agnon's most elaborate ancestral tale, *The Bridal Canopy* (*Hakhnasat kalla*), demonstrates that the harmonized pattern is a misleading façade. The main function of Agnon's ironic pretense stems, not from a mischievous impetus to ridicule his readers, but from a deep-seated consciousness of the troublesome and often inadequate answers provided by Jewish traditional sources to the perennial questions of the existence of evil, the suffering of the righteous, and the tragic history of the Jewish people. By creating a dissonance between the allusive text and its original source, Agnon succeeds in dramatizing the failure of the traditional sources to address satisfactorily the fundamental problems raised in his works.

The allusion is only one of Agnon's ironic techniques. What follows is by no means an exhaustive discussion of Agnon's parodic techniques; neither is it a comprehensive analysis of his parodic allusion. It should rather be understood as a suggestive introduction to a much neglected aspect of Agnon's ironic art.

The opening paragraph of *The Bridal Canopy* consists mainly of a laudatory presentation of Reb Yudel, the hero of the novel. The first sentence establishes that Reb Yudel was a devout Jew, "as he used to sit on the Torah, and the worship of God."[3] This

---

2. Hochman (1970), 50.

3. This and all the following references to Agnon's works are based on my own translation. The English version of *Hakhnasat kalla* is available as *The Bridal Canopy*, trans. I. M. Lask (New York: Schocken, 1967).

description echoes Mishnah Avot 1, 2: "Rabbi Shimeon the Righteous used to say, the world stands on [i.e., depends on] three things: the study of Torah, the worship of God and charity." Yet Agnon's text deviates from the original verse in a way that points up the troublesome aspects of Reb Yudel's apparently immaculate devoutness. First, unlike the world that according to Rabbi Shimeon "stands [*'omed*] on" these values, Reb Yudel is said to "sit [*yoshev*] on" them, implying passivity and indolence on the part of the Hasid, as well as a hint of unintended disrespectfulness regarding the holy Torah. In addition, our text omits the third factor cited in the original source: charity. Thus the allusion to Avot is in a way a backhanded compliment to the hero: It stresses that Reb Yudel follows only two of the three mitzvot mentioned by Rabbi Shimeon. The reason for Reb Yudel's inability to practice charity becomes clear in the description of Reb Yudel's poverty. The truncated allusion then undermines the implied praise for his indifference to such presumably mundane affairs as "trade and commerce." The laudability of poverty is counterbalanced by the inability to fulfill the mitzvah of charity.

Another ironic allusion that undermines the narrator's praise of Reb Yudel appears in the description of the Hasid's early rising to "serve his Creator." Apparently the allusion to the halachic tract *Orah hayyim*[4] intimates that Reb Yudel behaves strictly according to the prescription that a Jew should "rise up [lit. overcome himself] like a lion to serve the Creator so that he will wake up the dawn." But our Reb Yudel, rather than rising up like a lion, is awakened every morning by his rooster, Reb Zerah.

The description of Reb Yudel's early morning prayers contains an allusion to the *Zohar* that seems to corroborate the description of his piety; Reb Yudel is said to "rush to the study house" even before the break of dawn in order to "fashion a link

---

4. 1, 1.

between the day and the night [*midat yom be-midat layla*]." The injunction to start prayers at night and continue them into the morning is meant to link the sphere of *Tiferet* (associated with the day) with the sphere of *Malkhut* (associated with the night). According to the *Magen Avraham* the day is ruled by mercy (*hesed*), whereas the night reflects the dominion of judgment (*din*).[5] A covert allusion to Reb Yudel's continuous worship by day and by night appears also in the opening sentence, which refers to the first chapter of Psalms: "But his delight is in the law of the Lord, and on his law he meditates day and night."[6] The irony here does not stem so much from the incongruity between the original and the new context, but rather from the juxtaposition of Reb Yudel's "day and night" and his family's: "[there was] but a straw mat spread on the ground, and his family used to lie on it, and would not move it *neither in the night nor in the day* so as not to spoil their clothes" [italics mine]. It becomes clear that while Reb Yudel is busy modeling himself after the idealized worshipers of the Bible and the Kabbalah, his family pines away in the "dark, narrow and damp cellar," unable to distinguish between night and day. By highlighting the *practical* consequences of Reb Yudel's piety, the text questions the moral validity and social usefulness of this piety.

Although the unreliable narrator insists on Reb Yudel's poverty and piety as his major assets, the ironic allusions keep deflating this exalted presentation by intimating that these assets are mutually exclusive rather than complementary. Thus we are told that Reb Yudel's devoutness does not stem from any ulterior motives but is unflinchingly directed at a single goal: "to make a chair for the Shekhinah [the Divine Presence] [*la-'asot kise la-shekhinah*]." The idiom *kise la-shekhinah* alludes to the kabbalistic notion that ever since the destruction of the Temple, the Shekhinah rests on *kise ha-kavod* (the Divine Chair), which is the

5. 1, 3.
6. Psalms 1:2.

highest part of the Superior Chariot (*ha-merkavah ha-'elyonah*), and the link between the created and the emanated world.

What turns Reb Yudel's aspiration into a preposterously arrogant ambition is the fact that the man who wants to furnish the Shekhinah with a seat cannot even make a chair for himself or his family: "There was no bench to sit on, and no bed to sleep on and no table to eat on." The analogy between the mystical chair and the physical bench points up the incongruity between the exalted idea contained in the allusion and the context in which it appears. The description of the "dark, narrow and damp" cellar turns Reb Yudel's wish to play host to the Shekhinah into inadvertent blasphemy. Reb Yudel's obliviousness to his immediate reality and his total absorption in the higher or invisible realities emerge as absurd rather than praiseworthy.[7]

The absurdity reaches a peak in the description of Reb Yudel's spiritual meals. Instead of having a proper meal, Reb Yudel overcomes his hunger by the help of sacral texts alluding to food. His breakfast consists, for example, of the story of the manna with which he "used to ... feed his intellectual soul."[8] When he grows unbearably hungry, or as the text puts it euphemistically, "when his heart assaults him concerning the issues of food and drink, he overcomes it with a page of Gemara, as it is said in the Torah." An acquaintance with the original sources reveals that they do not by any means recommend the ascetic mortification in which Reb Yudel indulges. On the contrary, the story of the manna presents food as a human necessity accepted and provided for by God Himself.[9] What the story decries is the gluttony of some of the Israelites who preserved the manna for future use, in defiance of God's instructions.[10] But Reb Yudel

---

7. Dan (1975), 174.

8 According to the *Orah hayyim* (1, 5) it is customary to recite the story of the manna after the morning prayer.

9. Exodus 16:11–36.

10. Exodus 16:20.

equates gluttony with hunger, thus misinterpreting the moral lesson of the story. Furthermore, the conception of hunger as a basically negative drive that ought to be curbed undermines the significance of the miracle wrought by God. Similarly, Reb Yudel abuses the original sense of Proverbs 9:5, interpreting "lekhu lahamu be-lahmi" as "go wage battle against my bread." The biblical verse, however, quotes Wisdom as saying the exact opposite: "Come eat of my bread, and drink of the wine I have mixed." The explicit citation of the source in the text makes it easier for the reader to compare the text to the source it quotes and to identify the incongruity between the two.

The ultimate ironic jibe at Reb Yudel's exaggerated piety as well as at the narrator's unreserved adulation is not so much the misinterpretation of the original sources as the pragmatic use the hero makes of these sources. By using the sacral sources as substitutes for physical food and drink, Reb Yudel does precisely what he fears most: "He turns the Torah into a pickax to dig with," against the explicit instructions of the sages.[11] The original rabbinic injunction forbids the use of the Torah as a source of income. Reb Yudel's culinary use of the Torah is just as exploitative as its reduction to a lucrative business. Ironically, by feeding on the Torah, so to speak, Reb Yudel inadvertently desecrates the holy text.

The satiric implications, generated by the incompatibility between the original source and Agnon's story, reflect on the former as well as on the latter. The source, in other words, is just as vulnerable to the ironic sting as the alluding text. An immediate example presents itself in the name of Reb Yudel's rooster, Reb Zerah. The unreliable narrator, in his effort to stress that even the most mundane details in Reb Yudel's life are fraught with religious meaning, points out that the rooster's names were inspired by the verse "zarah ba-hosheh or la-yesharim."[12] Al-

---

11. Avot 4, 7.

12. Psalms 112:4.

though the truncated quote creates the impression that the subject of *zarah* (shine) is *or* (light), a glance at the original, rather ambivalent, biblical verse reveals that the subject of *zarah* can also be God. This suggests that the rooster is the namesake of God and that, like God, it shines like a light for the righteous. The application of the divine action to a bird is a travesty of the original verse, a result that obviously runs counter to the intention of both hero and narrator, but not necessarily to that of the implied author.[13]

Whereas the biblical verse uses "light in the darkness" in a metaphorical sense, promising the righteous man divine deliverance from suffering and misery, our text refers to "light and darkness" literally. The comic effect of transforming a figurative meaning into a literal one is compounded by the fact that in Agnon's text God offers neither literal nor figurative light to the righteous Reb Yudel, in blatant contrast to Psalm 112 and to Reb Yudel's delusions. Reb Yudel's *only* source of light is the rooster who wakes him up in the morning.

Another allusion that questions the applicability of religious theory to everyday life lurks in the words "ve-la-rash ein kol ki im tarnegol ehad" (and the poor man has nothing but one rooster). These words are evocative of Nathan the Prophet's description of Uriah: "And the poor man had nothing but one little lamb."[14] Nathan's parabolic description refers to Uriah the Hittite and is meant as a rebuke to King David who causes Uriah's death and appropriated to himself Uriah's wife, Bathsheba. Whereas the biblical prophet uses these words to chastise, our narrator uses them to praise. More important, the prophet perceives evil as a result of social and economic oppression; our unreliable narrator, by contrast, expresses no such consciousness. On the contrary, by praising poverty as a manifestation of righteousness, our narrator mutes and transmutes the prophetic an-

---

13. On the use of animals as parodic and satiric means see Paulson (1967).
14. 2 Samuel 12:3.

ger into a congratulatory paean. In addition to this ideological incongruity, there appears to be a generic incompatibility between the original source and our text. Whereas the original "poor man" is a fictional construct in a didactic parable, our "poor man" appears to refer to a real person. Yet the intertextual relationship between the evoked and the alluding text suggests that the latter may not be as realistic as first meets the eye. It suggests that our own "poor man" may be just as fictional as Nathan's "poor man," and that he too may serve a didactic purpose. The reflexive irony that is here merely foreshadowed becomes increasingly prominent as the novel evolves. By presenting horses in constant allusion to biblical and talmudic sources, Agnon not only parodies the excessive allusiveness of his own tale but also undermines its verisimilitude. He is basically reminding the reader that he is creating a fictional world, patented after the traditional didactic tale. What follows is a brief sketch of the major literary conventions of the Hasidic tale and their parodic treatment in the novel.

The Hero—The Perfect Hasid

The hero of the Hasidic folktale is, as a rule, a modest, devout, and innocent Jew of extremely limited means. The hero never lets economic concerns interfere with his complete commitment to God and the Torah. This element, however, is presented in *Hakhnasat kalla* with such preposterous exaggeration that the effect produced elicits laughter rather than veneration.

Reb Yudel's commitment to the Torah eclipses his basic obligations to his wife and family. He spends most of his time at the study house while his three unmarried daughters and exasperated wife pine away, famished and helpless (p. 8). Exhorted by his spiritual mentor, the Tsaddik of Apta, he reluctantly sets out on a charity campaign for his daughter but spends most of his time sharing Hasidic tales and legendary anecdotes with other Hasidim he meets on his way. Five months later, struck by remorse for having neglected his regular study of the Torah, he settles comfortably at a hotel, using up all the money collected for his daughter's sake. The incongruity between the hero's extreme dedication to the Torah and his indifference to his own family transforms the conventional positive characterization into a caricature of the protagonist. Reb Yudel mourns bitterly the destruction of the temple but does not blink an eye at the misery of his wife and daughters. The unreliable narrator lavishes praise on the pious properties of the hero, ignoring the latter's shady moral conduct and deceptive self-presentation as the rich and powerful Reb Yudel Nathansohn.

The exaggeration of the hero's spirituality reaches the limits of the grotesque in the description of Reb Yudel's magic transformation into sheer light: "And while he was talking with him that light grew stronger, until due to the light which fell on Reb Yudel, his body disappeared."[15] By exaggeration, incongruity, and omission of censure, Agnon subverts not only the stereotype of the perfect Hasid but also the normative value system of the Hasidic tale, which aims at glorifying one's complete and unflinching dedication to tradition.

The Figure of the Tsaddik

The juxtaposition of spirituality and materialism undermines yet another favorable stereotype in the Hasidic tale—the Tsaddik. The Tsaddik in the Hasidic folktale plays the role of what Vladimir Propp calls "the Helper"—he assists the hero by way of magic advice.

In Agnon's novel the Tsaddik of Apta, Reb Yudel's mentor, plays a rather minor role, invariably linked to the theme of deception and materialism. The Tsaddik helps Reb Yudel masquerade as a rich man and composes a letter in which he solicits donations for his protégé. When the miraculous engagement is concluded, the Tsaddik symbolically places his hand on the shin-

---

15. P. 347.

ing pile of golden coins, provided as dowry by the wealthy fathers. The letter of the Tsaddik is transformed in the course of the story into a highly coveted object, for which Reb Yudel is offered money and other valuables (p. 223). Another Tsaddik, mentioned in the story, is said to have depleted a whole district due to donations collected from the village Hasidim (p. 107).

In Agnon's "Ha-nidah" (The outcast), somatic functions such as eating and drinking, undertaken by both Reb Uriel, the Tsaddik, and his followers, are ironically presented as theurgic and mystical acts. The incommensurability of spirit and flesh undercuts the didactic orientation of the traditional folktale, which seeks to instill respect and faith in the Tsaddik. The treatment of the Tsaddik in Agnon's works parodies the conventions of the modeled reality and satirizes the norms of the social reality of the Hasidic community.

The Trial

The trial is a regular feature in the traditional Hasidic tale. The needy hero faces a tempting, easy but sinful way out of his misery. Thanks to his faith in God, however, he forfeits the easy solution, only to realize that he has just passed the divine test successfully. The trial is an important component in the traditional folktale that strives to explain the disturbing phenomenon of the suffering righteous man in a world ruled by a moral and omnipotent God. The trial concept defines suffering as a temporary educational process, at the end of which the hero is appropriately rewarded.

Hakhnasat kalla presents Joel's proposal to marry Pessele as a major trial and Reb Yudel's rejection of the proposition as a major victory of Satan's machinations. At work is a parodic reductio ad absurdum technique of the trial concept, which exposes the arbitrariness and glibness of the traditional convention. Joel does not propose a sinful way out, but rather a rational and practical solution to Reb Yudel's predicament. The trial is a specious one because Reb Yudel would not have failed in his commitment to

God. His only "sin" would entail a faster return to his hungry family.

A further distortion of the same traditional convention occurs in the metadiegetic story "Ha-rav ve-ha-oreah" (The Rabbi and his guest). The Rabbi clearly stands the test; he remains hospitable and patient vis-à-vis the maimed, blind, and bleeding beggar, but what about the latter? The Rabbi is fully rewarded for his inconvenience, but the wretched mendicant continues to suffer. Why was the sufferer punished? Why tortured for no apparent reason? The unreliable narrator does not see fit to refer to this problem. The device that triggers off the satiric effect at this point is the omission of censure. Withholding judgment at this problematic juncture exposes both the doubtful validity of the trial as theological concept and the biased viewpoint of the ancestral tale. The parodic treatment of the trial concept underlines the latter's partiality and relativity, thus virtually nullifying its didactic significance. The traditional folktale uses the trial convention in order to dramatize the principle of divine justice. The parodic double uses it in order to demonstrate the perennial and inescapable quirks of a blind, ruthless fate.

The Miracle

The miraculous reversal of the hero's fate from misery to glory is essential to the traditional folktale because it vindicates the traditional concept of divine providence. Agnon parodies this convention by alluding to the realistic causes of presumably supernatural events.

"The application of romantic mythical forms to a more realistic content," suggested by Northrop Frye as the basic structure of irony,[16] works as a powerful device in *Hakhnasat kalla*. The end of the novel presents the coincidental retrieval of the treasure by Reb Yudel's daughters as a miracle. The narrator leaves out at

16. Frye (1957), 223.

this point any reference to the realistic circumstances that
brought about the miraculous ending. But the reader, earlier informed of the many caves and crevices filled with the remaining
belongings of persecuted Jews (p. 272), cannot help but connect
the redeeming miracle with its lugubrious cause. The unreliable
narrator expatiates about God, who keeps his divine watch over
Israel, "His people" (p. 398), conveniently ignoring God's forgetfulness in this matter in other narrative contexts. The juxtaposition of historical realism and traditional fantasy exposes the
vulnerability of the traditional folktale. It underlines the fact that
miracles can happen only in literature and, consequently, punc-
tures the didactic message of the Hasidic tale. The sudden reversal of the plot, posits the miracle as a deus ex machina resolution
to an otherwise realistic story. The forced nature of the miraculous twist highlights its contrived artistry and artificiality, an effect that reminds us of the parodic effect in *Bi-lvav yamim* (*In the
Heart of the Seas*) of Hananya's magic transference from Europe to
the Land of Israel aboard his scarf. Similarly in "Ha-nidah" the
miracle of Gershom's death, presumably caused by the Tsaddik's
curse, is realistically explained by subtle allusions to his heredi-
tary disease and his mother's death. The miracle is dramatically
positioned at the forefront of Agnon's tale, only to be exposed as
literary ploy and naïve traditional apologetics.

The Happy Ending

The happy ending is crucial to the Jewish ancestral tale. It confirms the belief that justice is bound to prevail and that evil is no
more than an ephemeral illusion. In Agnon's parodies, the happy
ending offers a superficial solution to peripheral problems in the
narrative. The understated treatment of the problems, however,
only emphasizes their urgency and the tale's failure to confront
them. Pessele's engagement to her rich bridegroom is made possible by the miraculously found treasure. But what about the two
wretched sisters fighting each other for a loaf of bread? What
about Kalman, the poor tailor, and all the other paupers men-

tioned in the novel? The happy ending in the novel is disap-
pointing because it is too sudden and too concise. There is no
structural proportion between the succinct denouements and
the prolonged novel-spanning tales about competing leaders, ex-
ploited masses, arrogant and miserly ignoramuses, and penniless
men of learning. The structural and generic incompatibility of
the novel and its ending render the latter unbelievable, uncon-
vincing, and ridiculous—ridiculous mainly because it addresses
the fictional problems and eludes the realistic ones. The ending
does not resolve the contradictions and thematic tensions set up
by the novel, as Gershon Shaked would have it. On the contrary,
it underlines and amplifies them. The happy ending cannot
transform the work into a "comic legend"[17] because it does not
offer any solutions to the complex questions raised by the novel.
The incongruity between the conclusion and the rest of the
novel is not accidental but calculated, its effect not merely comic
but parodic. By appending the long and irrelevant "Poem of the
Letters" to the novel, Agnon offers in fact a parodic imitation of
his own ending, which is equally incommensurable with the
preceding chapters. The appendage of a happy ending to a problematic tale, such as the metadiegetic story "Mitato shel
Shelomo Ya'akov" (The bed of Rabbi Shlomo Yakov), is equally
parodic because it omits the critical implications regarding social
inequality in the community and elaborates on the hero's com-
fortable bed.

Conclusion

The "Poem of the Letters," so arbitrarily and artificially affixed
to the novel, in fact mirrors the novel's basic mode of composition. I stated earlier that the novel describes Reb Yudel's voyage
in pursuit of a dowry for his daughter. The fact of the matter is
that the description of the tales that the protagonist hears on his

---

17. Shaked (1976), 152.

way is far more extensive and predominant than the description of the voyage. The latter turns, consequently, into a compositional excuse for presenting additional tales. *The Bridal Canopy* is concerned not only with Reb Yudel and his daughters but also with the ancestral tale and the act of transmitting it. Above all it is a novel about the act of telling a story. The "Poem of the Letters," constructed alphabetically by order of the characters' names, imitates the novel's parodic attempt to mimic the conventionality of the ancestral tale. The subordination of narrative to a prescriptive ideology is ridiculed by the gross incompatibility of the alphabetical scheme with human life. The final implication is that the doctrines prescribed by the traditional narrative are valid in the world of letters, not in reality; their validity is theological, not ontological. The self-imitation of the novel's main plot line locks *The Bridal Canopy* in the vicious circle called by Friedrich Schlegel *Ironie der Ironie.* It is in Agnon's ironic self-consciousness that we notice his unique comment on Jewish tradition. In this sense he proves not the exception but the most sophisticated and subtle expression of the rule in modern Hebrew fiction: the dialectical movements of rebellion against tradition, by continuation of the latter's style. In this sense Agnon is closer to his predecessors than has been surmised. True, his parodies are less trenchant, more understated; they are reflexive as well as critical. His masterful wielding of irony, however, should not be mistaken for nostalgia or sentimentality.

9

The Anatomy of "Friendship": From Logical Constructs to Psychological Realities

Edna Amir Coffin

T he main trial of Job was not that of Job, but of the Holy One, blessed be He, as it were, because He had handed over His servant Job to Satan's power. God's trial was greater than Job's: He had a perfect and upright man, and He placed him in the power of Satan." This provocative and enigmatic passage plays two central roles in the short story "Friendship" (in Hebrew, "Yedidut"), from the collection *Sefer ha-ma'asim,* by Agnon: It provides cohesion for the text of the story and at the same time signals a shift from the plane of conscious behavior by a narrator who attempts to rationalize his actions, to the chaotic domain of the unconscious, where the narrator loses control over thoughts and actions.

In this chapter I shall examine the various strategies by which Agnon builds cohesion into a text composed of two main textual modes: one that operates on the narrative plane and is composed of a series of encounters and episodes around which the plot is organized, with familiar plot constituents such as participants and temporal and spatial elements; the other consists of general comments and pronouncements, which are not dependent on temporal or spatial constituents of text and are indirectly related to events that affect the participants. Like the Job passage they belong to a different type of discourse than the episodal one and constitute deviations from the main line of the plot. However, these deviations provide important referential clues that, although not constituting regular narrative events, serve to advance the plot in interpreting its significance.[1]

Like other stories in the collection of *Sefer ha-ma'asim,* "Yedidut" takes place in a universe of combined discourses that abounds in dreamlike qualities. We will examine its two main sequential textual units, one that precedes the Job passage quoted above and one that follows it. What distinguishes the first of the two is that it simulates an external reality within which the characters dramatize their concerns while a surrealistic environment is created by use of language props and discourse strategies. The narrator and readers move from episodes anchored in a realistic setting to a terra incognita that resembles a nightmare. "I now found myself in a street where I had never been before. ... I knew I had strayed to a place I did not know," the narrator tells the reader, upon entering this unknown territory. The shift from one environment to another signifies a change in the narrator's mental state, from a state where he can function and interact with others in a world governed by rules to a setting where he experiences a total breakdown, losing his sense of identity. The loss of a clear sense of identity is represented in the text through the narrator's forgetting his address and not knowing how to find his way home: "Today my wife came back from a journey and I

---

1. Gershon Shaked has an extensive discussion of the function of deviations in Agnon's stories in his volume *The Narrative Art of S. Y. Agnon.* He sees it as one of the basic structural patterns in Agnon's fiction. Discussing Agnon's strategies in using deviations as important narrative events, Shaked comments: "We should pay attention to the stories in *Sefer ha-ma'asim,* which are built on this structure ... having as their main concern a quest which is not realized because of a deviation. ... The deviation itself borders on the comic. Their accidental occurrence in the sequence of events in the explicit text brings about a comic reaction, however the hidden connections tying the events in the implicit text evoke anxiety" (p. 71).

cannot reach her," the narrator admits, "for the trivial reason that I had forgotten where I live." He also loses his ability to perform communicative acts and thus cannot effectively question others as to where his home is. Trying to form questions, the narrator experiences a loss of ability to speak: "I could not get the words out of my mouth." A condensation and dramatization of the narrator's existential dilemma is provided by the Job passage, which reveals the truth about the narrator's confused sense of self, exposing his need to shift responsibility onto others. When he extends the category of others to include the divine entity of God as bearing responsibility for his "sin," he is punished by being plunged into a nightmarish turmoil, which concludes only when he begins to gain awareness of his own obligations and duties.

The title of Agnon's collection of stories known as *Sefer hama'asim* can be translated as "The book of acts" or "The book of tales." The dual meaning embodied in the title points to Agnon's preoccupation with the relationship between words and actions, between text and actual experience, a relationship that is explored in "Yedidut." Although the author, in performing the telling of the story, is actually combining action and text through his narrator, his protagonist uses words to rationalize his failure to act. The truth is masked by words. The tension between word and action in "Yedidut" is finally resolved by a demonstration of the effectiveness of action over words. The protagonist comes closest to understanding the meaning of the concept of *yedidut* when it is defined for him through action, rather than by a verbal description or a prescription for action transmitted by words.

The Anatomy of a Journey

In "Yedidut" the first-person narrator embarks on a journey that is a simultaneous flight from and a search for intimacy, which is signified by wife and home. Such simultaneous contradictions recur in many of Agnon's stories and constitute their central themes. This story is told from a first-person narrator's perspective and at the outset informs the readers about the narrator's wife's return from a journey. Her return ends his solitude and, according to his initial proclamation, causes him joy. Ironically, the wife's return from the journey and the reunion of husband and wife serve to initiate another journey. This time it is the narrator's journey, which, not surprisingly to Agnon's readers, is brought about by the same event that made the reunion possible. It is this journey that constitutes the main body of the story and, like the previous one, leads to separation. At the narrator's instigation he and his wife set out to visit neighbors, who are perceived as potential intruders. The ambiguous target of the visit ("Let's go visit Mr. So-and-So or Mrs. Such-and-Such") takes on a specific shape as they set out to visit a certain Mrs. Klingel. She is chosen as the first target since the narrator feels that she is most likely to visit them. Mrs. Klingel is identified with irony as somebody who had once been a famous woman ("she had been principal of a school before the war") but has fallen from her high estate. Her status as a friend is perceived as self-serving for two different reasons: First, the wife remembers Mrs. Klingel when she was an "important" person and Mrs. Klingel likes to associate with people who "had seen her in her prime"; second, Mrs. Klingel seeks the acquaintance of those who have acquired a reputation and thus frequents the narrator's home. The narrator reveals more about himself in describing Mrs. Klingel than he does about her. He inadvertently admits to sharing a quality he despises in others as he is just as preoccupied as Mrs. Klingel with his own social status.

The visit is doomed to failure from the outset, as the target of the visit is a source of irritation for the narrator and predictably will again have the same effect. Mrs. Klingel enrages the narrator by telling his wife that during her absence he spent his nights in pleasure, and at the same time she turns to him and claims not to be telling his wife that pretty girls had come to visit him. The visit ends abruptly with the narrator losing his temper at this revelation/nonrevelation. He recognizes Mrs. Klingel's comments as a joke but reacts to them in a manner appropriate to the revelation of a secret, or to an insult.

The second encounter, in what constitutes a series of encounters in this story, is with a trio composed of a Hebrew teacher and two visitors. It is the narrator who chooses to greet the trio and to initiate a conversation with them. This encounter results in a renewed separation from the wife, as she does not wait but leaves her husband engaged in trite conversation with people in whom he has little interest and whom he does not respect. The encounter provides the narrator with a delay and serves to expose further his contempt for others and lack of sincerity in interacting with them.

At this juncture, noting the wife's departure, the reader begins to confirm suspicions that the true nature of the narrator's quest may not be to avoid intrusion by others but, instead, a desperate flight from home and all that it represents. The true intent is realized through the narrator's actions rather than his words. The visits and encounters are not sincere social interaction, as expected, nor are they strategies to ward off intruders, as the narrator claims them to be, but rather they take on the meaning of their actual consequences: a departure from home and eventually a separation from wife.

The Job reference appears at this point in the story. The message about Job is written by the narrator, who is both addresser and addressee, on an envelope or in a letter (the either/or possibility of the medium is included in the text and transmits the narrator's sense of confusion). The message is addressed to himself, and he reads it following his wife's departure and upon finishing it tears up the message, as is his habit with all written messages, before, during, or following the act of reading. The relevance of the message to the story is not immediately apparent. The change of medium from speech and the language of thought to the written word is significant, even though its meaning may not be immediately obvious. Not only is the text transmitted in a different medium but also it refers to a totally different context, one that is atemporal in nature and has claims to eternal and universal truths. It comes from a theological frame of reference and does not fit the narrative events of the story.

Following the reading of this passage, there is a shift to a fantasy world. The setting of night prepares the proper temporal environment of a universe of dreams and nightmares, in which the repressed elements of the psyche operate freely. The narrator can no longer call on his rational faculties to control his thoughts and rationalize his actions or even allow him to perform verbally. However, at this stage he becomes aware of the need to find his way home and be reunited with his wife. He reiterates this need at each of the three episodes that constitute the second half of the story. This portion of the text includes a full admission of the need to find self, home, and wife: "I've got to go home, I'm looking for my house, I've forgotten the name of my street, and I don't know how to get to my wife!" Although he has lost his sense of identity and belonging, the narrator has discovered the meaning of that loss, and the beginning of awareness and admission directs him in a quest for a way home. His awareness of his need—"I've got to go home"—saves him from totally losing himself in the chaotic world in which he finds himself.

The series of three encounters that takes place in this dreamlike scenario consists of two central episodes, for which one can find clear antecedents in the Job passage, and an interlude that serves both to separate and link these episodes. The first encounter is with a Dr. Rischel, a modern scholar of language and grammar. Rischel, aware of the confusion of the narrator, directs him in a path that takes him away from home and from which there is seemingly no return, and it is only a memory of a dream fragment that saves the narrator from such a fate. The last encounter is with a Mr. Jacob Tzorev who is accompanied by his son. Tzorev is a traditional father figure who points the narrator in the right direction and enables him to get home. Jacob Tzorev, in spite or because of his blindness, and in spite or because of the narrator's failure to fulfill social obligations, instructs his son to lead the narrator back home.

The interlude that separates those two encounters provides a link and a shift from one sphere to another. This interlude takes place in a post office, a center for communication where letters are sent and received, where addresses reside in a pool of names, and it proves to be of no value in helping the narrator find his way home. The impersonal figures in the post office are both unlikely support sources for the quest for true identity and direction and are also inappropriate adversarial targets for the narrator's anger, for they are characterized not so much by ill intent as by lack of intent. However, this interlude highlights the absurdity of the dilemma of the narrator who can no longer remember his way home and has lost the social mechanism to inform others of his dilemma. What he can do and does do is to lose complete control over his actions, and in a totally uncensored way he comes to express his need, admitting in public his loss of direction by shouting and revealing his absurd situation. Such a revelation in public constitutes another step on the way home, in spite of its unpleasant consequences.

At the end of the story, the narrator finds himself miraculously transported close to his home through Tzorev's clear direction for action addressed to his son. When words are translated into action, when true intent gives the text its full force, a light emanates from the combined father-son blind-sighted figure, which transports the narrator close to his home. The light from the blind man's eyes illuminates a truth and provides a lesson for relationship of the self with others. The narrator, who is now next to his house, must take the last step and enter his home to complete his journey. Nobody else can do it for him. Agnon thus leaves the reader at the conclusion of the story with a question mark that leads from one question to another. Will the narrator be able to take this last step, and once he does take it, will it be the beginning of another journey, as we are led to believe by observing that a conclusion to one journey was the initiation of another? Will he come full circle to a union that brings about the next phase of separation? Is life a dialectical process of a series of journeys which at one and the same time provides a conclusion and an initiation? Are these journeys a completion of some earlier journeys started in another lifetime? In other words, are they part of the human condition? The reader can address some of

these questions within the context of this story by closely examining Agnon's textual strategies and his techniques of analogy,
which endow the story with its metaphorical or even allegorical
qualities.

The Structure of the Story:
Logical Propositions and Psychological Dilemmas

One of the useful ways to examine this text is to look at its predicative content and view it as a logical discourse built on sets of
propositions. This approach does not deny other useful ways of
examining text but looks for the content and relationships of the
propositions to shed light on the narrative events.[2] Agnon successfully constructs a particular "logic" and truth condition to
define the fictional universe of his protagonist. It provides the
reader with insight into this disjointed, often confused and con-
fusing, dreamlike universe in which the protagonist is the main
actor. There is a method in the seeming madness of the narrator,
just as there is a method in the thought process of a dreamer or a
schizophrenic.[3] Along with examining the predicative logic and
presuppositions in the text, I shall also deal with the various
complex relationships between semantic entities in the text,

---

2. Another focus on the text of "Yedidut" is provided by a consideration of the
organization of the plot around speech events. For a full discussion of such a
perspective of the text, see the article "Do Words Conceal or Reveal Intent of
Verbal Expressions? Thought Process and Written Symbols in Agnon's
Fiction," Edna Amir Coffin, in *Agnon's Fiction in English Translation*.

3. Silvano Arieti, a noted psychiatrist, examined the language of fiction,
dreams, and schizophrenia and related their shared properties. His observations
are particularly apt for this discussion of the dreamlike qualities of the text and
the way in which it relates to the perceptions of reality of the narrator and those
of the reader: "When a dreamer dreams or a schizophrenic experiences delusions, they both think in a way that becomes understandable to us as an allegory
or a metaphor ... we must remember, however, that this world is metaphorical
only to us, not for the patient, who accepts it as reality" (*Understanding and
Helping the Schizophrenic*, p. 65).

both lexical and conceptual, which lend it cohesion. In examining the events that constitute the main discourse, I will highlight the logical predicates that give the first episodes their distinctive qualities, while examining the complex associative frames of reference of the last narrative events.

The Anatomy of a Visit

Background Considerations

The story begins with a set of propositions, revealing a familiar logical progression of cause and effect, which are included in a single sentential entity and are linked by the conjunction "and." The narrator begins with the sentence, "My wife returned from a journey, and I was very happy." The first of the two propositions included in the sentence is a simple factual statement. However, on closer observation, this statement reveals through its choice of lexical items that it is not devoid of meaningful presuppositions.[4] The conclusion of the wife's journey implies a previous existential state at which husband and wife were separated. The suggested responsibility for the separation is the wife's, as she is the one who undertook the journey in the first place and thus was the cause for the husband's solitary state. The second proposition, linked to the first by the neutral but potentially polysemic conjunction "and," reports the effect of the wife's return, which the narrator claims to have made him

---

4. Presuppositions are pragmatic inferences that are usually described as belonging to three possible cases: existential, factive, and categorical. The presuppositions in the opening sentence are examples of factive and existential cases. Factive presuppositions occur in sentences that contain predicates that express properties or relations involving facts ("My wife returned from a journey"), whereas existential presuppositions assume the existence of an object to which certain properties are attributed ("and I was very happy"). For discussion of presuppositions, see Alwood, Andersson, and Dahl (*Logic in Linguistics,* pp. 150–151).

happy. This proposition evokes a number of presuppositions as well about the narrator's claim concerning his state of bliss. Since he claims to be happy now, we infer that he was unhappy previously. Since it is the wife who is the actor in the first proposition, then the responsibility not only for the separation but also for his unhappiness is hers. Thus, a seemingly innocuous conjoined set of propositions in the opening sentence sets an emotionally loaded scene for the rest of the story.

The feeling of resentment and the assignment of responsibility for an unhappy state of affairs, all of which are not part of the explicit text, provide a common thread for the interpretation of the story. The narrator has to deal with and confront certain truths that he does not admit to himself. In contrast to what is expressed by the narrator and can be first assumed by the unsuspecting reader, the felicity of the narrator is not the responsibility of others but emanates from the self and the relationship of the self to the Other and others. This becomes clear to the reader upon retrospection as the story unfolds. It is at this point that the narrator begins to reveal his particular "logic" to the reader. The logical system that unfolds is a unique one and often stands in contradiction to accepted norms that operate in the external world that is familiar to the reader. The author, through his narrator, thus reveals to the reader the fictional universe in which the protagonist operates.[5]

The Initiation of a Visit

Immediately following his claim to being happy, the narrator modifies it: "but a tinge of sadness mingled with my joy for the neighbors might come and bother us." The cause for the sad-

---

5. Saul Kripke's and David Lewis's theory of "possible worlds," which are contexts built on a set of propositions within which these propositions are true, is very useful for considering fictional discourse entities as such "possible fictional worlds." Truth sets can be considered valid independently of other sets that may not agree with them.

ness, unlike the cause for the joy, is not some factual certainty but a possibility that the neighbors might come and bother the two. In a typical shifting of responsibility to others for his own mental and emotional state, the narrator contemplates the possibility of others interfering with the reunion, although there is no evidence to back this claim. Both implicit and explicit text can only validate the fact that the husband and wife are together at home but cannot validate the intentions of the neighbors to come and disturb them.

Is this supposed imminent intrusion the true cause for the narrator's sadness, or is it merely a cover? As the reader soon discovers, the protagonist, for whatever reasons, uses this potential visit as an excuse to instigate his and his wife's departure from home. By their leaving home, an intimate reunion will no longer be possible, and husband and wife will find themselves in an isolated state side by side. The conclusions that can be reached by the reader begin to diverge from those expressed by the narrator. Thus, two systems of logic, operating simultaneously, begin to give the text its full meaning and allow for contradictions to appear in the same statement without violating basic rules of discourse.

The narrator initiates the move away from home in the form of a suggestion/directive to his wife: "Let's go and visit Mr. So-and-So or Mrs. Such-and-Such, for if they come to us we shall not get rid of them in a hurry, but if we go to them, we can get up and be rid of them whenever we like." The lack of a specific target indicates a lack of sincere intentions.[6] The propositions are built on two "if … then" conditional sequences. If A or B comes to see us, then we cannot get rid of A or B in a hurry, but if we go to see A or B, we can get rid of them whenever we want. The

---

6. One of the felicity conditions for social interactions is that sincerity of intention be met. In any interpersonal interaction both participants have to be identified, addresser or addressee. An either/or identification of nonspecific entities does not fulfill such conditions.

contradiction built into the logical propositions reveals the hidden intent of the narrator. Using ordinary logic, which underlies social interactions, the reader can expect the following "if/then" propositions:

(–)*If* A does not want to see people,(–)*then* A does not go to visit people.

BUT

(+)*If* A wants to see people, (+)*then* A goes to see people.

A positive "if" statement entails a positive "then" statement, whereas a negative "if" statement entails a negative "then" statement. The narrator's logic, however, takes the following logical sequencing, which keeps the same basic propositions but switches the negative-positive pairing:

(–)*If* A does not want to see people, (+)*then* A goes to visit people.

BUT

(+)*If* A wants to see people, (–)*then* A does not go to see people. (They come to see him.)

The underlying presupposition of the narrator is that his wife's return home signals the resumption not only of marital obligations but also of social obligations. He is no longer in control of this aspect of his life. One of the interesting things in this passage is the use of the verbs "come" and "go." The coming of people to visit is perceived by the narrator as a true threat, and the going to see them is perceived by the narrator as the lesser of two evils. If rules of analogy are used, then the coming and going can be applied to the husband's and wife's coming and going: The coming home of the wife poses the real threat, and the going away from home is a way of warding off such a threat, an escape from the situation without confronting it. The rationalization of the narrator for going to see others is given in terms of his desire to maintain control over his actions and his time. He is unhappy with being the object or passive recipient of action and wants to be the initiator of events. This concern can be justifiably transferred by analogy to the narrator's perception of his marital situation.

The narrator's rationalization for undertaking the visit is presented in such a convincing manner that it can pass for a logical conclusion. There is a certain element of truth in his observation and the reader can sympathize with his concerns, no matter how much his comments raise questions concerning the intention for undertaking the visit. Such intentions can be seen as a subversion of the true meaning of a visit, which implies a voluntary social interaction, whereas for the narrator the visit becomes a selfish act devoid of any conditions of sincerity, meant to minimize the inevitability of relating to others. He is no longer alone and is faced with an obligation not only to his wife, but since the reunion reestablishes the two as a social unit, he faces interactions with others as well. Agnon sets the context that sets the plot in motion. He has also created the necessary underpinnings for the interaction between text and subtext. The reader has been challenged to consider the events as narrated by the protagonist and at the same time to observe the narrator dramatize and act out his true concerns. The two vantage points create a tension between the explicit claims of the narrator and the conclusions of the reader.

A summary of the introductory passage of the story can be viewed via these two textual dimensions:

1. On the explicit textual plane:
   Premises: Since the narrator wants to be alone with his wife, he and his wife must *leave home* in order to avoid the intrusion by neighbors. They should go to visit those who may come to visit them.
   Consequences if these premises are acted on: If the husband and wife go to see those who may come to see them, they will *no longer be at home.*

2. On the implicit textual plane:

Premises: Since the narrator does not want to be alone with his wife *at home,* he instigates a visit to neighbors, rationalizing this action to himself by his concern that the neighbors will come to see them and in addition that there is no way to control the duration of their visit.

Consequences if these premises are acted on: Narrator initiates a movement *away from home* and thus will be able to avoid the possibility of intimacy with his wife.

3. Reader's conclusions:

There is a serious gap between what is said and what is intended. The opening statement, "My wife returned home and I was happy," is now in jeopardy. Both approaches, whether we believe that the narrator wants to be alone with his wife, or whether we conclude that he wants to leave home so as not to be alone with his wife, bring about the same consequences of taking the narrator and his wife out of their home.

The Visit

"So we lost no time," the narrator resumes, as if to strengthen the argument that time is of the essence, "and went to visit Mrs. Klingel. Because Mrs. Klingel was in the habit of coming to us, we went to her first." The reference to time and the choice of a specific target for the visit transform it from a vague notion to a specific event, adding intentionality to suggestion. The question is, What are the explicit reasons for the choice of Mrs. Klingel, and do they diverge from the implicit intentions as understood by the reader?

The given reason is that she is the one most likely to visit them. However, as the reader finds other references to Mrs. Klingel in the text, it becomes clear that there are more compelling and pressing reasons that deserve consideration. She provides a constant source of irritation to the narrator, and he confesses to feeling some guilt and obligation to her. The feelings of guilt and obligation are inappropriate when applied to Mrs. Klingel, with whom he has little if any emotional involvement, but are particularly suitable for his sentiments toward his wife. In Mrs. Klingel the narrator finds a suitable substitute that allows him to vent his genuine strong sense of resentment, but directing it not at the true target of such feelings but toward another. This is a pure case of transference.[7]

Agnon provides a strong textual connection between the two female characters, even though they are described as oppositional entities.[8] Mrs. Klingel is old and the wife is young; Mrs. Klingel is an excessive talker, and the wife is silent. The reason given for an ongoing association with Mrs. Klingel is related to her contacts with the wife: "She clung to my wife as she clung to anyone who had seen her in her prime ... she was extremely friendly to my wife." However, the narrator admits that she became a frequent visitor in their home since she sought the acquaintance of anyone who acquired a reputation. By indirectly, but intentionally, advertising his own social status, he is unaware that he has admitted his part in the association with Mrs. Klingel. Details, such as the setting in which we find Mrs. Klingel during the visit, strengthen the connection between her and the wife.

---

7. The shifting of the feelings here from a real target to another one can be viewed as a case of transference, similar to that proposed by Freud. In *The Interpretation of Dreams,* Freud describes a process that he labels "transference," which occurs in dream formation. It involves the "transference and displacement of the psychic intensities of the individual elements, from which results the textual difference between the dream-content and the thought-content" (p. 338). In this segment of "Friendship" it is possible to describe the transference of the psychic intensities of the individual elements and the resulting textual difference between the sublimated subconscious-content and the thought-content overtly expressed by the narrator.

8. An interesting discussion of oppositions as one of the possible similarity relationships is provided by Linda Waugh ("The Poetic Function and the Nature of Language," p. 71). The oppositions here connect the two characters in this inherent relationship of similarity.

She receives the visitors seated in her bed, thus violating the rules of ordinary visits, which do not take place in the bedroom. There is no dimension of intimacy that justifies such a placement, except if it is viewed as part of the process of transfer. By placing Mrs. Klingel in bed, the author has made an undeniable connection with the wife. In addition, when the narrator contemplates what he exactly owes her in terms of social obligations, he blurts out a sentence that in no way makes sense, except if we are to apply it to his wife. "Is it because I have known her for so many years," the narrator muses, "that I am enslaved to her?" The wording "enslaved to her" when understood in a husband-wife context adds to the perception of the reverse roles in their relationship, since in Hebrew "husband" means an owner or enslaver, whereas he perceives himself as being enslaved.

Should the reader fail to establish the textual references connecting the two female figures, the narrator proceeds with the joke episode, which makes these ties manifestly clear. In telling the "joke" Mrs. Klingel performs the function of confronting the narrator with the possible causes for his anger and resentment at both his wife's departure and her return. Mrs. Klingel becomes the conveyer of repressed thoughts, the accusing voice of the silent wife. Masquerading as an older woman, Mrs. Klingel gives expression to the younger woman's complaints and to the censor's voice within the narrator himself. She is able to confront him not only in a different guise but also by using a joke mode of discourse to convey her accusation, and by pretending *not* to tell his wife about how her husband spent his nights when she was away. The negation becomes a form of strong affirmation.

The Anatomy of a Joke

There are three versions to the text we shall call Mrs. Klingel's joke. The three versions involve different addressers and addressees. In the first version Mrs. Klingel addresses the narrator's wife. In the second version, which follows it, she addresses the narrator, as if paraphrasing the joke. In the third version, the narrator addresses himself recalling the joke, choosing to paraphrase it as perceived by him. Each version then gets its full meaning not only from the propositional content of the text but also from the participants in the speech event.

Version 1: Mrs. Klingel to wife: "You were away, my dear, and in the meantime your husband spent his nights in pleasure."
Premise: Wife was away; therefore, husband was alone.
Premise: He spent his nights in pleasure; therefore, he was not unhappy.
Conclusion: It is not true that husband was unhappy while wife was away.

Version 2: Mrs. Klingel to husband: "I am not telling your wife pretty girls came to visit you."
Embedding proposition: I am *not* telling that ...
Premise: Wife was away; therefore, husband was alone.
Premise: Pretty girls came to visit; therefore, he was not unhappy.
Conclusion 1: I am *not* telling that ...
It is *not* true that husband was unhappy while wife was away.
Conclusion 2: What I am telling is that ...
It is true that husband was unhappy while wife was away.

The conclusions can be a two-step process as indicated above, or they can take the form of an either/or proposition:

Either I am not saying the following, but it could be true: "You spent your nights with pretty girls." Or I am not saying the following because it is not true: "You spent your nights with pretty girls."

Version 3: Reported speech of narrator to himself recalling the text of the joke:
"Your husband had visits from pretty girls; your husband took pleasure with them."

Premise: Pretty girls visited husband; therefore, husband was not
 alone.
Premise: He took pleasure with them; therefore, he was not unhappy.
Conclusion: It is not true that husband was unhappy while wife
 was away because he was not alone and spent his nights in
 pleasure.

We can see that the conclusions are the same for all versions, if
we do not take meaning of the performative embedding proposition (I am *not* telling) to be denial but rather that of an emphatic affirmative function. Although the text of the three versions does not constitute an exact repetition, the conclusions of
all three versions are the same and stand in stark contradiction to
the opening statement of the story: "My wife returned from a
journey *and I was happy.*" This accounts for the strong impact of
the joke on the narrator. The joke is also particularly effective for
the reader because it is based on a possible universe of stereotypic
and familiar behavior. Stated in terms of premises and conclusions, it can be described as follows:

Situation A
Wife is away; therefore, husband is alone.
Husband is free; therefore, he seeks pretty girls.
Conclusion: He spends his nights in pleasure.

Situation B
Wife is back home; therefore, husband is no longer alone.
Husband has obligations; therefore, he cannot seek pretty girls.
Conclusion: He no longer spends his nights in pleasure.

Situation A emphasizes sexuality and freedom from marital
bonds, whereas situation B emphasizes obligation and intimacy.
There are literally hundreds of jokes based on the tension created
between these two situations. Mrs. Klingel's comments echo
such jokes. Agnon, aware of the functions of jokes, which in

many ways resemble those of dreams,[9] uses this discourse mode to bring the narrator to a state of antagonism where he begins to lose control over himself.

The association of the dream and the joke is expressed overtly in the text. "Even in my dreams," the narrator says, "there was nothing to give me pleasure." The reader, going beyond the manifest text, can add a psychological dimension to the text, where again a denial of preoccupation with pretty girls and pleasure is transformed into an emphatic affirmative. The narrator was not alone in his dreams, although it is unlikely that pretty girls came to visit him in any other form. The object of his desire is repressed and finds expression in the realm of dream. The rude awakening from dream to a solitary reality may justify his claim that even in his dreams he had no pleasure but does not deny the presence of pretty girls in his dreams. The dramatic impact of the joke brings about a reaction that is suitable to an accusation.

The Anatomy of an Allegory

Having brought his narrator close to a confessional mode, Agnon switches his mode of discourse by introducing a condensed version of the events narrated in the first two chapters of the biblical Job story. The Job references are inserted into the recounting of the ongoing journey of the narrator, and the ruminations about Job serve to connect the narrator with the biblical tale. The narrator compares his own perceived trials and tribulations with the fate of the innocent Job, who was put to the test of faith by God and delivered to Satan. Like Job, the narrator has

---

9. Erik Erikson combines in his conceptual model of identity both group and ego identity (*Identity: Youth and Crisis,* p. 45). In his discussion he also quotes Freud, who, toward the end of his life in his *Outline of Psychoanalysis* (pp. 122–123), made the following observation: "What is operating in the superego is not only the personal qualities ... but also ... the standards of the social class in which they live and the characteristics and traditions of the people from which they spring."

been handed to the forces of evil without any divine intervention. The irony and absurdity of this comparision does not escape the attention of the reader. "On my way I put my hand in my lap," says the narrator, "and took out an envelope or a letter and I stood and read, the main trial of Job was not that of Job, but that of the Holy One, blessed be He, as it were, because He handed over His servant Job to Satan's power. God's trial was greater than Job's: He had a perfect and upright man, and He placed him in the power of Satan." He concludes this short monologue, revealing his contempt and attitude to those who wish to address him in any way, "Having read my words, I tore the envelope and the letter and I scattered the pieces to the wind, as I usually do with every letter, sometimes before reading, and sometimes while reading" ("Yedidut," p. 122).

Propositional Content of Text:

Sentence 1:

"The main trial of Job was not that of Job, but of the Holy One, blessed be He, as it were, because He had handed over His servant Job to Satan's power."

Premise 1: Job was God's servant. Job was in God's power.

Conclusion: If Job is to be tried, he should be tried by God.

Premise 2: God handed Job over to Satan. Job was in Satan's power.

Conclusion: Job was tried by Satan.

Premise 3: Job was God's servant. Job was tried by Satan.

Conclusion: God, through his servant Job, was tried by Satan.

Sentence 2:

"God's trial was greater than Job's: He had a perfect and upright man, and He placed him in the power of Satan."

Premise 1: God had a perfect man. He placed him in Satan's power.

Conclusion: He was no longer in God's domain and was being tried by Satan though not being his servant.

Premise 2: God abandoned his servant. God was tried, through his servant, by Satan.

Conclusion: God's trial is greater than Job's, as He is guilty of abandoning him and leaving him in Satan's power and of delegating the responsibility for the confrontation with Satan to Job and not to Himself. Job, being human and not superhuman, is not up to the task.

This cryptic message, which lies outside the main flow of the plot, can be related to the narrative events by analogy. The narrator interprets his own ontological state as analogous to that of Job. In his interpretation of the biblical drama the narrator sees his own state as determined by superhuman forces that control him. Like Job, he feels himself abandoned by God to be tested by Satan. Like Job, he becomes the object of temptation. Like God, he transfers responsibility to others. In the power of Satan, and thus becoming his servant, he follows his hidden desires and acts in an ungodly way. The heretical conclusions and the over-dramatic analogies reveal the narrator's perception of his existential state. He has a diminished notion of self caught between forces greater than himself that decide his fate. God and Satan are but voices rationalized as superhuman that strip the perceived self of responsibility for his actions. It is this diminution of the self that causes the narrator to lose his way and forget his true identity. In a mirror fashion, Agnon builds the rest of the quest as a journey backwards through a world stripped of recognizable road signs or orderly maps, as a kind of "Job through the looking glass."

The Anatomy of a Search

The concluding part of the story marks a change in style and in linguistic strategies. The object of the search is no longer defined as the narrator's repressed object of desire ("pretty girls") but is transformed to a metaphysical one ("home"). He admits to himself that he must find the way home ("I said to myself: I must find my wife"), but he finds himself in a predicament that he himself created, as he had strayed away from home and forgotten his address. For the first time he also admits his own responsibility for distractions from the straight path: "My thoughts had distracted me." This admission initiates the new quest. The discourse is no longer based on two divergent logical systems but moves into one that is replete with substitutions and references to textual and semantic structures connecting it to the earlier episodes.

The first encounter in this segment is with Dr. Rischel, who represents a new voice of temptation. Dr. Rischel offers his listeners "new ideas on grammar and language," a Western way of looking at language and text, which presents language qua language and does not look for meaning in historical and traditional context. Dr. Rischel's approach to language suggests two possible associations in the narrator's mind with the forgotten name of his street: "Sometimes I thought the name of the street was Humboldt and sometimes it was West Street." These either/or possibilities about to be uttered by the narrator are rejected as he becomes aware that neither will get him close to the target of his quest. Home is where his wife is and home is also where his cultural and historical roots are. Agnon thus adds another dimension to the concept of home by combining a sense of the self in relation to the Other as well as that of the self in relation to others who constitute the historical and cultural community to which he belongs.[10]

Dr. Rischel's theories of language and grammar affect the narrator in an adverse manner. He loses his ability to use language, both its external manifestation through speech and the internal process of the language of thought. The written form of language is also explored in this encounter: Two letters are found in the narrator's possession, both of which prove to be of no help to him in finding his way home. One is addressed to his old

---

10. Freud, in his well-known essay on the nature of jokes, noted the similarity of the technique of jokes with that of dreams. "As a part of the dream-work, I described the process of condensation. This process has a striking similarity to the technique of wit and, like the latter, it leads to abbreviations and brings substitutive formations of like character" (*The Technique of Wit,* p. 646).

home, which no longer can supply him with adequate answers, and one is addressed to Poste Restante, a modern impersonal definition that holds no promise of the full meaning of home. The linguistic environment provided by Rischel offers a view of language organized in paradigms. Agnon demonstrates the futility of such an approach to language, brilliantly describing his narrator in search of himself by resorting to association with words arranged in context-free categories: "I started reciting aloud names of towns and villages, kings and nobles, sages and poets, trees and flowers, every kind of street name: perhaps I would remember the name of my street—but I could not recall it." The name categories include geographical locations, figures of authority, men of science and arts, and objects from nature, none of which are realized in a meaningful context that ties them to reality.

Dr. Rischel, the tempter, instructs the confused narrator: "Get into the streetcar and come with me." He offers him a clear direction but one that the narrator recognizes will take him away from home. His salvation comes from the depths of the unconscious, by evoking the memory of a dream fragment. Although he is not able to recall his address, his recall of the dream leads him to action: "I jumped off the tramcar and left him." The dream memory has clear allusion to a nocturnal event from the world of biblical fiction. "I remembered that I had seen Rischel in a dream wrestling with me," the narrator recalls. Short as it is, the dream fragment evokes the biblical scenario of Jacob wrestling with the angel.[11] The narrator-Job-Jacob identification of the protagonist is matched by Rischel-Satan-angel identification of the antagonist. There is a clear development in the narrator's perception of himself, which shifts from that of the

---

11. The biblical passage reads as follows: "And Jacob was left alone; and a man wrestled with him until the breaking of the day. When the man saw that he did not prevail against Jacob, he touched the hollow of his thigh; and Jacob's thigh was put out of joint as he wrestled with him" (Genesis 32:24–25).

suffering Job to the wrestling Jacob, indicating a significant change in viewing himself as an object of action to taking on the role of an actor. Agnon successfully combines three separate discourses to build this encounter: the episodal discourse describing the sequential narrative events: the dream fragment, which shifts the reader to a different psychological reality; and the allusion to the biblical text, which again changes the domain of discourse.

Agnon uses the biblical Jacob, whose name is not explicitly mentioned, to provide an interesting textual connection with the final encounter in the story. That encounter is with Mr. Jacob Tzorev, an authority figure, who is accompanied by his son. The narrator-Jacob of the dream fragment provides a direct link through the use of the name Jacob to the authority figure of Tzorev and his son. The father-son figures represent separate complementary entities, of teacher and follower, of figures of authority and obedience, which are joined into one entity at the end of the story by blurring the referential system. When the connection between the two Jacobs is made, the three figures merge into one at the conclusion of the story, leading the reader to review the story's characters as a chorus of voices of one individual entity. Rather than separate characters, they are different attributes of the complex self of the narrator, mirroring his many inner contradictions and desires, his masculine and feminine attributes, which are in constant conflict.

Patterns of Cohesion

I end the consideration of "Yedidut" with the passage I started with, examining the triangular relationship within the Job story that gives the story its textual dynamics and supplies it with structural and semantic cohesion.[12] Triangles run through the

---

12. The concept of cohesion in text is examined in detail by Halliday and Hasan in their book *Cohesion in English*. Particularly useful is their discussion of the phenomena of ellipsis, substitution, and reference, which lend cohesion to text (pp. 142–225).

entire story and take on their configuration from the Job story. Echoes of the Job story can be found in the visit to Mrs. Klingel. She is seated with her three female companions, evoking the image of Job being comforted by his three companions. Like Job, she too has been the subject of a fall from grace ("When the world went topsy-turvy, she fell from her high estate"). In the following encounter, a male trio replaces the female trio found in the visit to Mrs. Klingel. The narrator becomes the Job figure, and the trio he encounters represent the companions. Agnon makes an explicit connection between the three female companions and the male trio, as he mentions that one of the trio "was the brother of one of Mrs. Klingel's three friends—or perhaps I am mistaken and she has no brother." The connection is clearly metaphysical, as the narrator professes not to know who any of Klingel's companions are and therefore he is not likely to know her brother, except in the sense of their analogous functions.

The Job passage follows sequentially and presents the classic Job–God–Satan triangle, which can be interpreted on either a theological or a psychological plane. In a simplified form this triangular relationship can be viewed as the self wrestling with problems of good and evil, or that concept can be extended to Freudian triangular metaphors of the ego, id, and superego. Whatever the representations are, it is the dialectical relations among the three forces that produce the dynamics of interaction in the story.

Following the Job passage, the narrator encounters Dr. Rischel. In this encounter the triangle is composed of two entities that are present and one whose presence is noted by its absence. The Job figure of the suffering narrator, which at the end of the episode takes on the qualities of the wrestling Jacob, is pitted against its adversary Dr. Rischel, who is first seen as a possible source of help but is then exposed as a tempter and a Satanlike figure. The absence of a Godlike figure is noticeable, and this ellipsis has a clear counterpart in the Job passage. "[God] ... ," the reader is told by the narrator, "handed over His servant Job to Satan's power. ... He had a perfect and upright man and

He placed him in the power of Satan." The narrator's encounter with Dr. Rischel is perceived as analogous to that of Job in Satan's power. God's absence is noted in both episodes. In the final scene a new trio emerges as consisting of the narrator, Jacob Tzorev, and his son. It has already been noted that the father-son figures complement each other in their relational attributes of teacher-follower and authority-obedience. The narrator is there to observe and learn from the example of this complementary relationship of the two, whose roles are clearly defined by traditional, recognized rules of civilized behavior, and whose sense of identity is defined not as solitary entities but in relation to each other. At the conclusion of the story the three merge into a unified entity, with the possibility that the lesson has been learned and internalized and the unity can be preserved. The alternative is disintegration, fragmentation, and the reemergence of the eternal triangles. The protagonist will find himself in a bind not only in his lifetime but beyond that time span. That fate is known to the narrator who comments: "If you come across someone and you do not know what connection there is between you, you should realize that you have not done your duty to him previously and you have both been brought back into the world to put right the wrong you did to your neighbor in another incarnation."

10

Homosexual Fantasies
in Mendele and Agnon

David Aberbach

Homosexuality, although not a major or overt theme in the fiction of Mendele Mokher Sefarim (S. J. Abramowitz) and Samuel Joseph Agnon, is nevertheless an unmistakable part of the characters that they depict. These characters, for various reasons and to varying degrees, are deflected from normal heterosexual attachments and are inclined, for this reason, to real or symbolic forms of perversion. Both writers thus give oblique insight into the nature of homosexuality, and some knowledge of theories regarding homosexuality is valuable, in turn, in interpreting their works.

Some of the salient features in the makeup of their central characters are hardly explicable, when taken together, except as possible signs of latent homosexuality: most strikingly, their often-strange dreams and fantasies in which sex roles are confused and identities reversed, and their constant search for and overvaluation of a strong man, or successful lover, as a model for identification and emulation. More generally, we can include their emotional immaturity, their fear of women and difficulty with them, the men being rather weak and passive in relation to the women who are dominant, at times cruelly so, leading to frequent expressions of sexual inferiority, frustration, and unwholeness. As both writers were, to varying degrees, practicing

Jews in a more puritan age than the present,[1] and homosexuality
is against Jewish law, neither could deal straightforwardly with
this theme: Mendele injects it with elements of ribald, even grotesque, fun, notably in *Mas'ot Binyamin ha-shlishi*,[2] whereas
Agnon's treatment of it is often characterized by a mocking, re-
coiling allusiveness.

It is true, of course, that Mendele and Agnon are different in
many ways. Agnon was more familiar than Mendele with
Western European culture and behavior. Mendele's anti-
traditionalism and social realism often contrast with Agnon's
neoromanticism and his adherence to tradition. Unlike Mendele, Agnon does not think in abstract, allegorical terms. Yet
Mendele's influence on Agnon may be seen not just in Agnon's
style and technique but also, to an extent, in his psychological
characterization; and this may be seen by comparing and contrasting the homosexual motif in their writings.

Mendele's *Susati*[3] and Agnon's *Sippur pashut*[4] provide paradigms for the family structures depicted in their works, which
sometimes produce a homosexual son:[5] in *Susati*, a father who
has died, leaving the anxious, indulgent mother to raise her only
son; and in *Sippur pashut*, a strong-willed, manipulative mother
and a weak father. In neither work, however, does the homosex-

---

1. On the harsh climate for the depiction of homosexuality in Western literature during the latter period of Mendele's career and the early period of
Agnon's career, see J. Meyers, *Homosexuality and Literature 1880–1930* (London: Athlone Press, University of London, 1977).

2. The travels of Benjamin the Third, 1878Y, 1896H. References to Mendele's
writings are from the one-volume *Kol kitvei Mendele Mokher Sefarim* (Tel Aviv:
Dvir, 1947). When two dates are given, the first refers to the Yiddish and the
second to the Hebrew text. Translations from the Hebrew are my own, unless
indicated otherwise.

3. The mare, 1873Y, 1909H.

4. A simple story, 1935.

5. See I. Bieber et al., *Homosexuality, A Psychoanalytic Study* (New York: Basic
Books, 1962). For a clear account of possible causes of homosexuality, see A.
Storr, *Sexual Deviation* (Harmondsworth: Penguin Books, 1977).

ual undercurrent emerge as a dominant perversion, but it remains as a clear, merely latent alternative in the absence of
healthy heterosexual bonds; in addition, the homosexual theme
in each work is illumined by other works by the two writers.

The central struggle of *Susati* is the assertion of masculine
identity: Israel, an orphan raised by his mother, unmarried, os-
tracized by his society as a *maskil,* unsuccessful in his bid to enter
the university, projects his frustrated yearning for manhood onto
the mare. The mare, a figment of his imagination in madness, a
reflection of his own self-image, is herself an allegorical representation of the Jews as a people in search of identity, having lost
their masculinity when they lost their homeland. Once a noble
prince, the mare has been unsexed in exile:

> In those days there lived a wise, good prince. This prince, while
> still a boy, would wander far from home, to see what went on in
> the world, and he became famous among the nations. The king
> of Egypt, a land defiled with the idols of magicians, sorcerers and
> wizards, got angry with the prince, who had come as a visitor to
> live in his country. He consulted his retinue and said: let us find a
> good way of destroying him. The magicians used their sorcery to
> turn the prince into a mare and made him do the hardest work,
> building Pithom and Rameses with bricks and straw.[6]

Israel's longing "to be a man" (pp. 309, 318) thus runs parallel
with the mare's longing to be turned back into a prince, and his
confused feeling for the mare betrays his unconscious perception
of himself. At one point, he weeps for the mare and is ready to
sacrifice his life for her (p. 313), but he is also infuriated that she
does not try harder to return to being a prince. When she groans
and kicks, as if struggling to go back to her former state, he is re-

---

6. P. 312. Compare this with Exodus 1. For images of the horse as a male symbol, see Swift's *Gulliver's Travels,* Bialik's "Avi" (My father, 1928), and D. H.
Lawrence's "St. Mawr"; perhaps the most famous clinical example is Freud's
case of Little Hans (1909).

lieved (pp. 313, 322). His reflections on the transmigration of souls, such as that undergone by the mare, transparently reveal the uncertainty of his own sexual identity: "If the mare is a prince, I, a male, in contrast, am a princess" (p. 315), and he fantasizes that in a former incarnation he might have been the Queen of Sheba. But he also wishes, or suspects, that he was Judas Maccabeus—this might be seen as an image of exaggerated masculinity compensating for the weakness in his male identity. Later, his fear-ridden temptation to identify himself with the Devil, and the sexual abandon that this entails, appear to express that side of him that seeks a perverse, distorted masculine assertion at the expense of others, by abandoning moral scruples.

Israel's sense of social and emotional emasculation reaches a climax during the night after he fails his oral examination for entrance to university, when he has continual nightmares of being a sacrificial cock: "Eyes watched me in reproach and anger, and the game began, a terrifying game! The players took their parts: some as donkeys, oxen or human beings, and I played the role of the rooster, bound at their mercy, a sacrifice for the Day of Atonement" (p. 320). This nightmare is a prelude to Israel's possession by the Devil, in which his social and sexual crisis becomes merged with his role as a symbol of the Jewish people. In the end, his problems remain unsolved, though he does recover his sanity and gain insight into his predicament.

Sippur pashut, Agnon's only novel telling of a youth growing up at home, is also a study of emasculation, with clear homosexual undertones. It, too, depicts an unstable family producing a son who is vulnerable to deviance and madness. The madness of Hirshl Horowitz, like that of Israel in *Susati,* derives largely from his suppressed, inward-turned anger, which finds expression in the nightmare of being a sacrificial rooster. Hirshl's murderous rage at his wife is clearly linked to his tortured bond with his mother, who has engineered this loveless marriage. Hirshl has no way of handling this anger other than turning it on himself. He develops an insane fear of slaughtering roosters and of being a slaughtered rooster. We are told by the narrator that Hirshl hides his knife at night in order to protect himself from his sadomas-ochistic impulses: "A man is not in control when he is angry. Suddenly he could get up and kill all the roosters in the world. Hirshl did well to hide his knife at night" (3:201).[7]

Like Israel, Hirshl in madness has a sense of disembodiment and of not being in control of his destiny: His sexual identity, too, appears to be distorted; Hirshl deliriously addresses trees as Israel addresses animals, as if they were superior creatures; when discovered raving in the fields, Hirshl pleads, "Don't slaughter me, I'm not a rooster."[8]

In his analysis of the rooster imagery in Agnon, Barukh Kurzweil calls attention to the fact that the word for rooster, *gever,* is the same as that for man:[9] Hirshl's terror at being a slaughtered cock could symbolize his fear of emasculation or his sense of having been emasculated. Kurzweil's interpretation is equally applicable to Israel in *Susati,* and it is likely that Agnon was influenced by this work in *Sippur pashut.*[10] Mendele appears to have been fully conscious of his use of the cock as symbol of manhood. During a temporary remission from madness, Israel is told of his behavior, of which he has no recollection and is, therefore, entirely unconscious: Encountering a rooster, he bowed down to it and addressed it as *gever,* a man of valor, im-plicitly contrasting it with his own self-perceived weakness and ineffectuality (p. 318).

In *Sippur pashut,* however, Hirshl's sense of emasculation, his sexual frustrations, and his suppressed rage at women appear to enhance his conscious homosexual leanings. He becomes partic-

---

7. Unless indicated otherwise, quotations from Agnon are taken from *Kol sippurav shel Shmuel Yosef Agnon,* 8 vols. (Tel Aviv: Schocken, 1953–1962).

8. 3:218.

9. B. Kurzweil, *Massot 'al sippurei S. Y. Agnon* (Jerusalem and Tel Aviv: Schocken, 1963), pp. 216ff.

10. See D. Aberbach, "Breakdown in Mendele and Agnon," *Proceedings of the Ninth World Congress of Jewish Studies,* Division C: Jewish Thought and Literature (Jerusalem: World Union of Jewish Studies, 1986), pp. 149–155.

ularly responsive to the touch of Jonah Toiber, the matchmaker who arranges his marriage. Toiber, from Hirshl's viewpoint, knows how to handle his life, in contrast with himself. Toiber's touch (3:180–181) is similar to that of Bluma (3:82–83), for whom Hirshl longs from a distance, and also of Hirshl's mother (3:100). His attraction to Toiber's touch continues after his marriage, and causes him guilt: "Isn't it a disgrace to me that when he takes my hand in his I want to kiss it. ... How smooth are Jonah's hands" (3:213). "Toiber's influence on Hirshl," it has been observed, "is like the influence of a woman."[11] When Hirshl undergoes psychiatric treatment, the hand of Dr. Langsam takes over: "The strong hand that held his hand as if inadvertently when he came in and when he went out was not soft like Toiber's, nor did he think that he needed to kiss it" (3:227).

The exchange of sexual identity in Agnon is generally treated as a sign of pathology, whereas in Mendele this phenomenon has a strongly comic side. Thus, in *Temol shilshom* (Only yesterday, 1945), in the throes of delirium after being bitten by the dog Balak, Yitzhak Kummer mixes male and female with seeming indiscrimination. In this state of being shattered, the lines of psychological weakness are clearer. In one fantasy, he thinks of the taxidermists Arzaf and Sweetfoot, who are characterized by their ability to live alone, apparently not dependent upon women, as Yitzhak is: "When Yitzhak managed to remember Arzaf's name, he found him in Sweetfoot's shack stroking Tzutzik's teeth, talking to him as if he were female, saying "ati" to him. Tzutzik was enjoying being coddled like a bitch" (5:597). The fact that the dog is treated as female is significant in the scheme of the novel, as dogs are often compared to people, and this might point to a homosexual component in Yitzhak's makeup that is corroborated in a juxtaposed fantasy involving Yitzhak's friend Rabinowitz. Rabinowitz (of whom I will say more later) appears to

---

11. A. Eshkoli, "Hagigim 'al *Sippur pashut* le-S. Y. Agnon" (Tel Aviv, 1977), p. 28.

Yitzhak, who expresses astonishment: "You don't know why you are astonished," says Rabinowitz. "It's because you've found me dressed in women's clothes." In *Shira* (1971), likewise, Manfred Herbst's craving for nurse Shira to be transformed into a man might betray a homosexual tendency: "He opened his mouth until the rows of his teeth stuck out and began to chatter against one another. He got up and screamed, 'And if you want to live, then live, only turn into a man'" (p. 164).

Mas'ot Binyamin ha-shlishi, in contrast, has none of the sordid pathology and hints of sexual deviation of Agnon's writings, but treats a "marriage" of men in the spirit of a Purimspiel. This allows Mendele to get away with a great deal that would have been otherwise inadmissible. The story begins in the shtetl of Bitalon, with the pious *luftmensch* Benjamin, a married man with children, undergoing a crisis of identity not unlike that of Israel in *Susati,* a crisis in which Benjamin, too, withdraws from his family. Likewise, intent on belatedly proving himself a man by making the hard trek to the Land of Israel, he devotes himself to an ideal of tough masculinity diametrically opposed to his nature. He adopts the figure of Alexander the Great—this recalls the Judas Maccabeus fantasy in *Susati*—as a male model of identification and, in order to combat his natural temerity, tests himself: "He decided to act bravely, to suppress his nature, to root out all fear from his heart. He forced himself to walk out alone at night, to sleep alone in his room, to go past the town limits, even though it wore him out and made him very scared" (p. 60).

Next he finds himself an ideal "wife": Senderl the Woman, malleable and ludicrous, henpecked, beaten, and effectively emasculated by his wife, careless of his indignities to the point of masochism, ultimately warmhearted and lovable. (He is called Senderl the Woman, as his wife puts him to work around the house and he often does women's chores.) Mendele depicts their friendship as a parody of a homosexual "marriage," perhaps the only way he could have portrayed it at the time: Senderl is Benjamin's "helpmeet," *'ezer ke-negdo* (p. 62), as Eve is to Adam (Genesis 2:20); and the biblical and rabbinic language of sexual desire and union—*teshukah, zivug, hityahadut*—is frequently used to heighten the tone of ribald farce. "My blood boils and I long for you" (p. 63), *ve-elekha teshukati* (Genesis 3:16), exclaims Benjamin to Senderl on proposing that they "elope" together; Senderl's agreement raises Benjamin's ecstasy to new heights in a parody of romantic love not unworthy of Groucho: "'My soul, the air I breathe, let me kiss you,' cried Benjamin as he hugged Senderl the Woman lovingly" (p. 64); and when Senderl pulls a bundle of coins, his life savings, from his pocket, Benjamin's joy is unbounded: "'Now, beloved of my soul, you deserve a kiss on every limb' (*kol ever me-evrei gufkha*), exclaimed Benjamin joyfully, embracing Senderl the Woman and hugging him" (p. 64).

On the morning of their departure from Bitalon, Senderl appears disguised as a woman, and once Benjamin ascertains that the bustling figure in skirts and kerchief is not his wife in hot pursuit, he brightens up and gazes at Senderl like a groom at his beautiful bride, *ke-khala na-ah be-'eynei dodah* (p. 65). They fairly sail along until Senderl tires, as a woman does according to the Talmud (Berachot 32b), *tash koho ki-nkevah* (p. 66). To his everlasting credit, Senderl had busied himself like a "woman of valor," *eshet hayil,* to prepare food for the way (p. 67), unlike Benjamin, whose preoccupations are masculine and spiritual—until he gets hungry. Each declares his inexorable attraction to the other, Senderl revealing that he was drawn to Benjamin "like a blind person … like a calf after the cow," and Benjamin: "Our marriage was made in heaven, you and I are body and soul" (p. 67). When they reach Kisalon, they stroll through the streets like a honeymoon couple, "like a bride and groom during the seven days of feasting after the marriage, alone together, walking in the gardens, enjoying one another's every word and glance" (p. 80).

This parody of marriage reaches its climax when the "newlyweds" unwittingly fall into the hands of *khappers,* this being Russia in the early 1850s. Unconsciously aware of the danger, they both have nightmares that betray their deepest fears, Benjamin of failing to live up to his masculine ideal, and Senderl of getting pregnant. Psychologically, these nightmares complement one another. Here is Benjamin's:

A horned viper appeared and examined me: "Are you Reb Binyamin of Bitalon? Please join me over there, there. ... Alexander the Great awaits you with his mighty army, he longs to see you." I lifted up my feet and ran ahead of the viper. A voice came from behind: "You run more swiftly than an arrow— may the Evil Eye not look upon you—and I cannot catch you." I looked back and saw—Alexander the Great. "My master the king!" I cried loudly, grasping his hand and squeezing it tight. Something smelled putrid, it was bad enough to make you faint. I woke with a crushed flea in my hand. (p. 81)

This is Senderl's nightmare: "I was no longer Senderl but, ex- cuse my saying it, a woman without trace of a beard. I was dressed like a woman, and my stomach, my stomach! May no Jew ever have such pain! 'It doesn't matter,' a man beside me comforted me. 'The first time is always the hardest'" (p. 82).

A mock marriage somewhat similar to that of Benjamin and Senderl is that of Mendele and Reb Leib in the story of "Bi- ymei ha-ra'ash" (Earthquake days, 1894H). As in *Mas'ot Binyamin hashlishi,* the latter pair abandons their families in order to journey to the Promised Land: "We made a covenant to live together and neither would abandon his mate" (p. 407). Leib, like Senderl, is the "female" partner, and when the bedraggled travelers visit the Zionist representative (based on Leon Pinsker) in Odessa to ask about emigration—the story is set in 1881, after the outbreak of the pogroms—Leib "bent and curtsied and twisted up his face as women do" (p. 410). Later, when Leib looks in the mirror, Mendele imagines that "Reb Leib the melamed fancied himself, like all ugly women. As they make themselves up in front of the mirror they say to themselves that they are beautiful and there is no one like them in the whole world" (p. 413).

There then follows a remarkable parody of the competitive- ness often found among homosexuals: Mendele becomes in- tensely distressed when he sees Leib in the company of a young woman who, in fact, wants him not as a lover but as a Hebrew teacher. Leib appears to be betraying not only his wife but also

Mendele, to whom he is "married," and who assumes the worst when Leib, dressed in his sabbath *kapote,* disappears with the woman: "To make things worse, I saw Leib's everyday *kapote* hanging on the wall, and she seemed sad, her sleeves crusted with mud like the sleeves of a woman's dress on sabbath eve" (p. 415). Leib returns from his rendezvous spouting Hebrew (the only time, incidentally, in the author's entire oeuvre that a character speaks Hebrew), full of excitement at being in demand as a Hebrew teacher. Here, too, as in *Mas'ot Binyamin ha-shlishi,* the climax is reached in a form of pregnancy: "At that moment Reb Leib was like a woman in labour struggling to give birth" (p. 415). Mendele sees that he has misjudged Leib, and now that Leib has found work, the "marriage" is dissolved.

Against the background of these "marriages" of men, the hilarious matchmaking done by Mendele's fellow bookseller, Reb Alter, in *Sefer ha-kabbtzanim* (The beggar's book, 1888Y, 1909H) seems to fit into a pattern. Reb Alter, seeing an opportunity to earn a hefty matchmaker's fee at the Yarmolinsk fair, hatches a match with excessive dispatch only to find that he has paired two grooms! This little tale, related with appropriate interjections of comic disgust is, in fact, the trigger for the main story of Fishke the Lame, his disastrous marriage and his love for Beila the Hunchback (Alter's daughter, as it turns out). Women in *Sefer ha-kabbtzanim* are either cruelly dominant and manipulative or fruitlessly yearned for, and divorce is a common motif. The bonds among men are more stable, such as those of Mendele and Alter and, in the end, of Mendele and Fishke. Mendele's attitude to Fishke is one of the most interesting features in this novel, changing as it does from amused pity at the start to genuine empathy and admiration, which is owing largely to Fishke's being in love, a state that Mendele has apparently never experienced.

This nose-in-the-sweetshop-window mentality is found frequently in Agnon's writings; and a homosexual element is involved, perhaps, in the hero's obsession with the lover, or former lover, of his beloved. In "Ha-rofe u-grushato" (The doctor and his divorcee, 1941), this obsession, which ruins the doctor's marriage, reaches its climax when his wife's former lover becomes his patient. The extraordinary care with which he tends the man, whom he hates, might indicate a homosexual attachment, and a narcissistic identification with him.[12] In a similar way, the ambivalent hatred of Moshe Pinchas for Reb Shlomo in *Shnei talmidei hakhamim she-hayu be-'ireinu* (Two scholars in our town, 1946), which Moshe Pinchas admits is irrational, may be partly homosexual in origin; he discusses the problem with his mother: " 'The man whom I hate wants to help me.' His mother replied, 'If he wants to help you, why do you hate him?' Rabbi Moshe Pinchas said, 'I hate him because he brings out this contemptible quality of hatred in me.' The old woman said, 'I don't understand what you're talking about.' He replied, 'I don't understand it either' " (6:23).

This identification is grotesquely confirmed at the end of the story when the doctor reveals that he chose to remain childless for fear that his children would look like the former lover. The evident fear of women and sex and the childlike dependence brought home most forcibly in the final sentence—the doctor sits up in bed and calls to his former wife as a child to its mother—might also contribute to these alleged homosexual tendencies. A similar pathological jealousy of and identification with the former lover, or lovers, appears in *Shira* (p. 26), for Herbst imagines that even a beggar has been with Shira, and in fact, when she tells him her violent, tragic life story, all he can think is, Which men did she know? (p. 63).

Samuel, the writer in *Oreah natah lalun* (A guest for the night, 1939), like the doctor, is obsessed with the lover of the girl to whom he is attracted. Kurzweil writes of his "demonic affection" for Yeruham Hofshi and observes that "no one in the novel arouses the Guest's envy more than Yeruham as he lives for the present, he engages in tough and manly physical labor, he has

---

12. "In all homosexual love, there is an element of narcissism." Storr, op. cit., p. 88.

his woman. The Guest, in contrast, cannot break away from the past, any ambition of his to work the land has come to nothing, and he lives alone, infatuated with Rachel from a distance."[13] Samuel's secret affection for Yeruham has a physical side: "Why do I like Yeruham? ... When he speaks, you feel as if a man were ploughing and the fragrance of the clean earth were rising all around him."[14] He is drawn to Yeruham's body, his eyes, and hair (4:84, 421).

Yitzhak Kummer, in *Temol shilshom,* is similarly obsessed by Rabinowitz, the former lover of his "beloved" Sonia. Rabinowitz is much that Yitzhak would like to be and is implicitly contrasted with Yitzhak as a model of success, in business and with women, and unhampered by psychological inhibitions. His secret: the constant striving to create new desires and to satisfy them, something that Yitzhak's personality seems to prevent him from doing. He tells Kummer:

> A man should get used to unnecessary things. If he has no great desire for these things, he ought to develop one. If you have superfluous lusts, you lust to satisfy them. In this way you increase the strength of your will and you don't sit idle, as lusts demand money and money demands action. If you force yourself to act and rid yourself of laziness, you build yourself up, and the land grows with you. (5:454)

In the context of Yitzhak's problems with women, all this is suggestive: Kummer's lust for woman is stifled by inner rage caused, as in the case of Hirshl in *Sippur pashut,* by unresolved family conflicts and imbalances that have made him vulnerable to homosexual impulses. These impulses may be symbolized by the dog Balak, and Baruch Hochman suggests that the dog bite leading to Yitzhak's death a month after his marriage is an external-

---

13. Kurzweil, op. cit., pp. 61, 62.
14. *A Guest for the Night,* trans. M. Louvish (New York: Schocken Books, 1968), p. 217.

ization of Yitzhak's deviance: "When Balak leaps at him from under Geronam's gaberdine, Yitzhak is presumably succumbing to his own rage and terror [toward women] and also to his wish that the violent old puritan take him as a man takes a woman. We feel it is no accident that Balak's assault comes so soon after Yitzhak's marriage."[15]

Another indication of latent homosexuality is the Agnon hero's attraction not to his peers as much as to men who, in contrast with himself, have succeeded in some form of masculine assertion, especially in business or public affairs. The most extraordinary relationship of this sort is with Mr. Gressler in "Pat shlemah" (A whole loaf, 1933).

> This Mr. Gressler was my acquaintance, one of my special acquaintances. Since when had I known him? Possibly since the days when I reached a maturity of knowledge. Nor do I exaggerate if I say that from the day I met him we had never ceased to have a liking for one another [lit, our love did not cease]. Now, although all and sundry like him, I can say that he prefers me to all of them, since he has taken the trouble to show me all kinds of pleasures.[16]

The suggestiveness of this passage—it could almost be mistaken for the admission of a young woman flattered by the attentions of an older man—is enhanced by the emphasis upon extreme hunger and heat, which pervade the story and could indicate the sexual craving of a man who is living apart from his wife. Also, at the beginning of the story, he is described first as moving with the crowd, then as breaking away on his own path. This could indicate perversion, which the rest of the story appears to bear

15. B. Hochman, *The Fiction of S. Y. Agnon* (Ithaca, N.Y.: Cornell University Press, 1970), p. 141.

16. Trans. I. M. Lask, in S. Y. Agnon, *Twenty-one Stories,* ed. N. Glatzer (New York: Schocken Books, 1970), p. 86.

out symbolically, especially in the scene of the overturned carriage:

> I stood up, took the reins out of his hands, and turned the horses off in a different direction. Since I am not an expert in steering horses, the carriage turned over on me and Mr. Gressler, and we both rolled into the street. I yelled and shouted, "Take the reins and get me out of this!" But he pretended not to hear and rolled with me laughing as though it amused him to roll about with me in the muck.[17]

The theme of unwholeness in this story and others could also symbolize homosexuality, as the psychiatrist Anthony Storr writes: "Heterosexual lovers habitually report that the partner with whom they are in love seems to fulfill their lives, to complete them, to make them whole. Homosexual lovers less often repeat such phrases because, inevitably, their lives lack this quality of wholeness."[18] In the restaurant, toward the end of the story, the narrator gives up on ever obtaining a "whole loaf." He sees a little boy eating bread similar to that which his mother used to bake when he was a little boy. He thinks to himself that he would give everything for a mouthful of this bread. Perhaps as a solution to his alleged homosexual leanings, he wishes to remain sexually innocent, like the children who populate the stories.[19] But when he hears Gressler riding along the street in his carriage, he calls to him. As to the lover in the Song of Songs, who is alluded to at this point, he receives no reply.

Strange dreams and fantasies could, among other things, have a homosexual meaning. The story "Yedidut" (Friendship, 1932) takes place immediately after the narrator's wife has returned to

---

17. Ibid., pp. 88–89.

18. Storr, op. cit., p. 89.

19. See D. Aberbach, *At the Handles of the Lock: Themes in the Fiction of S. J. Agnon* (New York and Oxford: Oxford University Press, 1984), pp. 66–69, where the motif of homosexuality in Agnon's stories is discussed in the context

their new home following a long absence. On his way to see her, he forgets where he lives. He meets an acquaintance, Mr. Rischel:

> "Get into a streetcar and come with me," said Rischel. I won-
> dered why he was giving me such unsuitable advice. He took me
> by the arm and got in with me. I rode on against my will, won-
> dering why Rischel had seen fit to drag me into this tramcar.
> Not only was it not bringing me home, but it was taking me fur-
> ther away from my own street. I remembered that I had seen
> Rischel in a dream wrestling with me. I jumped off the tramcar
> and left him.[20]

On the one letter that had his address and that he had torn up, the narrator had written that in the book of Job, the real trial was God's: "He had a perfect and upright man, and He placed him in the power of Satan."[21] An involuntary impulse to homo-sexuality—the satanic nature of which brings *Susati* to mind— may be evident as the narrator spends no time alone with his wife after her return, he forgets where they live, denies hysteri-cally any contact with women in her absence, and rides per-versely away from home with Rischel, who, wrestling partner that he is in the narrator's dream, might also be desired uncon-sciously as a sexual partner.[22]

In "Shevu'at emunim" (Betrothed, 1943), on the day after Susan reminds Rechnitz of their childhood oath to marry, he re-calls a fantasy in which he, like the narrator of "Yedidut," is rid-ing in a tram:

---

of the general emotional immaturity of the Agnon hero and the difficulties in his personal relationships.

20. Trans. M. Louvish, in Agnon, *Twenty-one Stories,* p. 76.

21. Ibid., p. 74.

22. The wrestling match between Gerald and Birkin in D. H. Lawrence's *Women in Love* is clearly intended by Lawrence as symbolic of a desired sexual encounter. See Meyers, op. cit., pp. 146–147.

Two young fellows got in and one sat on the other's knees. He heard them talking about Otto Weininger and his *Sex and Character*. The journey continued for an hour. And then, oddly enough, Jacob had found himself again sitting with Susan; and it was not yet eleven o'clock, although he had left Susan's house at ten, and she had accompanied him halfway, and he had even travelled for an hour on the streetcar, and spent an hour at home.[23]

Rechnitz's immaturity and his being something of a "womanly man," a theme of Weininger's book (as of *Susati*), might involve homosexual leanings, symbolized by the one boy's sitting on the other's knees. His inability to differentiate Susan from the image of her dead mother, whom he virtually regards as his own mother, supports this conclusion.[24] The motif of retarded time suggests regression or fixation on his part and difficulty in taking Susan as a man takes a woman.

Yet another fantasy with undertones of homosexuality occurs in the novella "Ad henna" (Thus far, 1952). The narrator, who, like most of Agnon's protagonists, lives alone, separated from his family, has a nightmare that alludes to the midrash on Exodus 2:24, with insinuations of homosexuality:

One night when I was lying in bed the executioners of Pharaoh came and fixed me in the walls of a brick house. I cried out from the walls, and the Holy One, blessed be He, took me out and put me to bed. And still the executioners were choking me. I made a great effort and they all fell down except for the official in the tax office who lived in the room opposite mine. ... He made a mistake and came into my room and got on my bed and lay on top of me and was pressing me. (7:68)

---

23. Trans. W. Lever, *Two Tales of S. Y. Agnon* (London: Gollancz, 1967), p. 69.
24. On the dead mother in Agnon, see Aberbach, *At the Handles of the Lock*, pp. 81–99.

Despite the humorous touch in the last illustration, a comparison between Mendele and Agnon suggests that the alleged deviance in their works is less severe in Mendele, as it is treated squarely in a semicomic, satiric vein, whereas Agnon, for all his comic genius, portrays it largely in a pathological light. It is interesting, too, that Agnon's picaresque novel, *Hakhnasat kalla* (The bridal canopy, 1930), which more than any other of his works shows the direct influence of Mendele,[25] particularly *Mas'ot Binyamin ha-shlishi,* avoids defining the relationship between Reb Yudel and Nuta as a mock marriage. Agnon, in addition, gives no complete biographical account that would help explain the persistence of deviance in his writings, though biographical parallels in fictional disguise may be detected throughout his works, central to which is *Sippur pashut.*[26]

Mendele, however, in *Ba-yamim ha-hem* (In those days) (1898–1899Y, 1903–1915H), gives a fairly clear biographical picture of the origins of problems that he addresses in his other works: his father's death when he was in his early teens, his mother's inability to support him and her remarriage, his consequent departure from home for the yeshiva of Slutsk, a prelude to his later life among beggars in the Pale of Settlement. He describes his indiscriminate hunger for friendship and love at the yeshiva, which may be taken to presage the male bonds that he portrays elsewhere: "The essence of Shlomele's soul was a mixture of love, eternal longing, affection and friendship. He was like a flame to a wick, reaching out to catch hold, indiscriminately, to everyone, and to live with him in love and friendship as

---

25. "No one writing in Hebrew in the 1920s concerning Eastern European Jewry of the early nineteenth century and using various plot features of *Hakhnasat kalla* could possibly do so without confronting Mendele psychologically and ideologically." A. Band, *Nostalgia and Nightmare: A Study in the Fiction of S. Y. Agnon* (Berkeley and Los Angeles: University of California Press, 1968), p. 130.

26. See Aberbach, *At the Handles of the Lock,* p. 217, index s.v. "biographical basis of writings," "life and career," "personality."

with his own soul" (p. 304). Significantly, Mendele admits that there was something wrong with these friendships, which he does not explain, though he conveys his view of the yeshiva as a moral swamp in which he had sunk and been besmirched. It is possible that the identification with beggars, which Mendele's characters share with some of Agnon's (e.g., Hemdat, Hirshl Horowitz, and Herbst) may have to do with the fact that beggars, being out of society's pale, can in theory live freely and, if they wish, in accordance with their deviances; in addition, they might symbolize emotional poverty leading to possible deviance.

To sum up: Certain obscure features in Mendele and Agnon become clearer if the possibility of latent homosexuality is taken into account. The patterns of relationships in their works that, although different in many ways, are recognized frequently to produce sons with homosexual leanings are particularly evident in Mendele's *Susati* and Agnon's *Sippur pashut*. It is suggested that they have caused, in part at least, the hero's emotional immaturity, his feelings of sexual inferiority and emasculation, and his fear of women, all symbolized most strikingly in the nightmares of being a slaughtered cock. It is further suggested that all this is linked with their postadolescent identification with various types of models of ideal masculinity, whether successful *hommes d'affaires* or men who succeed with women where they themselves fail, or, in madness, with exaggerated or distorted images of masculinity, and with their strange dreams and fantasies of sex changes or of men on top of one another. All these make better sense when taken as gestalt pictures of latent homosexuality. It is remarkable how much Agnon appears to have learned from Mendele, not just in imitation of the naïve and pious narrator who is, in fact, a sophisticated artist, but also in the psychological depiction of characters and their inner life, their dreams and fantasies.

11

Sleeping Princes, Beggars of Love

Miri Kubovy

What is the connection between the obscure insights and the open endings of Agnon's narratives? How can one say without lying, "My wife is not my wife and I am not her husband?" How can a man have a child by another man? Why didn't Noah save a pair of fish in his ark? What is the connection between loving Rembrandt and desiring married women?

It is questions such as these that this chapter will consider, in exploring the connection between two short stories of Agnon and their relation to his novel *A Guest for the Night,*[1] which alludes to both of them. I shall study Agnon's interpretation of desire and its repression in "Giv'at ha-hol" (The hill of sand)[2] and "The Doctor's Divorce."[3]

1. S. Y. Agnon, *A Guest for the Night,* trans. Misha Louvish (New York: Schocken, 1968); Hebrew: *Oreah natah lalun,* 1939, originally 1937–1938, in S. Y. Agnon, *Kol sippurav shel Shmuel Yosef Agnon* (Tel Aviv: Schocken, 1953–1962).

2. 1931, *Kol sippurav,* vol. 3: *Al kapot ha-man'ul,* pp. 351–389. The story is a later version of "Tishrei," which appeared in *Ha-poel Ha-tza'ir,* 22 November 1911, p. 9.

3. Trans. R. Alter, *Twenty-one Stories* (New York: Schocken, 1970), pp. 135–161; Hebrew: "Ha-rofe u-grushato" (lit., The doctor and his divorcee), *Kol sippurav,* vol. 3, pp. 469–490.

"The Doctor's Divorce"

A doctor meets a nurse named Dinah and is attracted to her particularly because he observes a deep sadness in her smile and
"that blue-black in her eyes" (p. 135). Eventually they marry.
But the reason for her deep sorrow remains hidden from the
doctor until, after long and persistent questioning, she reveals to
him that she had relations with another man in the past. From
that moment on the image of the wife's lover never leaves the
doctor; indeed, it obsesses him more and more. When, in the
story, the former lover becomes a patient at the hospital and the
doctor discovers his identity, he hovers over him, showering him
with attention and care, giving him medical checkups, treat-
ments, and presents. The doctor resists discharging him from the
hospital, afraid to lose him. Finally, the long-recovered lover has
to leave the hospital because there are no more beds and no more
excuses to keep him there. When he can no longer keep the
lover, the doctor gives him a checkup before letting him leave.
While doing this, he touches him and feels both revulsion and
guilt. He also feels like a criminal who is afraid to be caught. He
is going out of his mind; he cannot control himself and he runs
away from work in the middle of the day. At the same time the
doctor feels a deep sense of loss, and he has a dream. In the
dream the lover comes to him, saying: "What do you want from
me? Is the fact that you raped me any reason for you to have it in
for me?" (p. 155). After he tells the dream to his wife, she realizes that a divorce is inevitable. The story ends with the doctor
telling his friend that he still keeps in his heart Dinah's blue-
black eyes and her smile, and that at night, he often sits up in
bed, stretching out his arms, crying "Nurse, nurse, come to
me!" The bulk of the story is made of the doctor's confession to
a friend, in which he analyzes his relationship with Dinah and
his jealousy that finally leads to their divorce.[4]

---

4. Miri Kubovy-Manor, "The Nature of Jealousy" (Hebrew), *Moznayim,*
December 1986, pp. 24–47.

In my reading, from the point of view of the jealous doctor, the rival is both the object of desire with whom the doctor identifies and the hated enemy who had had his wife and thereby deprives him of happiness. The doctor becomes outraged and aggressive, blaming the lover for ruining his life. In retaliation for the persecution he feels, he captures the lover, deforms his body by stuffing him with food, and in his dream rapes him.

The changes from love to hate and back are based on an inherent ambivalence toward both Dinah and the lover. His behavior seems to be in line with the Freudian claim that ambivalence and paranoia serve the purpose of a "defense against homosexuality."[5]

Toward the end of the story the doctor realizes that his interest in the lover is independent of his wife. He is so alarmed by this revelation that when his buffer, his wife, is gone and he has to face up to his attraction to the lover, he terminates his relationship with both. He cannot live with the acute ambivalence toward the attractive-repulsive man through his beloved-hated wife. Not only does he suffer himself, but also he destroys both of them. The insight concerning the motivation and structure of his behavior almost comes to the surface of the doctor's consciousness, but only obscurely: "Before long I saw with my own eyes and I grasped with my own understanding what at first I had not seen and I had not grasped. At once I decided that I would grant Dinah the divorce. We had no children, for I have been apprehensive about begetting children for fear they would look like him" (p. 161).

It is thus the unconscious forces of desire and repression that determine and shape the narrative. The doctor relates his story by the telling of the same events over and over, explaining, disclosing, almost realizing, becoming afraid by the realization, obscuring it, covering up what he considers a crime, or worse, an

5. S. Freud, "Some Neurotic Mechanisms in Jealousy, Paranoia, and Homosexuality," *Sexuality and the Psychology of Love* (New York: Collier Books, 1963), p. 164.

abomination. In short, he interprets by telling and retells by interpreting. In Agnon, interpretation is an intrinsic part of the
story itself, an incomplete process of becoming. However,
Agnon's main skill is his coercion of the reader into continuing
the interpretation, so it is through and toward interpretation that
the endless becoming of the story moves.

"Giv'at ha-hol"

The story takes place in the days of the Second Aliyah.[6] It de-
scribes a failing relationship between a young poet, Hemdat, and
Yael, an attractive young woman who recently immigrated to
Palestine. At first Hemdat takes her for a frivolous, empty-
headed, loose woman, but then he finds out that she is a desti-
tute, struggling girl, plagued by many misfortunes and troubles.
Their relationship is platonic. At the beginning of the story
Hemdat sees himself as Yael's teacher, brother, or father. He
gives her food and money and also teaches her Torah and
Hebrew, so she can become a kindergarten teacher rather than a
manual worker. He defines his attachment to her as mere compassion and he wants to save her. When Yael makes attempts to
become physically close, Hemdat ignores them, when she gives
him the key of her room, he returns it to her, and when she tries
to discuss personal matters, he deliberately remains silent. "In
the past, while making love to young women, there was nothing
he liked better than to tell them about his affairs because these
stories, filled with ecstasy, attracted other young women to him,
but now that he is no longer involved with women, it would be
best to remain silent" (p. 352). Most of the time they meet in
Hemdat's room studying or eating elaborate meals. Sometimes
he even forces her to eat. Hemdat drives Yael into the arms of
another man, Shamai. For a while all three are friendly and
spend time as a threesome. Then, Hemdat begins to hate

6. The second major wave of Zionist immigration.

Shamai. At the end of the story, only when Yael moves in with Shamai and Hemdat realizes how serious their involvement is, he also realizes that he is deeply in love with Yael, but then, it is too late. He loses her to the other man and he is left alone on the hill of sand.

In my reading, Hemdat's artistic and romantic perfectionism and idealism[7] are only a pretext against marriage. His fear of marriage is camouflaging a deeper force, best described as absence, the key to which cannot be found because it is the hole itself.

The Hole as the Key

Agnon's art is about the inability truly to comprehend, explain, or tell: He tells his story through the obstacles not only of language but also of our very being. Although the text abounds with traditional literary forms such as parallelisms, repetitions, allusions, digressions, and irony, it never fully expresses its own meaning. Agnon's art is a network of substitutes for dormant, repressed dynamics that are never fully made present. There is never any real resolution. Agnon suggests that, at best, all an insight can achieve is to show us not the key but the *hole* in the lock, the *empty* mirror, the deprivation, the absence. All Agnon's art can do is pose the questions: Where is the misunderstanding? What is indicative of the repressed? Through the power of his questioning, Agnon creates contact with the unknown at the handles of the lock. The story "Giv'at ha-hol" appears in a volume of Agnon's writings called *'Al kapot ha-man'ul*.[8] This title is in itself a quotation from the Song of Songs 5:4, 5, 6: "My beloved put in his hand by the hole of the door. ... I rose up to open to my beloved; and my hands dropped with myrrh ... upon

---

7. Gershon Shaked, *The Narrative Art of S. Y. Agnon* (Hebrew) (Tel Aviv: Sifriat Po'alim, 1973), p. 169.

8. At the handles of the lock, *Kol sippurav,* vol. 3.

the handles of the lock. I opened to my beloved; but my beloved had withdrawn himself and was gone: my soul failed when he spake: I sought him, but I could not find him; I called him, but he gave no answer."

Agnon's figure of the handles brings to mind Freud's figure of the navel of the dream.[9] Lacan developed this concept into his theory of the "obscure insight," an insight that does not know its own meaning.

All of Agnon's insights and endings are, in fact, obscure and offer no solution. They are a condensed recapitulation of the complexity in the story as a whole. This textual system is encapsulated in one striking passage in the novel *A Guest for the Night:*

> The locksmith greeted me, clasping my hand joyfully, and I too rejoiced in him. First, because he would make the key for me, and second, because when I was a child I used to stand at the entrance to his shop, looking at the keys and locks, for in those days I longed for a chest with a key and a lock. When later, I gave up the idea of the chest I did not give up the idea of the key. ... I pictured the key in various shapes, but all the shapes were less important than its function and final purpose: the act of opening. Imagine it: In the center of the city stands a house, and that house has a door, like all the other houses, and on the door hangs a lock. Along comes a child from school, puts his hand in his pocket, takes out the key, pushes the key into the lock, and twists it this way and that, and immediately the whole house is open before him. What is there in the house? A table, a bed, and a lamp—namely, nothing the other houses do not have; but no other moment can compare to that moment of opening the house with the key that the child is holding. So now you can imagine how wonderful was that old man, who had a hundred keys and more hanging at his shop entrance. There are hidden stores of treasure that can be opened with a sentence, as when

---

9. S. Freud, *The Interpretation of Dreams,* chap. 2, *The Basic Writings of Sigmund Freud,* ed. and trans. A. A. Brill (New York: Modern Library, 1938), p. 199.

one says, "Open Sesame," I was not used to seeking things that were hidden from the eye, but only things that the eye could see, and I wished to have the key to them in my possession.[10]

Agnon is fully aware of the limitation of knowledge and insight. All that is possible, all that matters, is creating contact with the unknown by calling, "Open Sesame!" The key, the insight is the locus of the "unfathomable." It is the *hole* within the lock, before which one is situated. There are many keys that appear in the stories, but none is the right key itself. They are useless, displaced keys, duplicates of the original key that do not fit the lock, "negative keys," as Yael Feldman calls them. But they are far more negative than she implies. The real drama does not end in the void between the lock and the key. Even if the door were to open, a real treasure cannot be found; at best, it is reflected through us, but with the picture itself absent.

When Hemdat, who "abstained from women" (p. 377), desperately wants to tell Yael "the secrets of his heart," she doesn't want to listen and thus the secrets themselves never appear directly in the text. Hemdat and Yael go to "the hill of sand," which is also called "the hill of love," and sit on the mound. Yael takes the key of her room and hands it to Hemdat, saying: "What is pressuring me like that? The key. Yael took the key to her room and gave it to Hemdat. Hemdat put it in his pocket. Suddenly she got up and said, home. Hemdat walked her to her house and returned the key to her. Yael went in and shut her door and Hemdat's pocket became empty. ... Hemdat smiled to himself mocking his hope and he returned to his home" (p. 378).

As a result of his frustration, he cuts his beautiful hair and then shaves his scalp—an act of anger and self-hate. As in Samson's case the hair might symbolize potency. Yael almost goes out of her mind when she sees his bald head. She screams at him,

---

10. P. 98.

"How can a person be so foolish as to destroy the most glorious thing that he has." To her great revulsion, he makes her *touch what is cut off.* He makes her touch what horrifies her, the hair that is no longer there, *the absence,* an echo of his emptied pocket.

What prompts him to return the key? Why doesn't he enter? Just when he has a perfect chance, he deliberately avoids it. Like the doctor and the guest, Hemdat has a desire not to enter, thereby ignoring his sexual complexity, which he cannot face. His attraction-repulsion both to Yael and Shamai compel him to create triangles, thus avoiding direct contact.

The main point in our three texts goes far beyond the paradoxes and irony seen by most critics.[11] It is the story of the key that is the essence and the making of Agnon's narrative. Although irony prevails in the narrative, Agnon's message is not ambivalence in the service of playful irony but a faithful description of human existence, where blind, sleeping princes are obsessed with the obscure, tragically pursuing illusionary images, moving targets, projections that do not exist. The elaborate chain of keys that lead to other keys is a system of fallacies and deceptions.

Most of the characters in *'Al kapot ha-man'ul* find themselves on the threshold of love, too frightened to go in. Even if they

---

11. Yael S. Feldman, "The Latent and the Manifest: Freudianism in *A Guest for the Night,*" *Prooftexts* 7, 1 (January 1987): 36. The motif of the key has been discussed by Barukh Kurzweil, *Massot 'al sippurei S. Y. Agnon* (Jerusalem: Schocken, 1963); Arnold Band, *Nostalgia and Nightmare: A Study in the Fiction of S. Y. Agnon* (Berkeley and Los Angeles: University of California, 1968); Harold Fish, *S. Y. Agnon* (New York: Frederic Ungar, 1975), p. 44; David Aberbach, *At the Handles of the Lock* (Oxford: Oxford University Press, 1984); Naomi Sokoloff, "Metaphor and Metonymy in Agnon's *Guest for the Night,*" *AJS Review* 9, 1 (Spring 1984): 79–111. Feldman goes along with most other critics, who recognize the key as the ironic or grotesque symbolism of the novel. Esther Fuchs's *Cunning Innocence* (Tel Aviv: Tel Aviv University, 1985) is the most complete and accomplished study on irony in Agnon. Fuchs goes as far as to show that irony dominates absolutely all the genres in Agnon's fiction as the organizing principle.

had the key, the clue, something in their personalities hinders them from inserting and turning it: "I put my hand to the door, as one puts out his hand when he does not expect it to open."[12] Their hands are already placed on the door handles; they are at the most critical moment but are unable to commit the act of entering. The doors remain shut. They cannot consummate their love either emotionally or sexually. They simply stand on the "other" side of the door as voyeurs of their own lives. (Both the doctor in "The Doctor's Divorce" and Hemdat in "Giv'at ha-hol" stand behind closed doors.)

Lacan's definition of voyeurism seems to be particularly relevant to Agnon's text:

> What defines perversion is precisely the way in which the subject is placed in it. What occurs in voyeurism? ... What is the subject trying to see? What he is trying to see ... is the object as absence. What the voyeur is looking for and finds is merely a shadow, a shadow behind the curtain. There he will phantasize any magic of presence, for example, even if on the other side there is only an athlete. What he is looking for is not, as one says, *the phallus— but precisely its absence.* ...
> What one looks at is what cannot be seen.[13]

Hemdat, Who Are You?

In "Giv'at ha-hol" Yael asks Hemdat: "'What are you? ... I had a friend who used to say: I am not asking to what party you belong, what I am asking is what are you? I mean you yourself, what are you?' Hemdat pulled his head backwards and answered: 'I am a sleeping prince whose love arouses him to sleep again. I

---

12. *A Guest for the Night*, p. 7.

13. Jacques Lacan, *The Four Fundamental Concepts of Psychoanalysis*, ed. Jacques-Alain Miller, trans. Alan Sheridan (New York: Norton, 1978), pp. 182–183; emphasis added.

am a beggar of love whose bag tore and who places his love in a torn bag.'"[14]

In contrast with the fairy tale of the prince who awakens the sleeping princess and brings her back to life, Hemdat's love arouses him to "a new sleep." For Hemdat sleep is first and foremost repression: a numbness, a form of passivity. "New sleep" is "new repression" caused by his love. His love brings to the surface the problematic nature of his attraction to Yael and his homosexual desires that become active, paradoxically, only through her. These are issues with which Hemdat cannot come to terms. The "arousal to sleep" is the desire to ignore, the passion to be blind to what his previous dreams have told him. Agnon's heroes cannot overcome the void between the lock and the key because, in fact, they do not want to cross it.

The bag is torn apart, not only in the physical sense, but also in the figurative sense: It is torn apart by conflict. In spite of all his lofty, princely dreams, Hemdat can love only through his torn being, and that leads to the destruction of his love. By ignoring his love, he puts it away in the bag, but he cannot bury his desire. It haunts him from within the torn bag, which cannot hold it. The bagging is futile in that it prevents the actualization of the love, yet it does not give relief by controlling Hemdat's desire.

Like the bag that is the container of his love, Hemdat defines himself in terms of another container, the room he lives in.

---

14. "Giv'at ha-hol," p. 371. We find the motif of the beggar in many of Agnon's stories: There is a blind beggar in *A Simple Story* and *Shira.* In both, the beggar sings a song that had "no beginning and no end." When Shira is about to deliver, Herbst sees a blind beggar in the hospital. The beggar sings, "Flesh like yours will not soon be forgotten." This song is based on a sonnet by Shin Shalom, as stated by Hillel Barzel in *Sippurei ahavah shel S. Y. Agnon* (The love stories of S. Y. Agnon) (Ramat Gan: Bar-Ilan University, 1975), pp. 177ff. Herbst fantasizes that he and Shira disappear. They are both paralyzed: "What happened to the blind beggar from Istanbul now happened to Herbst. His limbs shrank until there was nothing left of him but sleep" (p. 418; trans. David Aberbach in *At the Handles of the Lock,* p. 136). There are beggars at the wedding in "The Doctor's Divorce" and in "The Last Bus."

Throughout the story Hemdat is constantly busy cleaning and rearranging his room. "If you didn't see Hemdat, look at his room" (p. 352). When Yael returns after a long absence, he invites her to come up to his room. She refuses. Again that evening the same thing happens. For him, the most important thing is the room itself. Instead of cultivating his relationship with Yael, he ceaselessly cleans and cultivates his container. A room, says Freud, is an established symbol of female genitalia.[15] Hemdat's desire to be in *his* room is another expression for his femininity and narcissism. His room is like an object of desire with whom he is having a relationship.

Most of the time Hemdat and Yael meet in his room, but when he goes to Yael's room or when he decides to go out and take on a secretarial job at a doctor's office in order to give Yael money, he is overwhelmed by fantasies of amputation and becomes completely paralyzed. When Hemdat goes to Yael's room, her roommate tells him that Yael has gone to the hospital to nurse her mother, whose arm might be amputated. She also tells him that Yael's mother has threatened to kill herself if the amputation should indeed take place. Hearing this, Hemdat becomes paralyzed. The same fears crush him when at the doctor's office he sees a worker whose arm has been amputated: "Hemdat sat in the place he was sitting and didn't move" (p. 373).

> He was terrified by a fantasy that his own arms would be torn off by birds. He went to sleep again wishing that a dentist would pull out his brain. A great sorrow came over him. Hemdat wanted to cry but he couldn't. Hemdat returned to his room and turned on the lamp. How long is this night. What he wanted to do he didn't do and what he did—it was as though it were not done. The day after, he avoided coming to the hospital. He slept throughout the day. He did not do a thing. He did not accomplish a thing. (p. 367)

---

15. Freud, *The Interpretation of Dreams*, chap. 6.

The paralysis is tightly linked in the story to a fear of castration, which is itself linked to the possibility of love.

Why is Hemdat terrified to the point of madness by the possibility of love? Like the doctor, Hemdat has an unresolved conflict with an implicit attraction to men, to whom he can relate only indirectly. This attraction is concretized by his driving Yael into the arms of another man. In both stories, at the beginning, the "other man" is only imaginary, and as the story progresses he becomes real and interacts with the protagonists, Hemdat and the doctor.

Hemdat entertains a fantasy of coming to Yael sometime in the future, when she will be married to someone else:

> After many days Hemdat will come back from far away weak and tormented and he will go to Yael. A group of children will meet him in the yard. They will all fall into their mother's lap. The children will say to Yael, Mommy there is a stranger here, Yael will say but it is Hemdat, and she will jump toward him with joy. And at night her husband will come from his business, and he will be sitting with them. Her husband won't be jealous of him since he is so weak. (p. 368)

The beloved woman who has a child by another man appears in other Agnon stories, and in all three works that are discussed here. The doctor is afraid that his child will resemble Dinah's lover; the guest is obsessed with Yeruham, the lover of his beloved Rachel. He is drawn to Yeruham's body, his eyes and hair, and doesn't quite understand his attraction, saying "Why do I like Yeruham?"[16] Yeruham and Rachel's baby receives the guest's key and his name.

Hemdat's problem is much deeper than only fear of commitment. Not only is he ambivalent toward Yael or *all* other unattached women, but also he has clear preference for married or engaged women. He starts to take a liking to the Mushlams (Mr.

---

16. *A Guest for the Night*, p. 217.

and Mrs. Perfect) only after their marriage, when he can operate in a triangle. At the time that Hemdat desires his friend's fiancée, he condemns such behavior and says, "A man should be happy with his lot and he should not covet what belongs to others." But despite this condemnation *Hemdat can love only when he covets someone else's wife.* The name Hemdat originates in the Hebrew verb "to desire, to covet," especially the unattainable, the impossible.[17]

The question "to what party do you belong?" exceeds the social and the political. If Hemdat had to define himself also sexually, how would he be classified? This matter of defining comes back later in the story when Hemdat is afraid to be found out as "one of the vegetarians."

Sexual Vegetarianism

Many scholars have observed Agnon's use of food as a sexual symbol.[18] Although they make connections between food and Eros, they do not show how structures of eating illuminate the essence of the problematic relationships or the attitude of the characters toward their own sexuality and sexual identity.

The entire relationship between Yael and Hemdat (as between the doctor and his divorcee) is characterized through food. Their denied sexual desire is displaced by a preoccupation with food. The seduction is conducted through meals and eating

---

17. "Thou shalt not covet thy neighbor's wife" is one of the Ten Commandments. Arnold Band (in a private communication) pointed out to me that Hemdat is not a real Hebrew name. It is a grammatical form that brings to mind the title of several rabbinic commentaries and sermons called *Hemdat yamim.* Having a name from religious literature is another illustration of the complexity of the character.

18. For example, Shaked, op. cit., especially p. 174; Barzel, *Sippurei ahavah shel S. Y. Agnon,* pp. 21, 26; and Yair Mazor, *Ha-dinamikah shel motivim bi-tzirat S. Y. Agnon* (The dynamics of motifs in Agnon's works) (Tel Aviv: Dekel, 1979), chap. 2.

rituals. Hemdat constantly invites Yael to eat with him and sometimes even forces her to eat. He is a vegetarian, but she likes only herring and meat. Finally, when she leaves him for Shamai, Hemdat "does not blame her," explaining, "She was hungry for bread and Shamai gives her both bread and chocolate" (p. 395). But the most telling of all about Hemdat's sexual conflict is his vegetarianism, which he himself considers an aberration and therefore hides.

"The Doctor's Divorce" does not mention the doctor's name or that he is a vegetarian. In the novel *A Guest for the Night* the doctor is called Kuba Milch (Milk), and this feature adds to his complex representation. The vegetarian doctor is looked upon with contempt by his community, and only people who cannot afford a regular doctor seek his help. The doctor is forever changing his position in the triangles he forms, from lover to husband, from husband to lover of his former wife, and to lover of his wife's former lover. In a way, Hemdat does the same. Like Kuba Milch, who cannot answer the "simple" question of whether he is the husband of his wife, Hemdat cannot bring himself to say whether he is vegetarian. In Hemdat's mind, eating meat is like committing one of the original sins associated with the flood. Yet he is very secretive about his vegetarian inclinations, as if they are even more sinful than eating meat. Admitting his vegetarianism is described almost in terms of coming out of the closet. His greatest horror is to be found out.

> Yael ordered a portion of meat and Hemdat ordered a dairy dish with a piece of fish. [According to the laws of Kashrut fish belongs neither to the category of milk nor that of meat.] Hemdat is a vegetarian, a vegetarian and not a vegetarian. He does not eat meat but he does eat fish. The truth is that he wanted to stop eating fish but was afraid to be found out as one of the vegetarians. The inn keeper returned, removed the large tablecloth and put on two tablecloths, one for Yael who eats meat and one for Hemdat who eats dairy food. Hemdat looked at the naked place between the two tablecloths, the profane body that crept into the meal. The owner asked Hemdat, while he was eating he said to

him: "If you are a vegetarian and you don't eat meat, why do you eat fish?" Hemdat answered: "Because fish was not a part of the sin of the flood." The inn keeper looked at him once and twice and he wondered "These guys, they have an answer for every question in the world. But what answer will they have at the Last Judgement. ..."[19]

Gershom Scholem comments[20] on the close connection in Jewish tradition between food and sex. In the Talmud we find the terminology of eating used figuratively to indicate sex: "I set the table for him."[21] "Fasting is used as a figure of speech to denote defective sexual relations in Kabbalah" (Scholem, op. cit., p. 151). There are images whose whole purpose is to turn profane acts into rituals of eating and drinking and sexual intercourse. The table as bed appears many times both in "Giv'at ha-hol" and in "The Doctor's Divorce." The table stands for a bed also in the scenes between the doctor and the lover. The locus of the battle is between meat and milk, between the two table-cloths, in what seems to be the place of refuge from sin. As Aberbach has noted, "to be 'between' is a desired state."[22] The doctor tells us, "Things were never so good for me as during the time between my betrothal and marriage."[23]

But the ultimate connection between the repulsion for Yael's sexuality and meat appears at the beginning of Chapter 2 of the story. Although Yael was very good-looking and attractive, "Hemdat used to say that she was not beautiful, but moreover, behind her back *he used to call her a piece of meat*" (emphasis added).

---

19. P. 393.

20. Gershom Scholem, *Pirkei yesod be-havanat ha-kabbalah u-smaleiha* (Jerusalem: Mossad Bialik, 1967), pp. 125, 134, 137.

21. Nedarim 20:B:21.

22. Aberbach, op. cit., p. 28.

23. My translation, *'Al kapot ha-man'ul,* p. 472.

In both *A Guest for the Night* and "Giv'at ha-hol" aberration and sexual ambivalence manifest themselves through phrasing that brings to mind truth tables in logic: A is not A. According to the doctor's account, his divorcee with whom he is still intensely involved is at the same time his wife and not his wife. He explains to his friend that his wife had to go somewhere else with her husband. The friend, puzzled and confused, says to the doctor: "'I really do not understand what you are saying. One thing or the other: if she is your wife, you are her husband, and if you are not her husband, she is not your wife. From what you say, on the other hand, I gather, you and her husband are two different people.' Kuba sighed and said: 'That's how it is: my wife is not my wife and I am not her husband.'"[24] Similarly, Hemdat is and is not a vegetarian. This Agnonian insistence that a thing is itself and not itself constantly brings into focus "the difference that inhabits language, a kind of mapping in the subject's discourse of its points of disagreement with ... itself."[25]

The issue of vegetarianism leads into the last chapter, the unraveling of the story, where Hemdat becomes aware of his desire, which intensifies the triangle to the point of exploding. Although he has an insight into his condition, he is unable to change it.

Reflections on
Rembrandt's Triangular Marriage Portrait

Agnon's stories organize themselves around the inescapable structure of the triangle, of which all three sides are equally indispensable. In the last chapter of "Giv'at ha-hol" we read how Hemdat is aroused by Shamai's attraction to Yael:

---

24. *A Guest for Night,* p. 417.

25. Shoshana Felman, *Jacques Lacan and the Adventure of Insight* (Cambridge and London: Harvard University Press, 1987), p. 21.

This strong excitement of Shamai's makes Hemdat happy. ...

Hemdat was happy when Shamai visited him. How attractive Shamai was when he was talking about Yael. When Yael was sick at the hospital he used to come every day to see how she was. He came from the country [*moshavah*]. He watched the hospital gates like a dog. But Yael couldn't stand him. She doesn't want to go near him. In the evenings Hemdat used to tell her all that Shamai had been doing for her. Alas Yael, are you ever ungrateful! (pp. 393–394)

Still another reflection of the triangle is symbolized through the glass covering Rembrandt's marriage portrait, which hangs on Hemdat's wall. This painting and Van Eyck's *The Betrothal of the Arnolfini* are the best-known symbolic marriage portraits in European art. The portrait shows the newly married couple displaying their ring as the symbol of their commitment. Whenever someone is looking into the painting framed under glass, his or her reflection appears in the middle between husband and wife. The very act of looking at the painting creates a triangle. The structure is permanent, but the constellation changes, depending on the person looking at it. First it is Hemdat who regularly uses the portrait as a mirror, positioning himself with his head in the middle. Then, it is Yael's image on her first visit to Hemdat's room (when she comes under the pretext of learning Hebrew), and finally it is the reflection of Shamai (p. 384). When the triangle in the story is about to break, Hemdat takes the picture off the wall. Each side of the triangle is taking turns looking into the painting and thus creates a triangle with the painting. But the main triangle is the one of the absent images of Hemdat, Yael, and Shamai, whose reflections keep changing in the glass covering the painting as they look at it. The painting reflects the story both as mirror and as thought. The core of the matter, the changing of triangles, takes place in the missing part, where there is no image, in the same way that the heart of the drama happens in the empty, naked place between the two tablecloths (p. 393). Agnon himself interprets part of the story by connecting the reflection on the triangular marriage portrait with Hemdat's problem: "In the past, at the time that the fiancée of one of his acquaintances was pursuing him [Hemdat], whenever he was looking at the painting, and he saw his own reflection between the couple, it seemed to him that he was the third party between them" (p. 353). And furthermore: "One of his friends used to laugh at him and say: 'your love for Rembrandt is not pure, there are ulterior motives to it'" (p. 354).

A Man or a Woman?

Only at the end of the story, when Hemdat realizes that he is losing Yael to Shamai, does he admit to himself that he loves her and considers her "his beloved" rather than his student, sister, or daughter. He goes with Shamai and Yael on a trip. In addition to the principal triangle, he further complicates matters by superimposing another triangle when he invites another lady, Mrs. Ilonit, to join them. Mrs. Ilonit appears earlier in the story as a woman who makes overtures toward Hemdat. She goes up to his room, grabs his arms, and starts dancing with him. While they are dancing, they have a heated discussion on sex roles, whereupon Mrs. Ilonit puts on Hemdat's pants, saying: "Men are blessed. The world was created for men." When she tries to have physical contact with Hemdat, he runs away with revulsion, believing she wants to rape him.

At this point in the story things become very confused. Although the plot moves quickly, no progress is made toward resolution. Shamai insults Hemdat, who, in turn, begins to hate Shamai and bad-mouths him to Yael. Yael tells everything to Shamai. Hemdat goes to mollify him. At the same time that Hemdat is trying to belittle Shamai in Yael's eyes, he is also convincing her that, like Shamai, he is not a suitable partner for her. Without fully knowing what he is saying, he tells her to run away from him because "a psychological condition is contagious." Hemdat finds himself lonely and sexually frustrated. "He was thinking about women and whenever he met one, he became depressed" (p. 397).

First he spends the nights walking aimlessly; then he locks himself in and won't come out of his room, waiting for Yael. One night he goes to the "hill of sand" and sees a shadow. He cannot decide whether it is a tree, a bush, or a person. He wants to be suspended between hope and despair, but suddenly he finds a moment of rest "that is [like] the rest between the baby's fall and his cry" (p. 397). As in "The Doctor's Divorce," this story ends in an insight. It is a paradoxical, complex insight, unclear to Hemdat, yet very informative: "The shadow moved and started to approach Hemdat. Hemdat sighed and said, 'Ah, a living creature. A man or a woman? A woman. ... Thank God it is not Yael Hayot, for if it were Yael Hayot, I would have taken it as a bad sign.' Yael Hayot passed by. She turned her eyes away from him. And Hemdat came down the hill" (p. 389).

Both stories end in a form of appeal. Hemdat says: "A living creature! A man or a woman?" The doctor stretches out his arms, shouting: "Nurse, nurse, come to me!" At the same time there is no clear resolution. The only conclusion is the recognition of the need of the unreachable other.

All of Agnon's endings are ambiguous. The story can never be completed because Agnon does not believe in absolute knowledge or understanding. Even at the end there is a clear intention to remain at the handles of the lock. The endings are like the unresolved dreams, the holes of the lock, and the empty mirrors: They do not know what they are telling us. Agnon's narratives are told through contradictions and constant questioning of their own artistic, linguistic, and ontological validity. At the end there is usually a moment when one thinks that one knows. Indeed, as the story progresses, one moves toward a certain knowledge, but can never fully comprehend the meaning of that knowledge. The implications are always too threatening and too complicated, and so, at any stage, even at the final one, we reach not a point of settlement but a dynamic of escape of knowledge.

Agnon's focus, like Lacan's, is on "*knowledge that can't tolerate one's knowing that one knows.*"[26]

In *A Guest for the Night* the doctor realizes that the problem lies within himself, yet, in spite of his insight, he is too helpless and confused to remarry his divorcee. When his friend suggests to him the idea of getting back with his wife, his last words, that might stand for Agnon's signature of the story, are "perhaps so, perhaps not." Hemdat is like a voyeur who cannot recognize his beloved in their last encounter on the beach. She seems to him like a blurry shadow, an obscure image. He cannot tell whether it is a man or a woman. When he finally identifies the shadow as Yael, the image—and the real woman—disappears. There is a fraction of revelation but it cannot be sustained. One could say that Agnon's endings "close [their] eyes after their revelation."[27]

It is true that the doctor and Hemdat deviate from social norms. In a conventional sense their behavior might be considered aberrant. However, in a deeper sense Agnon shows us how in effect they constitute the norm. Aren't we all offspring of the doctor or Hemdat, always dreaming of opening, but remaining at the handles of, the lock, forever, sleeping princes, blind beggars of love?

The gist of Agnon's narrative can be summed up in the guest's revelation in *A Guest for the Night:* "Finally, all my being ceased, except this pleasure, which did not cease. This may seem perplexing, for surely when a man's being ceases so do his sensations, and here was utter pleasure. Still more perplexing was the fact that this very complexity gave me further pleasure. And this was a novelty, for surely the more one questions the more one is in pain. And, wonderful to relate, even this novelty gave pleasure" (p. 93).

---

26. Jacques Lacan, Seminaire, 19 February 1974, unpublished, quoted in Felman, op. cit., p. 77.

27. S. Freud, *The Standard Edition of the Complete Psychological Works of Sigmund Freud,* trans. and ed. James Strachey (London, 1964), vol. 6, pp. 261–263.

12

A Personal Statement

Aharon Appelfeld

I am going to contribute a few words about my friendship with Agnon. Agnon became a legend in his lifetime, but many of us still remember him as a real person, walking in the streets of Jerusalem. For me, he was not only a great writer but a teacher who introduced me to my own world. Many dangers lurked in my path as a writer. Agnon, without knowing it, guided me. Hebrew literature was on the way to becoming a secular, parochial literature. Agnon opened, for all of us, new gates into our own being. He showed us that Jewishness is not an anachronism. It is possible to write about Jews in small towns and be a universalist. Jewishness is not an artistic obstacle—it is a richness to be sought.

I first met Agnon just after arriving in Palestine. It was in 1946 and I was fourteen years old. Our settlement was not far away from his home, and Agnon used to visit us often to ask questions and tell us jokes. We were totally disoriented, confused, and without words. What could a boy of fourteen do with so many memories of death? The experience was too great for us. The soul was incapable of assimilating so many scenes. Great catastrophes had left us dumb.

Agnon was the first person in Israel who gave me some details about my town. I was eight years old when I left my town. I was born in a town named Czernowitz. Until the First World War, it was part of the Austro-Hungarian Empire. A very Jewish town, and very assimilated too. In my home, for instance, it was forbidden to speak Yiddish. My parents admired the German language. For them, it was more than a language—it was a religion. My grandfather still maintained religious practice, but to inspire us with their belief was beyond them. With their own eyes, they saw the world around them collapse. But they did not believe that they could change anything. I can still see their sadness. It was not the sadness of the old, but of the defeated. The sudden Holocaust thrust us into the depths of suffering without distinguishing between the believers and the estranged. Perhaps for us, the children, it was easier. Our suffering was mainly physical and did not involve any soul searching. For our parents, it was the end of their world. Everything they believed in was suddenly destroyed. All they had left was their naked Jewishness.

Agnon knew my town quite well. It was not far from his town, Buczacz. I mention this fact because he was the first person in Israel who brought me back to my home. Like most of the youngsters who came to Israel as Holocaust survivors, I also wanted to run away from my memories, from my Jewishness. To build up a different image of myself. What didn't we do to change, to be strong? We concealed our bitter memories deep in the very depths of our souls—a place where no other eye, even our own, could get to them. So strong was this desire that we were able to do the impossible. We did not speak; we did not tell. It was an order which did not come from the outside. The little warmth contained in the few words we had brought from home evaporated. We acquired a handful of Hebrew words, which would serve us as a cover and camouflage, so that no one could detect the imprints of suffering.

Gradually, we lost the signs of suffering. We were like the youngsters from the agriculture settlements—absorbed in our daily tasks. People ceased asking us where we came from and how we managed to survive. And we were glad we were no longer bothered with questions. Of course there were the dreams at night, and these oppressed us greatly. And here the old terrors were upon us in full force, sharp and terrifying, as is only possible in naked nightmares. But the instinct for forgetfulness, if it may be called so, reached us even there. And we stopped dreaming. A wide expanse of life, without any fetters, was spread out before us, as if we had been born here. We were like one of the indigenous plants on the tops of the hills.

And so, the first months went by. It seemed as if we had forgotten everything. We grew up, and our bodies grew stronger. The calm of the earth, the breath of the trees, and the plenitude of clear blue skies shaped and renewed us. Everything that had happened to us, we understood, if we understood it at all, as a bitter experience about which one does nothing. Together with the smell of the earth, we absorbed the first written Hebrew words. The Jewish language, new to us, was absorbed clearly in our forgetfulness. We cast off, without any regret, the few words we had brought from home, as one casts off an old, worn-out garment. There was no better time than that. Something of the taste of childhood returned to us in a new form. The fearful movements of our bodies disappeared, and in their place was a flexibility unafraid of contact with other objects. It was a wonderful oblivion; it fed us with good things and gave us only what deep forgetfulness can give: release, ease, and freedom.

Agnon used to visit us, ask us a few questions, and disappear. Occasionally he would sit with a boy and ask him about his home and his parents. He was different from all the people on the farm. He looked like one of our lost uncles. Once, I remember, he said to a boy, "You should not forget your mother language. Yiddish is a beautiful language." He was a shy and strange uncle. Only in 1947 did one of our instructors tell us that the person under the tree was a famous writer.

The years 1946 to 1948 were the heroic years of the country. The land was full of activity, hope, and optimism. And despite the heavy war, festivity was everywhere. Even sadness became festive. Among the many slogans that were repeated very often was, "Never again like sheep to the slaughter." It was supposed to be a national slogan. Whenever the slogan was repeated, it brought to our ears the evil ring of accusation.

What had we not done to become normal-looking, brave, and strong? It was, first of all, a struggle against our weak bodies. As we could not punish our souls, so we punished our bodies. Surprisingly, our bodies did the impossible: They became strong and sturdy, and at the age of sixteen, we were ready to be mobilized. Our battle with ourselves succeeded. Some of us became brave soldiers. Then came years in the army, years of complete forgetfulness. We changed our names, lost our alien accent, and became part of a growing army. It was a strange army. Outside we fought with our enemies, but inside we fought with our feelings, with our nightmares and horrors. The external battle was not always the easy one.

The years passed, and life on the surface of consciousness continued. It was a life without dimensions, a life built in a sort of vacuum. We knew that something in us, warm and dear, had been lost along the way to this oblivion. Our parents, our families, scenes of childhood—without these, what indeed were we? The oblivion was so deep that when the time came that we were awakened, the shock stunned us, so far had we wandered from our true selves.

I turned to literature. Why did I turn to literature? Probably to open the darkness in me, to say something of my experience. Many dangers lurked in my way. Modern Israeli literature, created by our native writers, could not help me. It was a fresh and naïve literature that suited very well the heroic time of Israel's war of independence. But it was not my experience. At first I tried to run away from myself and my memories, to live a life that was not my own, and to write about a life that was not my own. But the hidden feeling told me that I was not to flee away from myself, and that if I denied the experience of my childhood in the Holocaust, I would be spiritually deformed.

Then came years of struggle, years to seek words and phrases that would fit my experience. Internally, the new words were not born. Help came to me from an unexpected source. It came from two people who had not experienced the Holocaust, but who had already foreseen the horrors during the declining days of the Habsburg monarchy: Franz Kafka and S. J. Agnon. I but glanced at the pages of *The Trial,* and the feeling that Kafka was with us in our anguish never left me. In Kafka's language I found, on the one hand, suspicion and skepticism, and on the other hand, deep yearning for meaning. My contact with Kafka's writing was, if I may say so, natural. I knew what he was talking about. It was not a secret language for me. I had come from the camps and from the forests, from a world that embodied the absurd, and nothing in that world was foreign to me. Another discovery showed me that behind the apparent generality of the non-place and non-time in his works, stood a Jewish man—like me, from a half-assimilated family whose Jewish values had lost their content and whose inner space was burned and hounded.

If Kafka gave meaning to my experience during the Holocaust, Agnon opened for me the gates and introduced me to my Jewish home and Jewish literature. In 1951, I met him again in Jerusalem and he immediately recognized me. We spent hours walking the streets. He was full of curiosity and hungry for details. What would I tell him from my experience? I was still totally disoriented. But he, for reasons unknown to me, took me on his walks through Jerusalem. Every walk became an enchanted chapter for me, chapters of Jewish history, Jewish literature, and Jewish memory.

"What are you reading?" was one of his first questions. "You should read the Mishnah. The Mishnah will teach you to think, to be sparing of words, not to use too many adjectives, not to intervene too much, and not to interpret."

I had not the nerve to tell him that I was trying to write. Once, after a long walk, he asked me, "Are you writing?" I could not escape the answer. "You should write only about your experience. If you are loyal to your experience, you will become a writer. You are the only one of your town who can become a Hebrew writer, and that is a great obligation."

If Kafka introduced me to my assimilated parents, Agnon opened the gates of oblivion and brought me to my grandparents, to my hidden home where belief was in full flame. As for myself, it took years for me to grow close to my experience, and afterwards, it took me years to accept it. Only when I reached the age of thirty did I feel the freedom to deal with it as an artist. Agnon gave me the keys to myself. If it had not been for Agnon, I would never have drawn a word from the dark recesses.

Artistically, I could not follow his path. He came from a Jewish world, from a full world, and I came from my own world. My real world was far beyond the power of imagination, and my part as an artist was not to open up my imagination, but to restrain it. Even then, it seemed impossible. Agnon understood my dilemma. He introduced me to a leading Hasidic teacher and to all the book dealers in town. He was a great lover of the Jewish book and a very good collector. Once he said to me that only he and Dov Sadan were real collectors. The others were just university professors. Just as I felt in Kafka the deep longings of the assimilated Jew trying to get to the core of his being, I found in Agnon a language that was most appropriate to my experience and my perceptions. I felt, and still feel, a close affinity to these concepts. The compulsion to return to myself, to the very source of my tradition derives not only from the obligation placed upon me by my past experience. I felt that without Jewish consciousness in the broad meaning of the word, I would remain on the surface of my experience. Agnon helped me to find my way home. Once he said to me, ironically as usual, "A writer should make his village the capital of the world. Once the capital was Dublin, now it is Buczacz."

Bibliography

Aberbach, David. *At the Handles of the Lock: Themes in the Fiction of S. J. Agnon*. New York and Oxford: Oxford University Press, 1984.

———. "Agnon and Jewish Nationalism." *L'Eylah* 21, Pesach Issue (1986).

Afek, Edna. *Ma'arakhot millim. Iyyunim ba-signon shel S. Y. Agnon*. Tel Aviv: Dekel, 1979.

Agnon, Shmuel Yosef/Agnon, S. J. *Ad henna*. Tel Aviv and Jerusalem: Schocken Books, 1952.

———. "Ad 'olam" ("Forevermore"). In *Elu ve-elu*. Tel Aviv: Schocken Books, 1974.

———. *Kol sippurav shel S. Y. Agnon*. 8 vols. Tel Aviv: Schocken Books, 1953–1962.

———. *Oreah natah lalun*. Tel Aviv: Schocken Books, 1968 (first published 1939).

———. *Temol shilshom*. Vol. 5 of *Kol sippurav*.

———. *A Guest for the Night*. Trans. Misha Louvish. New York: Schocken Books, 1968.

———. *Hakhnasat kalla*. Tel Aviv and Jerusalem: Schocken Books, 1964.

———. *Elu ve-elu*. Tel Aviv and Jerusalem: Schocken Books, 1964.

———. *Sefer ha-ma'asim*. Tel Aviv and Jerusalem: Schocken Books, 1932.

———. *Shira*. Tel Aviv and Jerusalem: Schocken Books, 1971.

———. *Twenty-one Stories*. Ed. N. Glatzer. New York: Schocken, 1970.

———. "Yedidut." Vol. 6 of *Kol sippurav*.

Alter, Robert. *After the Tradition*. New York: E. P. Dutton, 1969.

———. *Modern Hebrew Literature*. New York: Behrman House, 1975.

———. *Defenses of the Imagination*. Philadelphia: Jewish Publication Society, 1977.

Alwood, J., L. Andersson, and O. Dahl. *Logic in Linguistics.* Cambridge Textbooks in Linguistics. Cambridge: Cambridge University Press, 1977.

Arieti, Silvano. *Understanding and Helping the Schizophrenic.* New York: Simon and Schuster, 1979.

Band, Arnold. *Nostalgia and Nightmare: A Study in the Fiction of S. Y. Agnon.* Berkeley and Los Angeles: University of California Press, 1968.

———. "Ha-het ve-'onsho be-temol shilshom." *Molad* 1 (1967).

Bar-Adon, Aharon. *S. Y. Agnon u-tehiyat ha-lashon ha-'ivrit.* Jerusalem: Mossad Bialik, 1977.

Barzel, Hillel. *Bein Agnon le-Kafka: mehkar mashveh.* Ramat Gan: Bar Uryan, Bar Ilan University, 1972.

———. *Sippurei ahavah shel S. Y. Agnon.* Ramat Gan: Bar Ilan University, 1975.

Ben-Dov, Nitza. "The Dream as a Junction of Theme and Characterization in the Psychological Fiction of S. Y. Agnon." Dissertation, University of California at Berkeley, 1984.

Bettelheim, Bruno. *The Uses of Enchantment.* Harmondsworth: Penguin Books, 1987.

Brill, A. A., ed. *The Basic Writings of Sigmund Freud.* New York: Modern Library, 1938.

Brod, Max. *Franz Kafka: A Biography.* Trans. G. H. Roberts and R. Winston. New York: Schocken, 1960.

Brooks, Peter. *Reading for the Plot: Design and Intention in Narrative.* New York: Random House, 1984.

Casey, Edward S., and J. Melvin Woody. "Hegel, Heidegger, Lacan: The Dialectic of Desire." In Joseph Smith and William Kerrigan, eds. *Interpreting Lacan.* New Haven and London: Yale University Press, 1983.

Coffin, Edna Amir. "The Dream as a Literary Device in Agnon's Metamorphosis." *Hebrew Studies* 23 (1982).

———. "Do Words Conceal or Reveal Intent of Verbal Expressions? Thought Process and Written Symbols in Agnon's Fiction." In Leon Yudkin, ed. *Agnon's Fiction in English Translation.* New York: Markus Weiner Publishing, 1988.

Dan, Yosef. "Kabbalah, philosophiah ve-ironia be-piska shel Agnon." In *Ha-nokhri ve-ha-mandarin* (The foreigner and the mandarin). Ramat Gan: Massada, 1975.

_____, ed. *Ha-novela ha-hasidit*. Jerusalem: Mossad Bialik, 1966.

Davis, Robert Con. "Introduction: Lacan and Narration." In R. C. Davis, ed. *Lacan and Narration: The Psychoanalytic Difference in Narrative Theory*. Baltimore: Johns Hopkins University Press, 1983.

Diamond, James S. *Barukh Kurzweil and Modern Hebrew Literature*. Chico, Calif.: Scholars Press, 1983.

Erikson, Erik H. *Identity: Youth and Crisis*. New York: W. W. Norton, 1968.

Ezrahi, Sidra Dekoven. "Agnon Before and After." *Prooftexts* 2 (1982).

Felman, Shoshana. *Writing and Madness (Literature / Philosophy / Psychoanalysis)*. Trans. Martha N. Evans and S. Felman. Ithaca: Cornell University Press, 1985.

Freedman, H., trans. and ed. *Tractate Sanhedrin. The Babylonian Talmud*. Ed. I. Epstein. London: Soncino, 1935.

Freud, Sigmund. *The Interpretation of Dreams*. In *The Basic Writings of Sigmund Freud*. 2nd ed. Trans. and ed. A. A. Brill. New York: The Modern Library, 1966.

_____. "Leonardo da Vinci and a Memory of His Childhood." Vol. 11 of *The Standard Edition of the Complete Psychological Works of Sigmund Freud*. Trans. and ed. James Strachey. 24 vols.

_____. *The Technique of Wit*. In *The Basic Writings of Sigmund Freud*.

_____. *Totem and Taboo*. Vol. 13 of *The Standard Edition*.

_____. "The Uncanny." Vol. 17 of *The Standard Edition*.

_____. *Introductory Lectures on Psychoanalysis*. Trans. James Strachey. New York and London: W. W. Norton, 1977.

Frye, Northrop. "The Mythos of Winter: Irony and Satire." In *Anatomy of Criticism*. Princeton: Princeton University Press, 1957.

Fuchs, Esther. *Omanut ha-hitamemut: al ha-ironia shel S. Y. Agnon*. Tel Aviv: Tel Aviv University, 1985a.

_____. "Wherefrom Did Gediton Enter Gumlidata?—Realism and Comic Subversiveness in 'Forevermore.'" *Modern Language Studies* 15, 4 (Fall 1985b).

Geertz, Clifford. *The Interpretation of Cultures*. New York: Basic Books, 1973.

Greenson, Ralph R. *The Technique and Practice of Psychoanalysis*. Vol. 1. New York: International Universities Press, 1967.

Hagar, Sara. "'Temol shilshom': hithavut ha-mivneh ve-ahduto." In Gershon Shaked and Rafael Veiser, eds. *S. Y. Agnon: mehkarim u-te'udot*. Jerusalem: Bialik Institute, 1978.

Halkin, Simon. *Modern Hebrew Literature: Trends and Values.* New York: Schocken Books, 1950.

Halliday, M.A.K., and Ruqaiya Hasan. *Cohesion in English.* London: Longman, 1976.

Hochman, Baruch. *The Fiction of S. Y. Agnon.* Ithaca and London: Cornell University Press, 1970.

Holtz, Avraham. "Mi-shlemut la-'avodah zarah." *Ha-sifrut* 3, 2 (November 1971).

Joyce, James. *A Portrait of the Artist as a Young Man.* New York: Cape, 1968.

Jung, C. G. *Man and His Symbols.* London: Aldus Books, 1964.

Kafka, Franz. "The Metamorphosis." Trans. Willa and Edwin Muir.

––––––. *Letter to His Father/Brief an den Vater.* Bilingual edition. Trans. Ernst Kaiser and Eithne Wilkins. New York, 1966.

––––––. *The Trial.* Trans. Willa and Edwin Muir. New York, 1964.

––––––. "In the Penal Colony." Trans. Willa and Edwin Muir. In Nahum Glatzer, ed. *Franz Kafka: The Complete Stories.* New York, 1971.

Katz, Jacob. *Out of the Ghetto: The Social Background of Jewish Emancipation 1770–1870.* New York: Schocken Books, 1978.

Kirshenblatt-Gimblett, Barbara. "The Cut That Binds: The Western Ashkenazic Torah Binder as Nexus Between Circumcision and Torah." In Victor Turner, ed. *Celebration: Studies in Festivity and Ritual.* Washington, D.C.: Smithsonian Institution, 1982.

Kripke, S. A. "Semantic Considerations on Modal Logic." *Acta Philosophica Fennica* 16 (1963).

Kurzweil, Barukh. *Massot 'al sippurei S. Y. Agnon.* Jerusalem and Tel Aviv: Schocken Books, 1963.

––––––. "Temol shilshom." In Hillel Barzel, ed. *Shmuel Yosef Agnon: mivhar maamarim 'al yetzirato.* Tel Aviv: Schocken Books, 1982.

––––––. *Sifrutenu ha-hadashah: hemshekh o mahapekhah?* Tel Aviv: Schocken Books, 1958.

Lacan, Jacques. *Écrits: A Selection.* Trans. Alan Sheridan. New York and London: Tavistock Publications, 1977.

––––––. *The Four Fundamental Concepts of Psychoanalysis.* Ed. Jacques-Alain Miller. Trans. Alan Sheridan. London: Hogarth Press, 1977.

Lewis, David. *Counterfactuals.* Cambridge, Mass.: Harvard University Press, 1973.

Miron, Dan. "Domesticating a Foreign Genre: Agnon's Transactions with the Novel." Trans. Naomi B. Sokoloff. *Prooftexts* 7 (1987).

Mitchell, Juliet. "Introduction." *Feminine Sexuality: Jacques Lacan and the École Freudienne.* Eds. Juliet Mitchell and Jacqueline Rose. New York: Norton, 1985.

Moked, Gavriel. "Rivdei mashma'ut shonim ba-tekhnika shel ha-nidah." *Moznayim* 27 (1968).

_____. "Transendentsia, omanut u-mehkar mada'i: li-shney sippurim simliyim shel Shai Agnon—*Ido ve-'enam* ve-*Ad 'olam.*" *Shmuel Yosef Agnon: mivhar ma-amarim 'al yetsirato.* Ed. Hillel Barzel. Tel Aviv: Am Oved, 1984.

Muecke, Douglas. *The Compass of Irony.* London: Methuen, 1969.

Muller, John P. "Language, Psychosis, and the Subject in Lacan." In Joseph Smith and William Kerrigan, eds. *Interpreting Lacan.* New Haven and London: Yale University Press, 1983.

Patterson, David. *Abraham Mapu: The Creator of the Modern Hebrew Novel.* London: East and West Library, 1964.

_____. *The Hebrew Novel in Czarist Russia.* Edinburgh: Edinburgh University Press, 1964.

Paulson, Ronald. *The Fictions of Satire.* Baltimore: Johns Hopkins University Press, 1967.

Roskies, David G. *Against the Apocalypse: Responses to Catastrophe in Modern Jewish Culture.* Cambridge, Mass.: Harvard University Press, 1984.

Sachar, Howard M. *A History of Israel: From the Rise of Zionism to Our Time.* Oxford: Basil Blackwell, Vol. 1, 1977; New York: Oxford University Press, Vol. 2, 1987.

Sadan, Dov. *'Al S. Y. Agnon.* Tel Aviv: Hakibbutz Hameuchad, 1978.

Shaked, Gershon. *Ha-sipporet ha-'ivrit 1880–1980.* 2 vols. Jerusalem: Keter, Vol. 1, 1983; Tel Aviv: Hakibbutz Hameuchad, Vol. 2, 1988.

_____. "Helkat ha-sadeh ha-netushah." *Moznayim* 32 (1971).

_____. "Ha-ma'amin ha-gadol." In R. Weizer and G. Shaked, eds. *S. Y. Agnon—mehkarim u-te'udot.* Jerusalem: Mossad Bialik, 1978.

_____. *The Narrative Art of S. Y. Agnon.* Tel Aviv: Sifriat Po'alim, 1973.

_____. *Omanut ha-sippur shel Agnon.* Jerusalem: Hakibbutz Hameuchad and Keter, 1976.

Smith, Joseph H. "Epilogue: Lacan and the Subject of American Psychoanalysis." Joseph Smith and William Kerrigan, eds.

Interpreting Lacan. New Haven and London: Yale University Press, 1983.

Smolenskin, Peretz. *Kevurat hamor.* Vienna, 1874.

Sophocles. *Oedipus the King.* Trans. David Grene. In David Grene and Richmond Lattimore, eds. *Complete Greek Tragedies.* Chicago: University of Chicago Press, 1954.

Stanislawski, Michael. *Tsar Nicholas I and the Jews.* Philadelphia: Jewish Publication Society, 1983.

Tochner, Meshulam. *Pesher Agnon.* Ramat Gan: Massada, 1968.

Todorov, Tzvetan. *The Poetics of Prose.* Ithaca: Cornell University Press, 1977.

Tsemach, Adi. " 'Al ha-tefisah ha-historiosofit bi-shnaim mi-sippurav ha-meuharim shel Agnon." *Ha-sifrut* 1, 2 (1968).

Waugh, Linda R. "The Poetic Function and the Nature of Language." *Poetics Today.* 2a (Fall 1980).

Yehoshua, A. B. *Between Right and Right.* Trans. Arnold Schwartz. New York: Doubleday, 1981.

Zweik, Yehudith Halevi. "Tekufat Germania bi-yetsirotav shel S. Y. Agnon 1914–1924." Dissertation, The Hebrew University of Jerusalem, 1968.

About the Book and Editors

More than 100 years after his birth in Buczacz, Galicia, Samuel Joseph Agnon continues to hold a central position in modern Hebrew literature. For two generations Agnon enthralled Hebrew audiences with an immense flow of stories and novels, until his death in 1972. Even now, work found among his papers, unpublished in his lifetime, continues to be greeted with enthusiasm.

In spite of his enormous impact on the Hebrew-reading public and the acknowledgment that he is a writer of great stature, Agnon's reputation has not yet had as great an impact as it deserves. This is in part because his prose loses much of its tension in translation, and his language, perhaps more than that of most writers, is central to an appreciation of his work.

Agnon's themes are those of spiritual disintegration and decay as expressed through nightmare fantasy and symbol. These may be universal themes, but Agnon's originality resides in the way he relates them to the objective events of Jewish history. A palpable symbol of the appalling decline and disintegration of cultures in this century, the traumatized, evicted, or murdered Jew is highly evocative. Events have sapped his will to go on. In his encounter with the world and with God he is adrift and helpless. Beneath the dreamlike surface of many of Agnon's stories, where the fixed points of time and place dissolve, despair, tragedy, and violent death are commonplace events reflecting a pessimism of disturbing depth.

The fascination and enigma of Agnon's work is the inspiration for the studies that comprise this volume, illustrating the importance of this central figure of Hebrew literature. The careful research and detailed analyses of the experienced contributors included here, it is hoped, will finally bring Agnon's literature into greater prominence among the English-reading public.

David Patterson is emeritus president of the Oxford Centre for Postgraduate Hebrew Studies and an emeritus Fellow of St. Cross College, Oxford. He was Cowley Lecturer in Postbiblical Hebrew at the University of Oxford from 1956 to 1989. He is author of *Abraham Mapu: The First Hebrew Novelist, The Hebrew Novel in Czarist Russia,* and *A Phoenix in Fetters* as well as numerous articles and many translations. **Glenda Abramson** is Schreiber Fellow in Modern Jewish Studies at the Oxford Centre for Postgraduate Hebrew Studies and Cowley Lecturer in Postbiblical Hebrew at the University of Oxford. She is author of *Modern Hebrew Drama, The Great Transition* (with Tudor Parfitt), and *The Writing of Yehuda Amichai* and is editor of *The Blackwell Companion to Jewish Culture (from the Eighteenth Century to the Present).*

About the Contributors

David Aberbach is associate professor of Hebrew and comparative literature at McGill University and visiting professor at University College, London. He is author of *At the Handles of the Lock: Themes in the Fiction of S. J. Agnon; Bialik; Surviving Trauma: Loss, Literature and Psychoanalysis; Realism, Caricature and Bias: The Fiction of Mendele Mocher Sefarim;* and *Imperialism and Biblical Prophecy, 750–500 BCE.*

Aharon Appelfeld is a recipient of the Israel Prize. His works in English translation include *Badenheim 1939; The Age of Wonders; Tzili: The Story of a Life; The Retreat; For Every Sin;* and *To the Land of Cattails.* He was born in Czernovitz, Bukovina, in 1932 and now lives in Jerusalem.

Arnold J. Band has been professor of Hebrew and comparative literature at the University of California at Los Angeles since 1959 and is a senior Associate Fellow at the Oxford Centre for Postgraduate Hebrew Studies. He is author of *Nostalgia and Nightmare: Tales of Nahman of Braslav* and has been president of the Association of Jewish Studies.

Nitza Ben-Dov is associate professor in the Department of Hebrew and Comparative Literature at Haifa University. She is author of *Agnon's Art of Indirection: Uncovering Latent Content in the Fiction of S. Y. Agnon* and of numerous articles on Hebrew literature.

Edna Amir Coffin is professor of Hebrew language and literature at the University of Michigan. She is author of *Modern Hebrew, Level 1 and Level 2* and *Hebrew Encounters 1 and 2* as well as numerous articles on Hebrew language and literature.

Esther Fuchs teaches Hebrew literature, modern and biblical, at the University of Arizona at Tucson. She is author of *Israeli Mythogynies: Women in Contemporary Hebrew Fiction* and *Sexual Politics in the Biblical Narrative.*

Anne Golomb Hoffman is professor of English and comparative literature at Fordham University. She is author of *Between Exile and Return: S. Y. Agnon and the Drama of Writing* and is currently at work on *Inscriptions of Difference: Gender and Body in 20th Century Jewish Writing.*

Miri Kubovy is professor of Near Eastern languages and civilizations and director of modern Hebrew at Harvard University. She is also a member of the Harvard Center for Middle Eastern Studies. She has translated three books and published numerous articles on modern Hebrew literature.

Naomi Sokoloff is associate professor of Hebrew in the Department of Near Eastern languages and civilization at the University of Washington. She is author of *Imagining the Child in Modern Jewish Fiction* and coeditor of *Gender and Text in Modern Hebrew and Yiddish Literature.*

Judith Romney Wegner is visiting associate professor and Blaustein Scholar of Judaic Studies at Connecticut College. She is author of *Chattel or Person? The Status of Women in the Mishnah* as well as articles on comparative aspects of Jewish and Islamic law.

Index

Halliday, M.A.K., 166n
"Ha-malbush." *See* "Garment, The"
"Ha-nidah," 68, 138, 140
"Ha-rav ve-ha-oreah," 139
"Ha-rofe u-grushato." *See* "Doctor's Divorce, The"
Hasan, Ruqaiya, 166n
Hermann, Leo, 34, 35
Hirsch, Samson Raphael, 112
Hochman, Baruch, 117, 180
Holtz, Avraham, 49n, 68, 73, 76

"Ido and Enam" ("Ido ve-'enam"), 6, 37
"Ido ve-'enam." *See* "Ido and Enam"
Interpretation of Dreams, The (Freud), 33, 157(n7)
In the Heart of the Seas (*Bi-lvav yamim*), 140
Introduction to Psychoanalysis (Freud), 92
Ishmael, R., 76
Israel, literary renaissance in, 2–3

Jaffa, Agnon in, 28–29
Jerusalem, 7, 33–34, 54
Joyce, James, 36, 54
"Judgment, The" ("Das Urteil") (Kafka), 37, 38–39

Kafka, Franz, 26, 59, 60(n15), 61, 211, 212
  influence of, 6, 32–39, 43, 44
Katz, Jacob, 112
Kirshenblatt-Gimblett, Barbara, 57
Kripke, Saul, 152n
Krochmal, Nahman, 3
Kurzweil, Barukh, 4, 45n, 68, 70, 74, 92n, 173, 179

  on Jewish tradition, 36, 37, 42, 43, 124–126, 129

Lacan, Jacques, 192, 195, 206
"Last Bus, The," 196n
Lawrence, D. H., 183(n22)
Letter to His Father (Kafka), 60(n15)
Lewis, David, 152n

Maimonides, Moses, 3
Malamud, Bernard, 90, 102–103
Mann, Thomas, 89
Mapu, Abraham, 110
Mas'ot Binyamin ha-shlishi (Mendele), 170, 175–177, 178, 185
Mendele Mokher Sefarim, 27, 28, 30, 40, 41, 110
  homosexuality in, 169, 170, 174, 175–178, 185–186
Meredith, George, 13
"Metamorphosis" (Kafka), 34, 38, 59, 61
Midrash, in literature, 3–4, 6
Miron, Dan, 46, 62(n19)
"Mitato shel Shelomo Ya'akov," 141
Mitchell, Juliet, 56n
"Modern Love" (Meredith), 13
Moked, Gavriel, 10n
Muller, John P., 50(n16)
Musil, 36

Narrative Art of S. Y. Agnon, The (Shaked), 144n

Oreah natah lalun. See Guest for the Night, A
Outline of Psychoanalysis (Freud), 161n

"Pat shlemah." *See* "Whole Loaf, A"